THE END OF THE LINE

MORALITY AND SOCIETY

A Series Edited by Alan Wolfe

KATHRYN MARIE DUDLEY

THE END OF THE LINE

Lost Jobs, New Lives in
Postindustrial America

THE UNIVERSITY OF CHICAGO PRESS

Chicago and London

The University of Chicago Press, Chicago 60637
The University of Chicago Press, Ltd., London
© 1994 by The University of Chicago
All rights reserved. Published 1994
Paperback edition 1997
Printed in the United States of America
03 02 01 00 99 98 97   2 3 4 5
ISBN: 0-226-16908-1 (cloth)
ISBN: 0-226-16910-3 (paperback)

Library of Congress Cataloging-in-Publication Data

Dudley, Kathryn Marie.
    The end of the line : lost jobs, new lives in postindustrial America / Kathryn
Marie Dudley.
        p.   cm.—(Morality and society)
    Includes index.
    1. Plant shutdowns—Wisconsin—Kenosha—Public opinion.   2. Public
opinion—Wisconsin—Kenosha.   3. Automobile industry workers—
Wisconsin—Kenosha.   4. Unemployment—Wisconsin—Kenosha.
5. Ethnology—Wisconsin—Kenosha.   6. Chrysler Corporation.
I. Title.   II. Series.
HD5708.55.U62K463   1994
338.6'042—dc20   93-6041
                                                                                              CIP

In memory of
Mark Minetti (1958–1988)

We all have expectations. We look outward through a little chink in our armor, one conditioned by our background, our experience, our doubts, and our faith. The true ground of hope is not our expectations, however, no matter how grand or humble. It lies in the hubbub, which upsets our expectations and reorders our perceptions. We are constantly being challenged therefore to become more inclusive, mature, and enduring in our love.

JOHN A. BUEHRENS AND F. FORRESTER CHURCH,
OUR CHOSEN FAITH

CONTENTS

ACKNOWLEDGMENTS

The End of the Line is in many ways a book about my hometown. I grew up several miles north of Kenosha's auto plant, in the neighboring city of Racine, Wisconsin. As teenagers caught up in divisive high-school rivalries, most of us would have taken offense at the suggestion that the two cities had anything of any importance in common. Only in retrospect, as the mass shutdowns and layoffs of the 1980s delivered one blow after another, did it become apparent that our greatest similarity, and increasing liability, was our industrial heritage. I had been living in New York City for a number of years before I realized that Racine and Kenosha are part of the "rust belt"—that great swath of middle America razed by the decline of the rubber, steel, and automobile industries. This understanding came to me slowly, not through news stories or scholarly articles, but from my visits home.

Vast chunks of Main Street had fallen to the wrecking cranes, and the boarded-up windows of factories and shops appeared on every block. But the specter of a ghost town went hand in hand with a good deal of talk about economic revitalization, the new marina, hotels, condominiums, and shopping malls. Rust belt America, I soon realized, is not a static landscape of slag heaps and desolate smokestacks. It is a cultural drama of communities in transition and ordinary people struggling to find a place for the past in the present. When the closing of a local machine-tool factory forced my grandfather into early retirement, I saw in his loneliness why the loss of an industrial job can be so devastating. Friendships built up over twenty years on the shopfloor gradually fade away, and with them the sense of community that gives us all a meaningful place in the world. My grandfather is not alive to read this book; I can only hope it conveys my appreciation for the life he lived.

Many people have helped to make this book possible. I am especially indebted to Jack Ward, Joanne Steagall, and the dedicated staff of job counselors at Kenosha's UAW-JDTC Dislocated Workers Assistance Center. Without their help, this book would not exist. My heartfelt thanks and lasting respect goes to the autoworkers who volunteered to participate in this research. I wasn't able to quote every worker's words directly, but everyone I spoke with shaped the outcome of this book in great and small ways. Despite considerable stress and some initial misgivings, these men and women took the emotional risk of sharing their experiences with me, as together we explored the meaning of the shutdown in their lives. Their contribution to this project is a testimony to the strength with which they face a largely unforgiving world.

Friends and family in Racine and Kenosha made the arduous task of beginning a community study infinitely easier. Sally Orth offered early assistance by putting me in touch with sympathetic educators who steered me through layers of administrative bureaucracy. I conducted research in the high schools with the approval of John Hosmanek, superintendent of the Kenosha Unified School District, and Jackson Parker, director of Educational Research and Development for Racine Unified. My sister and her friends, Hedy Pflugrad and Cindy Carr, opened doors to several social networks that allowed me to meet a much wider range of autoworker families then might otherwise have been possible. My brother gave me rolls of film that measurably enhanced my visual memory and hence the descriptive passages in this book. Grace Meyer good-naturedly put up with an anthropologist in her house during the spring and summer of 1989. During the last phase of my fieldwork, Bill and Sara Jensen welcomed me into their home as they have so often before. Cindy Weiss, best friend of long acquaintance (note I did not say *old* friend), kept my spirits up with generous humor and wise counsel. Many thanks go to my father, who for weeks on end let me borrow the car. Useful financial support for this project came in a grant-in-aid of research supplied by Sigma Xi, the Scientific Research Society.

Katherine Newman was everything I could have wished for in a thesis adviser. She has been an inspiration, a constructive critic, and a wellspring of moral support. I count myself among those fortunate graduate students who can, in times of terror or despair, rely on the equanimity and sound judgment of their advisers. When such virtues are combined with intelligence and compassion, the only appropriate acclamation is "awesome." Thus, with unabashed admiration I thank my awesome adviser for her strong guidance of my graduate career and her unwavering belief in this project. Many people have read this work in one or several of its incarnations. Herbert Gans, Elaine Combs-Schilling, Martha Howell, and David Koester offered valuable suggestions at the dissertation stage. Cathy Wanner, friend and intrepid colleague that she is, plowed through the entire manuscript on a moment's notice, not once but twice, and her challenging questions helped clarify many points. I am much obliged to Alan Wolfe and Douglas Mitchell for the confidence they expressed in this book from the outset and for their sure handling of the revision process. Rick Fantasia offered incisive criticism at a crucial point, and the book has benefited enormously as a result. Mark Hertzberg at the Racine *Journal Times* and Bill Siel at the *Kenosha News* helped to compile the wonderful set of photographs included in the book. Alice Bennett's judicious editing provided the polish and finishing touches.

This book is dedicated to Mark Minetti, my friend since the sixth grade, who died the winter the plant closing was announced. Mark was the son of a factory worker, and when we were in high school, many of our late-night conversations were edged with the anxiety of wanting to honor family expectations while still being true to ourselves. A star gymnast, Mark often dreamed of a career in dance but eventually began working with his hands, designing furniture in New York City. One of the last times we met, he was working on a desk made of cherry wood and had just sanded down the surface to a rosy glow. He invited me to run my fingers across it, and as I did I knew that neither of us, standing there in a loft in Soho, had left our hometown very far behind.

Trying to understand experiences that are at once personal and cultural calls for a kind of passionate detachment that is, I think, almost impossible to sustain alone. Susan Robertson, my psychotherapist, has been a constant source of emotional support and thoughtful analysis, and always an exasperating master of the third instance. She has helped me maintain a creative balance between a sense of personal limitation and hope in the world's possibilities. Special thanks is reserved for my mother. Her evidently unshakable conviction that I usually know what I am doing has seen me through many times when in truth I have not. The courage to explore and respect different ways of life springs from this sturdy faith, and for it I am forever grateful.

The Tradition of Opportunity

The morning of January 27, 1988, began like any other. Joe Gordon was driving a small utility vehicle on his usual rounds through the sprawling assembly plant. He had just picked up a load of machine grindings to take to the disposal area when he happened to glance out the long expanse of factory windows. Spreading out around the building were a dozen or more county sheriffs. Joe pulled his tug around and got out to take a better look. The uniformed officers seemed to be looking for something as they fanned out across the ground. Only in retrospect would it be clear that they were there because officials were afraid there would be labor trouble.

As Joe turned to finish his run, he was summoned to answer an urgent telephone call. As a shop steward and executive officer, he was used to being called away from the job on union matters, but intuition told him today's call was not routine business. The shop chairman started to talk as soon as Joe picked up the receiver. He was calling an emergency meeting and wanted all executive board members at the union hall right away. The conversation, Joe recalls, ended there:

> So I'm thinking, this doesn't sound good at all. And just then we had the radio on in the office, and it said Governor Thompson's in town and Chrysler's gonna make an announcement. I took it as bad right there. I just jumped in the car, drove down there, and came in. . . . And everybody in this hall was just sitting with their heads down. Half the [union's executive] board was here already when I walked in. They said, "That's it, it's over: they're closing the place down."

Iacocca falls from favor on the sign at a tavern near the main plant. After Chrysler's "rescue" of AMC, the sign read "Lee Iacocca for President." Photo by Charles S. Vallone and the Racine *Journal Times*.

Joe pauses and looks down at his hands. In every interview I have done with the autoworkers here in Kenosha, there comes this moment when the emotional impact of the events they are describing—often slowly and deliberately, in matter-of-fact tones—simply overwhelms them. Sometimes there are tears. But usually there is silence, as now.

"I was devastated," Joe says at last, his initial feelings still close to the surface. "I remember sitting there that day thinking: the bottom just fell out."

I hold in mind the image of a man in free fall, and I ask Joe why he felt that way. What concerned him most?

"I guess the reaction is you always look at yourself first. And I thought, *now* what's going to happen? Now I'm without a job. I got a family. I gotta start all over again. And it wasn't panic, it was just, like, *there's nothing there.* You know, I was in a void. Emotionally, I felt bad. Probably two hours into it, I was on the verge of tears cuz then I started thinking about everybody: *there's nothing left.* This town, it's a ghost town. You might as well take the signs down on the interstate, you know?"

Joe smiles wanly when he says this. It's a running joke among dislocated autoworkers around here, a variant of "Will the last one to leave town please turn off the lights?" There's another joke the unemployed tell, and I think of it when Joe smiles. A man falls off the top of a building, and as he passes each floor he reassures himself by saying, "So far so good; so far so good; so far so good . . ." Workers like to tell this one when somebody asks how they are doing or how a job interview went. They play along by saying "So far so good," and then they tell this joke—on themselves.

Outside the union hall this macabre humor would win few comedy awards, but around here, it gets a lot of laughs. When I first heard these jokes, I wasn't sure whether to laugh or look seriously sympathetic. I felt uncomfortable laughing at people's misfortune, but I quickly learned that my puzzled expression was offensive. The teller of the joke would study my reaction, then give me an accusing look. If I couldn't "get it" and laugh along, what made me think I could understand what they were going through? The idea is, when you're really in this situation, when you *really* understand how it can stretch a person to the limits, you've got to laugh or cry. There are no neutral emotions.[1]

Glory Days

Joe Gordon isn't alone in feeling that the sudden loss of his job ("there's nothing there") is connected to a loss of identity for the city as a whole ("there's nothing left"). All the autoworkers I've talked with feel this way. And with reason. When Chrysler stopped building cars in Kenosha, Wisconsin, a way of life came to an end.

From the early 1900s onward, generations of workers in the city's rapidly growing "motor car" factory were able to link personal aspirations and rising incomes to the promise of prosperity in America's manufacturing industries. Before and after the Great Depression, the auto plant was the major source of employment in town. Boosted by Defense Department contracts during World War II, the auto plant (Nash Motors at the time) doubled its workforce within four years, bringing employment at the plant to a high of 7,300 by 1945. In 1954 Nash merged with the Hudson Motor Car Company to create the American Motors Corporation (AMC). Kenosha instantly became the major center of production for a company that, by 1960, claimed 7.2 percent of the domestic car market.[2] AMC earned its place in automotive history with America's first mass-produced compact car, the sturdy, economical Rambler. When this car hit the market the Kenosha plant surged into high gear. Round-the-clock shifts soon provided jobs for well over 15,000 autoworkers, almost 40 percent of the city's total labor force.[3] During the 1960s, AMC became the largest single employer in the state of Wisconsin.

These are the glory days autoworkers recall when hats are doffed and eyes grow misty at the local bars. There was a feeling of being at the center of the action, nationally and internationally. United Auto Workers Local 72 had the largest membership of any union in the state, making it one of the most powerful constituencies to be reckoned with by state and local politicians of any ambition. Since Kenosha remained the hub of AMC's assembly operations, Local 72 also wielded considerable clout on the shopfloor and frequently threatened systemwide work stoppages when its demands were not met. Workers' earnings were steadily rising, always a step or two ahead of inflation. The postwar pie was sweet, and big enough to pass around in generous portions.

Kenosha's African American and Mexican American workers, arriving in the city with the great migration of southern farm labor in the late 1940s and 1950s, also saw their fortunes rise. Like the ethnic minority groups before them, these newest "immigrants" were often given the least desirable factory jobs. But Local 72, working in partnership with the National Association for the Advancement of Colored People (NAACP), eventually saw to it that minority-group employment was expanded to all areas of the auto plant, and other factories soon followed suit.[4] Meanwhile, the second and third generations of Old World immigrants could take pride in family trajectories that were astonishingly steep. New homes in the suburbs, new norms of domesticity for women, and passels of children in station wagons were all, amazingly enough, within reach. Back in the old country, who would have dreamed all this was possible?

Making cars was something America seemed especially good at, and we were doing it right here in Kenosha. I remember when my grandfather drove home with his brand new Rambler. We all tumbled out of the house to see it, and neighbors strolled down the sidewalk to admire its aqua exterior and matching upholstery. As I bounced up and down in the driver's seat, wiggling the steering wheel to and fro, I heard my grandfather talk off-handedly about how his good friend down at the auto plant had inspected this car and set it aside especially for him. My grandfather was a tool bin attendant at another local factory, and to me at age six this car was evidence that he knew the most important people in town.

The future Kenosha's workers imagined, for themselves and for their families, was tied to prevailing expectations about the place of automobile manufacturing in the United States economy—and the place of America in the world. From the end of World War II through 1973, these expectations had a real basis in fact. In 1946 the average fifty-year-old man who worked full time had an income of $15,257 (in 1987 dollars). By 1973 a man of the same age and employment status was earning, on the average, $30,578. Families saw their incomes double, from an average of $14,830 in 1947 to $28,890 in 1973.[5] As economist Frank Levy points out, the rapid expansion of the postwar middle class was fueled almost entirely by this dramatic upsurge in real earnings. Rising incomes, sustained by strong economic growth and the increasing productivity of labor, put a middle-class lifestyle within reach of a larger proportion of the population than ever before in our nation's history.[6]

Upward mobility could largely be taken for granted. Industrial workers like Joe Gordon didn't have to elbow their way up the occupational ladder to see the value of their paychecks grow. The whole country was riding an up escalator, and workers could "get ahead" in real economic terms simply by standing still. This was true regardless of educational level. Although there has always been a wage gap between those with four years of college and those with a high-school education, both groups saw their earnings rise after World War II. In fact, as college graduates flooded the labor market in the 1960s and early 1970s, the wage gap between educational groups narrowed to a point that prompted some social critics to question the highly touted "investment value" of a college education.[7]

Rising incomes also eased the economic dislocation caused by industrial change. Despite recent attention to the "new" postindustrial society, the shift toward service-sector employment actually began in the late 1950s.[8] Then as now, service jobs paid most people considerably less than they could earn in manufacturing or other goods-producing industries. Workers who lost factory jobs in the 1950s often took as much as a 20 percent cut in pay if they found new employment in the service sector.[9] Yet even at this lower rate of pay, dislocated workers could expect to see their earnings grow over time and might eventually recoup their previous standard of living.[10]

The fact of market-driven upward mobility contravenes cultural wisdom. America's "success ethic" has always portrayed economic advancement as a matter of individual effort, hard work, and perseverance. It is the overcoming of obstacles, the spit shine, and personal gumption that we highlight when explaining our accomplishments, not the overall state of the economy. This is because economic actions are also, in a fundamental sense, *moral actions*.[11] How we act in the marketplace expresses and reinforces our commitment to basic cultural values like equality of opportunity, honesty, fair play, craftsmanship, thrift, and the repayment of debt. The American dream is more than a statement about limitless opportunity in the land of free enterprise. It is also a story about moral order—about what we owe our families, friends, and communities. Moreover, the success ethic spells out in no uncertain terms what society owes us in return for the hard work we do, and we measure the value of what we do in light of these expectations. Above all, the American dream tells us that success and happiness require work. They are not supposed to come as the surprise inside a crackerjack economy.

The plenty of the postwar years has affected the national psyche profoundly. Three decades of virtually unbroken wage growth have shaped the aspirations and expectations of several generations of Americans. During these years it was possible to believe that everyone was participating in the tradition of opportunity. There were still marked inequalities—between men and women, for example, and between blacks and whites—but the "rising tide," in President Kennedy's words, really did seem to be "lifting all boats," even if a bit unevenly. Within the framework of the American dream, most people could feel that they were working hard and truly deserved the good things that came their way. The Joe Gordons who made a down payment on a single-family house in the suburbs had no reason to doubt that they were just as entitled to a middle-class style of life as the schoolteacher who moved in next door. Hard work could mean punching the clock or cracking the books, and both conferred a sense of self-worth.

[handwritten margin note: always been a myth?]

Who Are the Real Middle Class?

During the 1960s and 1970s an intense debate arose in the social sciences over whether the new American affluence did, in fact, extend downward to include members of the so-called working class. Some commentators ventured to suggest that a "classless society" was well within reach, and that the working class would soon disappear altogether. Others hastened to decry the myth of working-class prosperity or *embourgeoisement* and the related notion of cultural homogeneity in the suburbs. Still others plumbed the depths of workers' psychology to show that working-class life, even at middle-income wages, wasn't always a bed of roses. Much of the disagreement among these social observers centered on the thorny issue of whether class position was a matter of income, occupation, or lifestyle. Nevertheless, most were concerned to determine whether everyone was sharing in the American dream, not whether everyone *should* be so fortunate.[12]

Definitions of what it means to be working class and how this differs from being middle class are notoriously porous. In general, the distinction is based on income (how much money you make) and lifestyle (how you spend your money). More academic, if not political, definitions stress the conditions of the work done (wage or salary, supervised or managerial), the sector of the economy within which it is done (goods-producing or services), and the skills required to do it (manual or mental labor). All these definitions tend to involve structural considerations—where a worker is located in some social, political, or economic system—and classify people according to an academic theory about the class structure rather than in terms of the way they classify themselves. When self-reports are considered, a curious picture emerges. As sociologist David Halle discovered in his study of an industrial chemicals plant, production workers think of themselves as workingmen on the job who enjoy a middle-class lifestyle at home.[13]

In this book I focus on the cultural meanings that ordinary people draw upon to understand their place in American society. The definitions of "class" that emerge from my conversations with people in Kenosha do not fit comfortably into a theory about "the class structure." Indeed, my work suggests that the issue of who is or is not a member of the middle class is now hotly debated *outside* the ivory tower. The economy and the occupational structure are changing dramatically, and people have strongly held, often competing, opinions about what this means for the class structure and the future of American society. The basic premise driving the success ethic—an expanding economy— has ground to a standstill. The stable world system that gave postwar America a steadily growing middle class has, since the 1970s, turned volatile and unpredictable. People are unsure where they stand in today's economy, and many fear that their present positions are far from secure. The American dream, for a substantial percentage of the population, has become an illusion.

More and more Americans are finding that hard work doesn't pay off the way it once did. A college education doesn't guarantee a middle-class lifestyle, and a factory job is no longer a ticket to upward mobility. The United States is in the midst of an economic crisis, triggered by the OPEC oil shocks of the 1970s and perpetuated by the overvalued dollar of the 1980s and soaring levels of debt in the 1990s. The consequences of these global events for American workers have been severe. Wages stopped growing after the first oil embargo in 1973 and have been stagnating ever since. The average worker makes no more today than twenty years ago, and many have even lost ground since the 1970s.[14] The up escalator has come to a halt.

Current macroeconomic trends are well documented by economists and political scientists.[15] Their research allows us to see how global events shape the market economy within which we earn a living and pursue our dreams. But an understanding of wage rates, industrial shifts, and employment patterns cannot in itself tell us how people experience and make sense of economic change. Few scholars have asked how the American dream has fared during this period of stagnation and decline in the standard of living people have come to expect.[16] The tradition of opportunity is based on the assumption of a growing economy, and its central tenet—the belief that anyone willing to work hard can get ahead—often proves false under conditions of economic contraction. For Americans like autoworker Joe Gordon, today's economic restructuring has resulted in a crisis of expectations. The old rules are not working: promises are broken, and the dreams of a lifetime have ended. For others—like the business managers, schoolteachers, and local politicians I met in Kenosha—the current slowdown is temporary, a necessary adjustment the nation must make as it turns the corner into the twenty-first century. This book explores the cultural factors that give rise to these different ways of experiencing and interpreting economic disorder.

The American dream has come under intense scrutiny before. In the early 1950s, sociologist Eli Chinoy asked a group of autoworkers how they reconciled their limited opportunities for advancement in the factory system with America's ethic of success. How do production workers cope, he asked, with the reality of their place in the social and economic order, given a set of cultural expectations that ties feelings of self-worth to upward mobility? *Automobile Workers and the American Dream* has become a sociological classic and remains an outstanding example of cultural analysis.[17] Rather than blaming forces beyond their control or berating themselves for not rising higher in the company, Chinoy's autoworkers transformed the ethic of success in ways that enhanced their self-esteem. Financial security, not personal advancement, was the moral goal they valued and measured themselves by. In the 1950s and for the next two decades, this definition of success was entirely viable. But today, when economic security has become as hard to achieve as occupational advancement, can the American dream survive?

Plant Closings as a National Ritual

The toll taken by the current restructuring of the United States economy is not limited to lost jobs, sagging tax revenues, boarded-up shops, and vacant lots. With it comes the singular fact of uncertainty—not knowing what the next blip in the stock market will augur, what the balance-of-trade figures bode, or what the next day's news will bring. With the future uncertain and the economic foundation of past political coalitions in disarray, industrial centers like Kenosha have become the locus of intense conflict over alternative visions of the common good. A shrinking manufacturing base has made a hardscrabble life for trade unions, and as their memberships fade away, so too does their imprint on local politics and community life. New lifestyles and political coalitions have emerged to take their place, and the economic climate of old rust belt towns is changing.

The cultural implications of these changes are profound. For dislocated workers trying to find work in the new labor market, experience is no longer a guide to what the future may hold. Poring over the want ads and seeing nothing but column after column of seasonal, part-time, and minimum-wage jobs does not instill hope in workers who seek a smooth transition back to their former place in the social structure. The relocation of workers in today's economy is not a straightforward process of people moving from one fixed location in the labor market to another. As workers are pushed out of vanishing slots in the occupational structure, the structure itself is shifting and in flux. For millions of American workers who are faced with finding a new job in this changing economy, it isn't always clear how to get back into the workforce or what cultural rules prevail. Like Alice tumbling down the rabbit hole, these displaced persons quickly discover that following all the instructions and scraps of information they come upon can be dangerous and disorienting. Yet we have much to learn from their sojourn, for these culturally displaced persons are us.

Coming to terms with the collapse of the postwar order is a cultural problem that confronts every American, not just those in the rust belt industries. The social transformation under way is not simply an economic trend reflecting America's changing place in the world: it is also a cultural process. Many of the cultural symbols, beliefs, and values that once fortified a sense of moral order in our capitalist economy have been cast into doubt. When United States firms eliminate thousands of high-paying jobs in the industrial heartland and then employ workers at lower wages in plants built across the border or overseas, we can no longer assume that the interests of American companies are synonymous with the interests of the nation. When, in the rubble of a demolished plant, traditional manufacturing towns lose the central institution that has held them together for generations, the out-migration of working people can turn entire neighborhoods into caldrons of crime and despair. As loyalty to company in exchange for job security becomes an elusive will-o'-the-wisp for a majority of American workers, can we be surprised that preoccupation with short-term gain has replaced larger concerns about the well-being of future generations? When daily life on Wall Street or inside the Beltway is steeped in scandal and broken promises, the notion that anyone of honest character can succeed in the United States seems embarrassingly jejune. Even Horatio Alger's bootstrapping—the enduring faith that hard work will be rewarded—seems to have given way in the national consciousness to a renewed respect for the wily wisdom of Tom Sawyer painting the fence: the best way to get a job done is to persuade someone to do it for you.

Cultural systems respond to uncertainty and ambiguity by attempting to clarify and articulate the prevailing rules. "The cultural tradition of a people—its symbols, ideals, and ways of feeling," sociologist Robert Bellah observes, "is always an argument about the destiny its members share. Cultures are dramatic conversations about the things that matter to their participants, and American culture is no exception."[18] Economic change has meaning for every member of American society, not just those who are traumatized by it. Thinking of culture as a "dramatic conversation" leads us to wonder how an event like a plant closing is viewed by people in the community who do *not* stand to lose their jobs. A growing ethnography of plant closings shows us that dislocated workers often develop biting critiques of American industry in the aftermath of a shutdown.[19] Yet virtually no attention has been paid to the other side of these cultural conversations: the side that does not mourn the loss of old line-manufacturing and is, in fact, glad to see it go. As my research in Kenosha demonstrates, there are plenty of "urban entrepreneurs" out there who want to transform America's industrial landscape into a very different place. These self-proclaimed visionaries have also developed a symbolic language for expressing their understanding and tacit approval of deindustrialization.

The legitimation of industrial decline, like its critique, is a ritualized mode of communication. Both strands of contemporary discourse transmit cultural meanings that help people make sense of what is happening to the places where they work and live. The current debate over the "vanishing middle class" is a form of cultural ritual because it dramatizes something about the moral order. Ritual, in the words of sociologist Robert Wuthnow, is "a symbolic-expressive aspect of behavior that communicates something about social relations . . . [and] assists in *articulating* and *regulating* the nature of social relations" (italics added).[20] Plant closings, I argue in this book, provide the occasion for an important kind of ritual communication in American society. Every participant and bystander in a local plant-closing drama is drawn into a national "conversation" about cultural values. How should labor be valued? How do people demonstrate their moral worth? Who has the right to make decisions that will affect the whole community? What kind of country was America in the past, and where are we going in the future?

As a catalyst for ritual communication, a plant closing symbolizes different things to people in different social positions. The Chrysler plant closing dramatized a deep cultural antagonism that has long divided the city of Kenosha. At the time of the closing, an urgent need arose to articulate these opposing positions with as much persuasive force as possible. What was, and continues to be, at issue is something much greater than the six thousand jobs Chrysler eliminated. At stake is the future of a whole way of life and how social relations will be organized in a postindustrial world.

*read Horatio Alger's stories?

PART ONE

What Happened to the American Dream?

Hey Lee *—who?.*

Hey, hey Lee, why did you lie?
Several thousand workers now left behind to die
They bust their backs for you, hard as they can
If your sales are down, don't blame Japan
And where is the worker's protection plan?
Hey, hey Lee, can't you make a stand?
So you turn your back and you walk away
Hey, hey Lee, that ain't the American way

Chorus:
Kenosha had a dream
That the plant would live on
And the people would grow strong
Kenosha had a dream
But then Lee lied

Newspaper said new car sales are down
How much longer can Chrysler keep you around?
Now you're thinking of takin' a dollar an hour away
Will Kenosha's doors be open longer that way?
How could you ever think that way?
Hey, hey Lee, give up some of your big pay
Governor Thompson even trusted you
Hey, hey Lee, you let him down, too

(Repeat chorus)

CHAPTER ONE

Kenosha Had a Dream

Early settlers streamed to the western shore of Lake Michigan with dreams of developing major centers of commerce. Frontier literature made sweeping claims about many a small village or port, promoting these fledgling outposts as the new rivals of Philadelphia, Boston, or New York. Such visions of greatness were not unreasonable in the 1830s. Chicago was little more than a fort in the wilderness, and fewer than 1,700 people lived around the harbor of Milwaukee.[1] When claims were laid at Southport, Wisconsin, in 1835, anything seemed possible.

The bustling village of Southport was incorporated as a city within a county in 1850. The new city and county were both named Kenosha after *kenozia,* an Indian word for "pike," the freshwater fish that teemed in the city's natural harbor and river inlets. Settlers from New England constituted over 70 percent of the county's original population. By the turn of the century, however, this Yankee-British core was almost equaled in size by an immigrant-derived combination of Germans, Scandinavians, Irish, and other northwestern Europeans.[2] Millions of artisans, craftsmen, and farmers came through Ellis Island with the first wave of European immigration. These immigrants came to an America steeped in the ideology of Manifest Destiny and the spirit of unrestrained progress. Westward expansion and the savage treatment of native peoples went hand in hand with a belief in the limitless potential of the industrial revolution and the moral claims of democracy.

3

The Jeffery plant, about 1901. Automaking in Kenosha began at the turn of the century when Thomas B. Jeffery purchased the Sterling Bicycle factory and converted it into a motor car assembly plant. Photo courtesy of the Racine *Journal Times* archives.

The Making of a Company Town

Drawing upon a wealth of skilled immigrant labor, the automobile industry made an early entrance into Kenosha's economy.[3] In 1902 Thomas B. Jeffery began producing his Rambler motor car in one of Kenosha's bicycle shops. Public response to the Rambler was overwhelmingly positive. Annual production rates at the Jeffery plant soared from 1,500 cars in 1902 to a remarkable 13,513 in 1914, the year Henry Ford inaugurated the first assembly line.[4] With a growing workforce at the plant and supplier companies springing up all around it, Kenosha's future was becoming firmly linked to the fortunes of a single industry. In the early part of the century, few could imagine an outlook brighter than this. The automobile was, after all, the wave of the future.

The Jeffery Company was purchased by Charles Nash when he resigned as the president of General Motors in 1916. The Kenosha plant soon stepped up production to crank out the new Nash automobiles along with military trucks for the Great War. By 1919 Nash Motors was the seventh largest automaker in the United States.[5] Nash opened additional plants in Milwaukee and Racine, Wisconsin, but the bulk of production always remained in Kenosha. And Kenosha was booming. In the 1900s the city was a small commercial port; two decades later it had become one of the state's largest industrial centers, ranking third behind only Milwaukee and Racine in the size of its industrial output. The city was rapidly developing a "monoeconomy" based on the manufacture of durable goods. The number of Kenoshans employed in manufacturing increased from 1,000 in 1890 to an astonishing 13,000 workers in 1920. Three out of every four were employed in manufacturing, and most of these workers labored in durable goods and primary metals industries.[6] With a workforce of 4,125 men, Nash Motors was the largest employer in town. Jokingly called "Ke-*Nash*-a" by its citizens, Kenosha had become the quintessential company town.

The rapid metamorphosis from village port to auto town could not have occurred without a bottomless pool of cheap labor. Between 1900 and 1930, eastern and southern Europeans flooded into Kenosha at such a phenomenal rate that the city swelled to four times its former size.[7] Most of the new immigrants had been peasants or poorly paid laborers in their homelands, and they were drawn to Kenosha in hopes of finding work at one of its many factories. Some learned of employment opportunities in the area from the enthusiastic letters of family and friends. Many were recruited by industry representatives who greeted the hordes of job-hungry immigrants as they stepped off the boats in New York and Chicago.

Russians, Italians, Poles, and other southeastern Europeans entered the ranks of factory labor at the bottom of the ladder, while descendants of the city's "old immigrants" moved up into supervisory and managerial positions. A similar process of ethnic succession occurred in the city's residential patterns. With the arrival of the "new immigrants," earlier ethnic groups began their exodus to the suburbs. The housing they left behind was in poor repair and primitive even by the standards of the day. Streets were unpaved, and the closely spaced houses often lacked central heating, electricity, or indoor plumbing. New immigrants accepted this inferior housing out of necessity to be within walking distance of the factories where they worked. Not surprisingly, the heaviest concentration of foreigners could be found living in the neighborhoods that ringed Nash Motors and other large factories.[8]

The clustering of immigrant communities in a few central city neighborhoods presented a serious challenge to the existing political order. Kenosha operated on an aldermanic system of government, which meant that representatives to the city council were elected by the people living in aldermanic districts or wards. As old immigrants left the city for more attractive areas, new immigrant leaders found it easier to organize political coalitions and elect their own representatives to public office.[9] The political progress of new ethnic groups depended almost entirely on the ward system, since this pattern of district-by-district voting enabled them to make the most of their numbers by capturing small units of government.

Successful old immigrants looked on these signs of progress with grave misgivings. Ethnic favoritism and other political skullduggery were thought to be rife within the new immigrant wards (surely not the case when the old immigrants were in charge!). Dissatisfied with the existing system and concerned about the growing political power of new ethnic groups, leading civic groups and women's clubs organized to press for change. In 1920 old immigrants won a "city manager" form of government. Under this new system of representation, the city council would be elected at large on a nonpartisan basis, which virtually destroyed the power of ward politicians. The city manager system was regularly challenged by ensuing local referenda, with the strongest pressure for repeal coming from new immigrant voters. But not until the 1950s, when most immigrants were naturalized citizens and thus eligible to vote, would the city manager form of government finally be repealed and replaced once again with the old ward system.

The ethnic conflicts that shaped city politics also played a role in the development of the local labor movement. In the early part of the century the Kenosha Trades and Labor Council (chartered by the American Federation of Labor in 1902) was not eager to unionize the masses of new immigrants who toiled in the city's most labor-intensive factories. Typical of the union movement in America before the Great Depression, early trade unions in Kenosha largely comprised skilled workers of British, Irish, German, and Scandinavian descent. There was little impetus for change until 1928, when a particularly violent strike erupted at Kenosha's Allen-A textile plant. New immigrants in desperate need of work refused to join union knitters in a walkout. The failure of this strike impressed on union leaders the dangers of a partially organized labor force and the urgent need to address this situation.[10]

Nothing did more to convince workers of the need for unity than the depression. The economic fallout in Kenosha was especially severe, leaving no ethnic group unscathed. Production figures at Nash Motors tell much of the story. From a peak of 138,169 units in 1928, production collapsed to 14,973 in 1933, a harrowing decline of almost 90 percent in less than five years.[11] Throngs of jobless men stood outside the factory gates each morning, desperately hoping for a day's work at the current rate of thirty-six cents an hour. Most were turned away, since Nash's hiring policy gave preference to former employees and married men.[12] Those fortunate enough to work held their jobs largely at the discretion of their supervisors. The humiliating practice of "basketeering" was common as anxious workers tried to curry favor with their bosses by bringing them baskets of fruit or garden produce.

In September 1933 the AFL chartered a group of Nash workers as Federal Union 19008.[13] Charlie Nash was strongly opposed to the idea of a union in his plant. Adopting the strategy of General Motors, Ford, and Chrysler, he tried to circumvent workers' right to organize by setting up a company union. Meanwhile, Nash was also attempting to institute a piecework system in his final assembly department. One of the first sit-down strikes in the automobile industry occurred in November 1933, when one hundred Nash workers spontaneously refused to work under the new system. Nash retaliated by locking out his entire workforce and threatening to throw the keys to the plant into Lake Michigan. A union rally was held that evening at the Italian American hall. More than 1,500 workers attended and joined Local 19008 on the spot. By midnight several hundred new union members were setting up picket lines around the plant. Under continuous pressure from the National Labor Advisory Board (NLAB), Nash eventually reached a settlement with Kenosha workers.

This settlement notwithstanding, union officials found it impossible to compel the company to honor its oral agreements and bargain in good faith. It took another strike, joined by Nash locals in Racine and Milwaukee, and additional intervention by the NLAB before workers received a satisfactory contract, in writing, in April 1934.[14] The success of these labor struggles was symbolized by the sleek new Nash Lafayette. When this classic roadster was introduced to the public in 1934, autoworkers at Nash could proudly claim that it was the first car in America to be built entirely by union labor. In that same year, Kenosha's Local 19008 and other auto company unions petitioned the AFL executive council for a national autoworkers' union. When the new international United Auto Workers (UAW) was subsequently formed, the Kenosha union was rechartered as UAW Local 72 in November 1935.[15]

The Rise and Fall of AMC

When the United States entered World War II, Kenosha's major employers received substantial government contracts for defense work. Federal dollars pouring into the manufacturing sector enabled the city to shake off the last vestiges of depression-era sluggishness. Doing its part for the war effort, Nash converted to the production of military aircraft engines in 1942. In four years employment doubled, bringing the plant's workforce to a new high of 7,300 by 1945.[16] As the demand for workers soared and as more and more men were recruited into the armed services, women began entering the labor force in great numbers. By 1944 there were over 7,500 women working in Kenosha, most of them in manufacturing industries. Within four years, women's wartime employment doubled the number of women in the labor force before 1940.[17]

Nash Motors merged with the Hudson Motor Car Company to create the American Motors Corporation (AMC) in 1954. Kenosha became the new company's major manufacturing center. Production skyrocketed as American Motors introduced its innovative series of compact cars. By 1960 AMC employed 14,000 workers, twice the number employed during the early 1950s. AMC distinguished itself in 1958 when it came out with the economical Rambler, named in honor of Thomas B. Jeffery's original Rambler built in Kenosha half a century earlier. In the early 1960s the Kenosha plant could boast of being the single largest assembly operation by volume in the United States. So large was AMC's local workforce that four out of every ten adult workers in Kenosha had a job at the auto plant.[18]

American Motors was ahead of the times with its popular line of small economy cars. From the late 1950s well into the 1960s, these cars found a market among cost-conscious youth and families looking for an affordable second car. Yet, as auto industry analysts are fond of saying, AMC may have been too far ahead of its time.[19] The 1960s and 1970s were years of steadily increasing sales for the domestic auto industry. Newly affluent American families were itching to splurge on gas-guzzling roadsters with snazzy tail fins or new station wagons with staid wooden paneling. Frequent trade-ins for the latest and priciest models became a critical status marker in suburbs all across the country. Before the first oil shock, conspicuous consumption seemed the aim—fuel economy hardly mattered.

Nonetheless, the market for compact cars was growing, albeit slowly, during the 1960s and 1970s. But the competition posed by small-car manufacturers abroad—first Germany and then Japan—plagued American automakers from the start. An overvalued dollar and foreign expertise in compact car technology proved daunting, if not insurmountable. Even though AMC was well positioned to compete in the compact car niche, it was handicapped by two factors related to its relatively small size: a limited distribution network and the concentration of its assembly operations in Kenosha.[20] To produce new car models every year, an auto company must be able to shut down production at least once a year to retool. General Motors, Ford,

Fig. 1. Aerial view of Kenosha's two auto plants. Photo courtesy of the Racine *Journal Times* archives. Under the American Motors Corporation, and later under Chrysler, assembly operations involved two plants located two miles apart. The lakefront plant appears in the background (*top*), and the main plant is in the foreground (*bottom*).

and Chrysler were able to do this fairly easily by rotating the shutdown periods at their many assembly plants. AMC, with its major assembly operations divided between two plants in Kenosha, could not afford to shut down for model changes as frequently as the market demanded (fig. 1).

In 1969 American Motors acquired the Kaiser Jeep Company. With this purchase AMC added to its lineup a civilian truck based on the design of the rugged World War II all-terrain vehicle. In the long run this application of four-wheel-drive technology would prove to be the company's most valuable asset and contribution to the industry. Unfortunately, however, as AMC's management shifted its attention to the new Jeep line being built in Toledo, Ohio, it began to let the company's core car business decline. This was an untimely business decision: the United States soon found itself mired in the recession of the early 1970s, and the public demand for economical, high-mileage cars was on the rise.

AMC's efforts to navigate the crosscurrents of an increasingly unpredictable global industry created a volatile situation in Kenosha. Year-to-year variations in production demands led to wide swings in employment levels at the plant. From 1960 to 1980, employment at AMC rose and fell by as many as five to ten thousand workers.[21] These massive fluctuations exacted a severe toll on the community's overall economic stability, primarily because the bulk of the local labor force was concentrated in the manufacturing sector. Virtually all of Kenosha's industrial employment—including that at AMC—was in the durable goods sector, which in itself comprised more than 90 percent of the county's total manufacturing employment.

changing employment rates (handwritten margin note)

Mirroring national trends, the occupational distribution of workers employed in Kenosha changed dramatically from 1960 to 1980 (see fig. 2). The greatest change occurred in the manufacturing sector. In 1960 manufacturing industries employed about 50 percent of Kenosha County's total civilian labor force. By 1980 employment in manufacturing had plunged by ten percentage points. In direct contrast, the service sector showed a pronounced increase over the same two decades.[22] Twenty years of declining employment in manufacturing did not, however, have an appreciable impact on the concentration of employment in the durable goods sector, which includes employment at AMC. By 1990, with the shutdown of the auto plant, total manufacturing employment in Kenosha plunged to 27.5 percent of the labor force, even though durable goods continued to account for 71 percent of the workforce in manufacturing.

Facing certain collapse in the late 1970s, AMC entered into part-

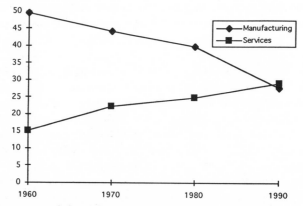

Fig. 2. Percentage of the civilian labor force in manufacturing and service industries, Kenosha County, 1960–1990. Based on United States census data and on data compiled in Southeastern Wisconsin Regional Planning Commission, *Kenosha County Overall Economic Development (OEDP) Plan—1985 Update*, 2d ed., Community Assistance Planning Report 74 (Waukesha, Wis.: SEWRPC, 1986), p. 107, plus 1990 SEWRPC data.

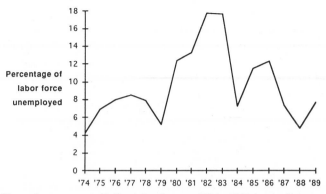

Fig. 3. Unemployment rates in Kenosha County, 1974–1989 (annual averages). Data from Wisconsin Department of Industry, Labor, and Human Relations, Employment and Training Policy Division, Bureau of Labor Market Statistics, Annual Civilian Labor Force Estimates—Service Delivery Area (SDA).

nership with Renault, the French automaker. In 1978 the two companies signed a master agreement in which AMC became the exclusive distributor of Renault products in the United States and Canada. Renault gained distribution rights to Jeep products in France and other overseas markets. Renault also agreed to invest $150 million in the Alliance, AMC/Renault's jointly produced car, in return for a 4.7 percent share of the company. As AMC's losses continued to mount in the early 1980s, Renault poured an additional $400 million into the struggling company and eventually became its major shareholder with 46 percent of the stock. Autoworkers refer to this period with lascivious irony as their company's "French adventure." Kenosha was still a company town, but its fate now seemed to rest uncomfortably in the hands of a fickle Parisian paramour.

The recessions of late 1970s and early 1980s hit Kenosha especially hard. Unemployment rates reached a high of 17.8 percent in 1982. As figure 3 shows, employment at the plant rebounded somewhat when it began manufacturing the Alliance in 1983 and the Encore in 1984.

The Alliance was selected by *Motor Trend* magazine as its 1983 "car of the year." This industrywide recognition helped boost sales, and AMC earned about $15 million in 1984, allowing it to capture a 1.8 percent share of the domestic car market. AMC posted its first profitable year since 1979—a minor miracle for this struggling automaker but a drop in the bucket compared with General Motors' profits, which topped $4 billion in the same year.[23]

11

AMC's shrinking market share loomed in the background even as increased production of the Alliance and Encore was a boon to Kenosha's economy. Thousands of autoworkers were called back to work in 1983–1984, and the drop in the local unemployment rate was striking. Celebration of this revival was clouded, however, as many in the community became aware of how disposable the Kenosha plant must look to decision makers in France and Detroit. Kenosha was AMC's only car manufacturing plant in the United States. Jeep trucks were built in Toledo, Ohio, and additional automobile production was slated to begin in 1987 at the state-of-the-art factory under construction in Brampton, Ontario. AMC owned its main plant in the center of town, but the lakefront plant was leased by a Chicago-based corporation, and that agreement was due to expire in February 1989.

Other ominous signs were gathering on the horizon. AMC's three-year contract with UAW Local 72 would be up for renegotiation in September 1985. This agreement was generally perceived—by the company and other business analysts—as the least competitive labor contract in the auto industry. The 1982 negotiations had produced several "pattern-plus" (better than the industry average) provisions for Kenosha autoworkers. When viewed strictly from the standpoint of costs to the company, these pattern-plus features seemed unwarranted and excessive. Under the 1982 agreement, hourly workers at AMC were the most highly paid autoworkers in the country. As of January 1985, an assembler at AMC made $13.38 an hour: this was 55 cents an hour more per hour than workers earned at Ford; 56 cents more than at GM; and $1.65 more than at Chrysler.[24] The worker-to-steward ratio in Kenosha was also eight times the industry average. In 1983 the company offered workers a raise of 25 cents an hour if they would agree to cut their worker-to-steward ratio in half, but the union rejected this offer.

Most vexing to AMC management, however, was the $133 million in outstanding debt owed to workers as a result of the Employee Investment Plan (EIP) negotiated in the 1982 contract. Under this plan Kenosha autoworkers agreed to defer raises, casual days, and cost of living adjustments (COLA) to allow the company to "invest" workers' forgone pay in new product development. The EIP agreement stipulated that these "investments," averaging about $9,000 per employee, would be paid back, with 10 percent interest, by 1988. How this repayment was to be made would be a subject of the upcoming 1985 contract negotiations.

For Kenoshans who pondered the "noncompetitive" elements of this contract in light of Local 72's reputation for intransigence, it began to seem increasingly unlikely that the next round of contract talks would yield anything other than a stalemate and a shutdown. Perhaps most troubling of all were industry rumblings picked up by those with an ear to the ground: tooling for Kenosha assembly of new models of the Alliance and Encore had been canceled, and no new cars were forecast for Kenosha after 1986.

A Whole New Ball Game

Two months before the 1985 contract negotiations were scheduled to begin, American Motors set a deadline for concessions by UAW Local 72 in Kenosha and UAW Local 75 in Milwaukee. The company was demanding nonnegotiable cuts in hourly wages, paid days off, and the ratio of union representation. Union leaders were willing to grant concessions, but they argued that these would have to be achieved through collective bargaining—not by company ultimatum. With the support of the general membership, union leaders agreed to open contract negotiations one month early, on June 11, 1985. On June 12, however, the key negotiator for AMC announced that if the unions did not agree to concessions by June 28, AMC's Wisconsin operations—the Kenosha assembly plant and the Milwaukee stamping plant—would be shut down. The unions steadfastly refused to comply with this demand, insisting that they could not be expected to bargain in good faith with a gun to their heads. When June 28 came and went with no change in the unions' position, AMC issued sixty-day plant closing notices to workers in Kenosha and Milwaukee.[25]

The issues involved in AMC's threatened plant closings went well beyond local labor-management disputes. Renault, with a controlling interest in American Motors, was determined to protect its multi-million dollar United States investment, even if it meant scrapping thousands of American jobs.[26] As the 1985 negotiations unfolded, however, debate within the community rarely focused on the broader international picture. The emphasis was on what the Wisconsin locals had not conceded and on what business incentives the state and local governments had failed to offer. Company officials frequently complained that it was "inconceivable" that AMC, the nation's smallest car company, should have to pay its workers higher wages than the Big Three—ignoring the fact that Renault's control of AMC largely invalidated this simplistic view.[27]

After fifteen days of "negotiations" in which the company held firmly to its initial demands, in June 1985 a final contract proposal was laid before Locals 72 and 75. The company stood behind its

13

threat to close the plants if concessions were not made. The union bargaining committees were given until midnight to reach a decision on the company proposal, which was essentially the same list of demands the unions had rejected in early May. The bargaining committee for Local 72 was warned that a rank-and-file vote would be held on the company's offer even if the committee failed to recommend its ratification.[28] Between the proverbial rock and hard place, committee members voted to recommend AMC's proposal to their unions.[29] The concessions contained in the new contract cut the wages of an assembler from $13.56 to $12.95 an hour, slashed the number of paid union stewards and officers from 167 to 28, repealed eight paid holidays a year, and extended the "loan" period of the Employee Investment Plan from 1988 to 1991.

Having won the labor contracts it desired, AMC withdrew its plan-closing notices and turned its attention to securing tax breaks and other government blandishments. A much-publicized search for a better "business climate" sent the Wisconsin legislature scrambling for ways to compete with other states for the new plant the company said it was planning to build. Toward the end of 1985 Governor Anthony Earl appointed his predecessor, former governor Patrick Lucey, to head a state economic development team charged with the mission of keeping AMC in Wisconsin. American Motors was considering a state-of-the-art plant that would employ at least 2,500 workers.[30] As the Lucey team began putting together an incentive package for building such a plant in Kenosha, state legislators geared up to debate the wisdom of providing a single manufacturer with state-backed loans amounting to $600–700 million.

These ventures were immediately suspended in March 1986 when it became known that the Chrysler Corporation was interested in using the excess production space in Kenosha for its aging line of luxury cars. Before agreeing to such an arrangement with AMC, however, Chrysler wanted a reduction in worker job classifications, a step that would entail another round of bargaining with the union. Reducing the number of job classifications involves collapsing the pay levels for different kinds of auto work. In addition to cutting costs—by paying lower wages for a wider range of jobs—it gives a company greater flexibility in making manpower moves that fill vacant jobs with "qualified" workers—that is, those with the same job classification.

Assured that job classification talks would not require reopening the 1985 contract, Local 72 agreed to negotiate with AMC in hopes of bringing Chrysler work into the plant. Management argued that satisfying Chrysler's demands would mean reducing job classifications from 166 to 35. Since Chrysler's interest in Kenosha was a welcome event to both parties, the union was able to keep AMC at the bargaining table and working toward a compromise, in notable contrast to the situation a year before. Eight days of vigorous bargaining in June 1986 resulted in an agreement that reduced the number of jobs classifications to 46. A week later Chrysler announced it would be transferring production of at least 50,000 its Fifth Avenues, Dodge Diplomats, and Plymouth Gran Furys to Kenosha in early 1987. In one stroke, 2,900 jobs were created. With the understanding that this line of cars would be built in Kenosha for at least two years, the Wisconsin legislature unanimously approved $3 million in funds to train AMC workers in the new Chrysler production techniques.

Later that summer, Chrysler indicated its desire to transfer another line of cars to Kenosha, this time its subcompact models, the Dodge Omni and Plymouth Horizon. AMC pressed Local 72 for further negotiations to reduce labor costs because of the slimmer profit margin on the subcompacts. Here, however, Local 72 drew the line. Flatly refusing to engage in new contract talks, union leaders asserted that the concessions they had already agreed to were more than sufficient. Local 72 held this stance until January 1987, when AMC again approached the union with a request to reopen the 1985 contract. This time the deal looked much sweeter. The newly elected governor, Tommy Thompson, had come up with a way to provide AMC with a state loan of $195 million for renovating and expanding its Kenosha plant.[31] In exchange for this loan, AMC would promise to bring a new Jeep model to Kenosha in 1989. Meanwhile, excess production capacity in Kenosha could be used to build Chrysler's luxury and subcompact cars. This elaborate plan would create 6,500 new jobs.

With the governor's plan on the table, American Motors insisted that Local 72 would have to accept additional cuts and a wage freeze, a five-year agreement, changes in the seniority system, mandatory overtime, and further reductions in the number of stewards. Union leadership countered that their current contract was more than adequate. A vote taken by the general membership to decide if the union should reopen its 1985 contract registered firm support for the position taken by the leaders. After this rank-and-file vote, negotiations on the proposed amendments to the 1985 contract got off to a rocky start. Bargaining jolted along over the month of February, producing little in the way of compromise on major issues. Then on March 9, 1987, in the midst of round-the-clock negotiating sessions, Chrysler chairman Lee Iacocca broke the stalemate by announcing that Chrysler intended to buy out Renault's controlling share of AMC.

15

This stunning eleventh-hour proclamation instantly suspended contract-amendment talks, and plans for expanding the Kenosha plant were put on ice indefinitely. In August 1987 AMC shareholders approved the merger with Chrysler, and AMC's Kenosha, Toledo, and Canadian operations were renamed Chrysler's Jeep-Eagle Division. For $1.1 billion, Lee Iacocca had acquired the nation's fourth largest car maker and its original Kenosha factory, the oldest operating auto assembly plant in America.

When Chrysler shifted production of the Omni and Horizon to Kenosha in the summer of 1987, employment at the auto plant bounced up to 6,100 workers as 4,000 people were called back to work. Kenosha was beside itself with relief and feelings of goodwill toward Lee Iacocca, the man who had appeared out of nowhere to pull the town back from the brink of disaster. The message that went up over a tavern near the auto plant expressed the sentiments of many: "Lee Iacocca for President!" it boldly proclaimed in block letters on a lighted marquee. Two weeks after Chrysler's show-stopping announcement, a full-color, 127-page supplement appeared in the *Kenosha News,* cheerfully titled, "American Motors and Chrysler: A Commitment to Excellence."[32] The supplement was packed with full-page advertisements sponsored by local businesses and community groups, welcoming Chrysler to Kenosha and celebrating what all hoped would be a long and prosperous relationship. Comprehensive articles by a *Kenosha News* reporter made up the body of the piece, offering Kenoshans thumbnail sketches of the key players in the Chrysler deal as well as a panorama of their city's place in the history of the American automobile industry.

Yet in a town that had long ago learned to look a gift horse in the mouth, the mood of grateful optimism was fragile at best. The consolidation of the two companies resulted in swift managerial restructuring, and more than one hundred white-collar employees in Kenosha were let go.[33] Industry analysts warned that the acquisition of AMC left Chrysler with excess production capacity and that the closing of one or more of its plants was inevitable. As early as October 1987, rumors started to spread that the Kenosha plant would be the most likely casualty of any corporate belt tightening. At the same time, Chrysler signaled its desire to start immediate contract negotiations with Local 72, almost a year before the old contract was due to expire. To many autoworkers, the situation was beginning to look grimly familiar. The threat of a shutdown lurked behind every action the company took. Moreover, it was agonizingly clear that even if deep concessions were made, there was no guarantee that a shutdown would not occur anyway. In this tension-filled climate, the union stonewalled. In response to Chrysler's invitation to begin negotiations in late 1987, Local 72 announced that there would be no contract talks until workers were repaid the $15 million in EIP money still owed them by AMC.

Meanwhile, autoworkers were operating in top form. The quality ratings received by the workforce in Kenosha were consistently higher than those in Chrysler's thirteen other assembly plants around the country. Kenosha workers rarely logged production deficits, and the number of repairs required at the end of their lines was almost always the lowest in the Chrysler system. When Kenosha broke a fifteen-year company record for the lowest production deficit rate, management stopped the assembly line to give workers a coffee break in their honor.[34] Few autoworkers were prepared to hear the announcement that came early in 1988. On January 27 a Chrysler spokesman announced that auto production in Kenosha would be discontinued by June 1988. Only the Motor Division, which employed about 900 workers, would remain open. The rest of the workforce, about 5,500 autoworkers in all, could expect to be without jobs come midsummer. The following day, the sign above the local tavern carried a new message: "Lee Iacocca Lied to Us."

CHAPTER TWO

Keep Kenosha Open!

When news of the Kenosha plant closing hit the national media, the Reverend Jesse Jackson was the only 1988 presidential candidate to communicate with Local 72, offering his immediate support. Within days of Chrysler's announcement, the Jackson campaign organized a massive rally in the parking lot of Kenosha's main plant. Over four thousand predominantly white autoworkers turned out in subzero weather to hear this black man speak, and what they heard was a resounding echo of their own feelings.

"The issue is workers in Kenosha and workers in Detroit against the multinationals!" Jackson thundered. "Stop putting profits over people, and put America back to work!" Driving the spirit of resistance home to labor, he continued: "We have to put the focus on Kenosha, Wisconsin, as the place, here and now, where we draw the line to end economic violence!" And linking contemporary labor issues to the powerful legacy of the African American struggle for civil rights, he asserted that "Kenosha could become a national symbol and rallying point for economic justice, just as Selma, Alabama, once was for voting rights."[1]

In March, despite UAW international prohibitions against endorsements by local unions, the membership of Local 72 voted to endorse Jesse Jackson's 1988 bid for the presidency.[2] Jackson's highly publicized visit to Kenosha was the catalyst that enabled Local 72 to put its own media campaign in motion. Autoworker Fred Shultz explains how this happened:

> The [Jackson rally] generated publicity on Chrysler that was astronomical. There was a barrage of newspaper people and

18

Over two thousand Kenosha autoworkers gather in sub-zero weather to hear the Reverend Jesse Jackson speak at a rally outside the main plant.

Jackson tells workers that they were the victims of "corporate barracudas" and urged them to fight for economic justice. Photos by Paul Roberts and the Racine *Journal Times*.

cameras that got national attention. Then Jesse helped set us up on an international basis with the BBC and some of the Canadian and Mexican stations. I was also instrumental in getting some information out about how Chrysler was treating its employees here in the plant. And it helped put a lot of hype on Chrysler, in order to embarrass them.

The notion that a major corporation can be "embarrassed," or "shamed" under the glare of public scrutiny is really quite remarkable. It assumes a popular consensus about the values and obligations that bind people together as a society, and it extends these ethical precepts to include not just individuals, but the actions of big business as well. Kenosha's autoworkers believed that the American people were on their side and that the power of public opinion could force Chrysler to honor its commitments and keep the plant open.

Fighting Back

Local 72's media war was perceived as fighting fire with fire. If Lee Iacocca had acquired his power by projecting an all-American image, then autoworkers would blow his cover by disseminating the truth. Jesse Jackson's presidential campaign seemed the perfect vehicle for doing just this. Fred explains why he committed an enormous amount of personal time and energy to traveling around the country, speaking out on Jackson's behalf, and telling people about the Kenosha situation:

> Chrysler has, for the last nine years, went around the country telling everybody we're the American company. The American people bailed them out when they were in trouble, and [the company] had lived with all of their commitments based on the American worker, and they really cared, and that's how they got the loan. I was there basically to tell them that Chrysler was no different from any other corporation, [and] that their sales had to be stopped in order to make them recognize that they had a responsibility to all the workers and not just their own pocketbooks. About that time Iacocca's wages was announced. So it really helped to generate a lot of press with that.

Indeed, 1988 was a year of record profits for United States automakers, up more than $10 billion from the industry's low point in 1982.[3] How could Detroit executives claim they needed to close plants when they were making money hand over fist? Lee Iacocca's $23 million salary gave the autoworkers exactly the moral leverage they desired. If Iacocca was willing to "give up some of his big pay," they argued, the Kenosha plant could be retooled, and thousands of jobs would be saved.

Joe Gordon was among the delegation of union representatives who went to Chrysler's annual stockholders' meeting, held in New York City the week after the closing was announced. The union delegation hoped to make a personal appeal to Chrysler's board of directors and, by showing their willingness to consider new contract concessions, persuade stockholders to join them in their fight to keep the Kenosha plant open. When the contingent arrived at the posh big-city hotel, they were promptly informed by the security guards that they could not even enter the building, let alone address the meeting in progress.

Undaunted, the group set up a picket line outside the hotel. In the blink of an eye, international press correspondents and New York camera crews descended. This was Joe's first taste of the kind of street theater the American media expect of newsworthy demonstrations. Reporters had definite ideas about what would—and wouldn't— make for a good thirty-second spot on the evening news. As Joe eventually came to realize, reporters were not interested in finding out what this labor dispute was about—they had their own story to tell:

> It was more or less the media was playing us against him. Boy, they loved it. They said, "How many people are you going to have here? Are you going to picket?" When [Iacocca] was coming out of the room, they all ran over to us [and yelled], "There he is! There he is! Are you going to scream? Are you guys going to chant? Are you going to lay down in front of him? Are you going to throw something? *What* are you going to do?"
>
> They were trying to egg us on. But we stayed over to the side. We did wave [to Iacocca] and said, "Would you come over here and talk to us?" But [the media people] could have intervened, if they were real honest about it. They could have said, "Well, I'll tell you what: we'll go in there and we'll ask the questions for you that you want to ask. We'll invite him to come out and talk to you, or we'll say, why don't you let these people in?" They wouldn't do that for us. They *liked the division* because their story was here's Iacocca and here's Local 72.

[handwritten margin note: Role of the press]

In the early days of Local 72's campaign against Chrysler, autoworkers felt they could take media slights in stride. Their attention was focused on the long-range goal: generating enough public pressure to make Lee Iacocca reverse his decision. So what if the press didn't always portray the autoworkers in the best light? Workers had dealt with these community attitudes and stereotypes before, and they seemed minor things to worry about now. Surely everyone saw how vital it was to stop the shutdown and save jobs. So what if the television cameras went to the local bars to interview people who spoke their mind freely, if unconventionally? At least their message was getting out to the American people. Even if the media did have their own agenda, at least they were showing the country what kind of man Lee Iacocca really was.[4] And that, after all, was what Local 72 most wanted to do.

Creative minds, and a hearty bunch of workers willing to stage a protest on a moment's notice, gave Local 72's media campaign a delightful touch of the outrageous. Hearing that Lee Iacocca would be in Chicago, two busloads of workers were quickly organized to picket the hotel where he was staying. Demonstrating in near-zero temperatures, they carried signs that read, "Thou Shalt Not Lie" and "Iacocca, Be a Hero, Save Kenosha."[5] Dozens of Local 72 members traveled to the Greater Milwaukee Auto Show to picket and hand out leaflets about the shutdown. Union leaders purchased space on billboards in Detroit and on buses in Madison to carry messages to Iacocca and Governor Thompson, urging the one to change his mind and the other to file a lawsuit against Chrysler. Learning that Lee Iacocca would be at the winter Olympics in Calgary, Local 72 dipped into its war chest to hire an airplane that circled the site trailing a banner that read "Keep Kenosha Open!"

More than sixty workers picketed the hotel in Milwaukee where Lee Iacocca was holding a hastily called press conference in mid-February. Huddled outside in the cold, they listened to a live radio broadcast of Iacocca's pitch to the media. To their amazement and horror, Iacocca was announcing Chrysler's intent to establish a "trust fund" for its Kenosha employees. The fund was to be financed through company contributions of the net profit on all cars and trucks sold in Wisconsin during 1988. Based on sales figures from 1987, the company estimated that the fund would amount to $20 million. Autoworkers were quick to denounce Iacocca's offer as "damage control" and a "neat public relations ploy." They saw the trust fund as a last-ditch effort to thwart a union-led boycott and discourage public interest in a state lawsuit. The trust would not replace a lost payroll of $800–900 million, and it included no provision for returning the $133 million still owed to workers under the Employee Investment Plan they had negotiated with AMC. Nor would it do anything to ease the costs to taxpayers as unemployment benefits, welfare payments, and added social services began to drain city and state coffers.[6]

22

Chrysler chairman Lee Iacocca announces the creation of a trust fund for Kenosha autoworkers, financed by profits made on all Chrysler vehicles sold in Wisconsin. Photo by Charles S. Vallone and the Racine *Journal Times*.

The shop chairman said Lee Iacocca's performance reminded him of an old Jesse James movie:

> Jesse James rode into town and robbed the bank, just like Iacocca came to town and robbed us of our new plant and our new product. As he rode out of town with the posse in hot pursuit, he looked over at his brother Frank and smiled, opened his saddlebag and threw a little bit of money behind him. The next thing you know, the posse was back there fighting over the money. And that's just what you saw today from Mr. Iacocca—a Jesse James performance: come to town, steal our new plant, steal our new product, and then throw a few dollars behind him on the way out of town.

The establishment of the trust fund, however, did appear to have its intended effect. There was a perceptible shift in the attitudes of local and state officials, who began to talk more openly about reaching an out-of-court settlement with Chrysler. Their responses expressed "cautious optimism" that the company had taken a "step forward" and suggested that "it might be too cynical" to believe that Chrysler's motives were entirely mercenary.[7]

The Lawsuits

In March 1988 Local 72 opened talks with Chrysler on the contract that would cover Kenosha autoworkers when their 1985 agreement with AMC expired in September. A critical component of these negotiations concerned Local 72's status within the UAW international and whether the Kenosha local would be included as a full member of the UAW council.[8] As matters stood, the UAW vice president in charge of the international's Chrysler department had recently denounced Chrysler's labor relations as "the worst in 30 years."[9] The automaker was facing strike threats at many of its key supplier plants over the proposed sale of its Acustar parts manufacturing division. Local 72 had already declared it would join a strike and "do whatever it takes to make sure Lee Iacocca's image becomes tarnished."[10] Labor tensions reached the snapping point when Chrysler announced it would be transferring a line of cars from a plant in Detroit to one in Mexico to make room for the Omni and Horizon cars it was taking out of Kenosha. This news prompted the UAW vice president to threaten Chrysler with a suspension of national negotiations, adding that if these talks were derailed, "the chances of a strike in September would be 95 percent or better."[11] The membership of Local 72 reacted with a quick and overwhelming vote authorizing union leaders to declare a strike if it became necessary.

Out of this heated atmosphere came the surprising announcement that the Kenosha plant closing would be delayed. Originally scheduled to close in July 1988, the plant was now slated to continue producing Chrysler's subcompact and luxury models until the end of the year.[12] In a statement explaining the reason for the extension, Lee Iacocca pointed out that sales of the cars being built in Kenosha continued to be strong, and therefore current production arrangements would be satisfactory for the time being. Iacocca took pains to emphasize that this revised production schedule was only a temporary reprieve. At year's end, luxury car production would cease and the subcompacts would go to Detroit. Let there be no doubt about it, he stressed; assembly operations in Kenosha were unequivocally coming to an end.

After reaching a contract settlement with Chrysler in May 1988, Local 72 decided to drop the federal lawsuit it had filed against the company earlier in the year. This legal challenge had been based on the assumption that Chrysler intended to close the plant without discontinuing the subcompact cars it was building in Kenosha. Although the company said it planned to discontinue its luxury models when the plant closed, there were persistent rumors that these models would be resurrected and moved to underutilized Chrysler plants in Mexico and in Windsor, Ontario. The Omni/Horizon line was being shifted to Chrysler's old Jefferson Avenue plant in Detroit. Autoworkers believe that Detroit's mayor Coleman Young was putting pressure on Chrysler to maintain employment levels at this aging factory until a new plant, under construction nearby, was completed. The union's lawsuit alleged that this transfer of work involved a misuse of federal funds.[13]

Union officials pointed out that even had their lawsuit been won, it would not have prevented Chrysler from moving work out of Kenosha. The threat to sue had served its purpose as a bargaining chip during contract negotiations, they argued, giving the bargaining committee the leverage it needed to win an additional $200 million in benefits for the Kenosha workforce.[14] Union officials were optimistic that effective pressure was being applied on Chrysler by the UAW international. They attributed Kenosha's six months of additional assembly work to the strike threatened by the international, which appeared to be preventing, or at least delaying, the transfer of cars to Mexico. Nonetheless, the shop chairman reminded workers that though they could feel good about the contract they had achieved, the fight to save their jobs was not over. The only way car production could be kept in Kenosha, the leader of Local 72 believed, was for the governor and local officials to seek a court injunction against the transfer of cars to Detroit while the state's breach-of-contract lawsuit was in litigation.[15]

Autoworkers had every reason to believe that state and local officials would seek a court injunction to keep jobs in Kenosha. The city council and county board had voted unanimously to pursue all means of legal redress,[16] and the governor had thrown his weight behind a state-sponsored lawsuit.[17] Addressing union members as a guest speaker that spring, Governor Tommy Thompson told autoworkers that he was "damn serious" about a lawsuit. He vowed that he was not afraid to file it, even though many had advised him to drop it, saying that "if companies cannot keep their word, we don't want them in Wisconsin!" The union hall was festooned with cheerful banners that read, "We Love You Gov. Thompson." The governor was given a special plaque thanking him for his "efforts to retain and to bring new work to the community and the Kenosha facilities."[18] Members of Wisconsin's congressional delegation also went on the warpath, charging that Chrysler had agreed to continue production in Kenosha for five years in exchange for substantial financial assistance from state and local governments.[19] In taking steps like these, politicians in Kenosha and Wisconsin joined an increasing number of local and state officials around the country who have begun to insist that the plants they subsidize must remain in business, in place, for as long as they are profitable.[20]

The state lawsuit was never filed. In the fall of 1988 Chrysler offered the city and county of Kenosha a plant-closing deal. This "memorandum of understanding" consisted of a package of community benefits, contributions, and reimbursements valued at nearly $200 million. In exchange for this plant-closing package, Kenosha officials would agree not to sue the corporation. The governor of Wisconsin told local officials that the decision was in their hands—if they still wanted to sue, the state would go forward; if they didn't, the lawsuit would be dropped.

At a public "town hall" meeting in September, Kenosha's politicians agreed to forgo a lawsuit and accept the memorandum of understanding.[21] Autoworkers who dearly wanted to see the plant reopened were outraged by this "sellout." Save for the offer of direct reimbursements to the city and county, virtually all the "concessions" featured in this plant-closing package were, item for item, reiterations of terms the company had already agreed to in its contract with Local 72. In the eyes of most autoworkers, the common council's decision to forgo legal action—and thus allow the plant closing to proceed—was a betrayal. The meeting grew so heated and potentially violent that politicians had to be escorted out of the building by police. Shots were fired at the mayor's house, and aldermen who voted against the lawsuit received death threats.

The Politics of Place

We tend to think of the decline of manufacturing as a kind of linear evolution from an industrial past to a postindustrial future. From a cultural standpoint, however, this is not an orderly or smooth transition. It is not simply a matter of people moving from one form of work to another, with a few unemployed scattered along the way. Dislocated industrial workers, their families, and their communities are struggling to preserve a way of life against the threat of social disorder. What we see is not a value-neutral evolution in technology, but a battle for culturally contested terrain.

In traditional manufacturing towns in the Midwest, the cultural debate about industrial change often finds its clearest expression in the political arena, as competing interpretations of a pivotal event like a plant closing vie for cultural legitimacy. The changing occupational structure in these rust belt towns has generated dramatic shifts in the political power of local interest groups. The old blue-collar coalitions have largely given way to a new breed of politician: young middle-class professionals who have a radically different vision of the city's future.

The debate over deindustrialization in these communities is fundamentally a debate about who is going to control the future. Whose interests will be uppermost on city hall's agenda? Whose cultural values and lifestyle preferences will be taken into account as plans are laid for economic development? And who, when push comes to shove, will be considered most qualified to lead these gritty lunchbox towns into the twenty-first century—a century in which computers, telecommunications, and fax machines will be as central to industry as assembly lines and steel mills were in the past?

When the last cars ever to be made in Kenosha bumped off the line two days before Christmas 1988, many workers cried quietly, and many gathered to record the event with video cameras and pocket Instamatics. To them it seemed certain that without the auto plant, Kenosha had no future. The old blue-collar world they knew had come to an end, and it seemed impossible to imagine another in its place. Many of the cultural rules and expectations that world had been built on were now in doubt. The sense of being cast into a "Loony Tunes" cartoon was captured by a hand-made drawing placed on the hood of the last car coming down the line. Carrot in hand, Bugs Bunny says with a rabbity grin, "That's all, folks!"[22]

The autoworkers' pessimism was not, for the most part, shared by the rest of the community. In the months before the closing, the city elected a youthful new mayor who billed himself as the "man for the time." To many in Kenosha's white-collar middle class, this former marketing executive was the perfect tonic for the unions' prophecies of doom and gloom. "We are at a crossroads," the newly elected mayor said of the plant closing. "There is the fork of danger, and there is the fork of opportunity. We are moving along the fork of opportunity."[23] The mayor's gospel of civic self-assurance has been matched by a mood of buoyant optimism on the part of city officials, business leaders, and development boosters. "Sooner or later it was going to happen to us," the city spokesman declared after the shutdown. "We're shifting from a more blue-collar to a white-collar community."[24]

Viewing this shift as highly desirable, local officials have made economic development and diversification a top priority, determined to turn a potential crisis into an opportunity for redevelopment. At the time of the shutdown, the unemployment rate stood at 3.5 percent, and state job service analysts were predicting that the dislocation of 5,500 autoworkers would boost that rate to 12 percent within the next year.[25] The loss of an estimated $130 million in annual payroll and $1.2 million in city property taxes was bound to create serious hardship for small businesses throughout the area. New business development has been actively courted with an array of incentives and tax breaks. The city council and county board are prepared to pour millions of dollars into tourism and promotional marketing. Political and business leaders are convinced that these pro-growth, supply-side strategies are the only way to ensure economic recovery.[26]

A year after the shutdown, the successful results of this approach appeared to be springing up everywhere. Real estate sales were brisk. Shoppers were packing the malls and factory outlet stores. Out-of-town developers expressed keen interest in the area. Local business firms were expanding, and unemployment had been held below 5 percent. By January 1990, many proclaimed that Kenosha had become "Boom County."[27]

Kenosha's politicians and middle-class professionals believe that aggregate growth in the private sector will eventually benefit everyone in the community.[28] Even so, some professionals privately concede that the city's fortuitous location between Milwaukee and Chicago accounts for a major portion of the new development it has enjoyed. Ten million people live within seventy-five miles of Kenosha. Escalating land values and a large traffic volume in the metropolitan corridor have spurred new growth of all kinds.

Illinois home buyers have flocked to Kenosha, where housing and living costs are still significantly lower than across the state line in adjoining Lake County.[29] Retail stores continue to pop up along the interstate highway, and new companies are rapidly filling Kenosha's industrial parks. With dog racing illegal in Illinois, the construction of a greyhound track in Kenosha County is expected to draw almost two million visitors a year.[30] When the auto plant closed, forty acres of prime lakefront property became available for private development. Within days of the decision not to sue Chrysler for a breach of contract, the common council approved a $14 million bond to seed the construction of a $41 million marina. Investors estimate that 70 percent of the six hundred boat slips in the new Southport Marina will be rented by Illinois residents.

The decline of manufacturing leaves its most permanent mark on the urban landscapes it is irrevocably changing. As economic restructuring alters our roles in the marketplace, it also reorganizes our sense of "place" as it transforms the character of specific places. Place is a kind of cultural artifact that dramatizes, in the rise and fall of various landscapes, the conflict and cohesion of the social groups occupying that geographic space.[31] Political conflict and cultural antagonism are expressed and experienced in the kind of built environments that rise out of the rubble of deserted factory towns.

28

A yacht club and a factory cannot coexist in the same place, not because such a juxtaposition is physically impossible, but because these uses of space represent different cultural identities. The new Kenosha, like urban areas all across the country, is being designed to project an image of contented consumption and respectable leisure—the promised rewards of a professional-managerial lifestyle.[32] Banished forever from the center of town is the image of sweaty, brutalizing labor—the tavern on every corner life of the old blue-collar community.

CHAPTER THREE

Dollars and Diplomas

At thirty-eight years old, Steve Miller had eighteen years' seniority at the auto plant. In another twelve years he would have been eligible for early retirement. Without this goal to work toward, Steve feels confused and disoriented:

> It's really hard to describe the feeling that you have when all of a sudden you don't have a job anymore—especially after all them years. You're under pressure every day, and you just don't know how you can relieve that pressure. You're kinda in limbo. You're kinda hung out at the end of the pole to dry. It's a tough situation. You don't know where you're gonna go, or what you're gonna do for a living. I worry about the kids, how I'm gonna get them through college. It's rough . . . it's pretty bad.

For industrial workers at the peak of their working lives, job loss instantly nullifies the principle of seniority around which so much of their life has been structured. It used to be that seniority protected you from the waves of layoffs so frequent in the volatile auto industry. And every year worked at the plant built up "equity" in the substantial retirement package you could plan on receiving at the end of thirty years. But a plant closing forecloses this sense of working toward a secure future. In the Kenosha shutdown, many workers were under forty and thus too young to qualify for the special retirement benefits Chrysler agreed to give older workers dislocated by the plant closing.[1] Two years shy of forty, Steve feels his eighteen years of seniority are now almost worthless:

30

Protesters jam the meeting room where Kenosha's county board and city council convened to vote on Chrysler's offer of a plant-closing settlement package. Photo by
Charles S. Vallone and the Racine *Journal Times.*

I'll get partial pension when I'm sixty and no insurance. But
if I was forty years old, I could get my partial pension when
I'm fifty-five *and* insurance. If they wouldn't have closed
down, in two more years, then at least after fifty-five, I'd have
my insurance. But they cut it off at forty years of age, and
anybody that was under forty [gets] nothing.

Workers know that a partial pension is better than no pension at
all, but they share an overriding feeling that they are the victims of a
cruel hoax. After all, they weren't banking on a partial pension. Many
pushed themselves to continue working at the auto plant year after
year because the promise of retirement benefits made it seem worthwhile. Most had every intention of staying until they reached that
goal. It is as if they have charted the course of their lives with a com-
pass fixed steadily on the north pole and have come halfway round
the world only to discover someone has moved the goal.[2]

Connie Miller shares her husband's feeling of constant pressure
since the closing was announced. She worries whether Steve will find
a decent job, one that can support a family of four on a single income
and allow them to maintain their present lifestyle:

> I could think about finding a job too, you know, but we really feel strongly about the mom being home with the kids. [Our daughter] is a year and a half. We don't want anyone else raising her. That was one of the nice things about Steve working at the plant—and probably for other people, too—that it enabled me to stay home with the kids and only work very part-time. Instead of like having to go and work some dumb job, and ship them off to a day care and let someone else raise them. We just don't believe in that.

Women like Connie belong to a generation for which the nature of family roles is far more open to individual choice than ever in our nation's history. Connie herself worked in the auto plant for several years before her son was born and has always planned to return to work when her daughter starts school. But as a mother, she feels strongly that her proper social role, if not moral obligation, is to stay home while the children are young.

Actions that may seem economically counterproductive—such as turning down a promising job offer, staying at home with young children, and holding out for largely nonexistent factory work—make sense when understood as a last line of defense against the psychological trauma inflicted by involuntary job loss.[3] Next to the family, employment is the dominant social institution in working people's lives. The workplace is more than just a place where we earn money. Through its organization and rules, it structures our daily lives by providing certain unavoidable categories of experience. In this sense work meets enduring human needs for time structure, activity, social contacts, participation in a collective purpose, and knowledge of one's place in society.[4] Steve and Connie Miller are struggling to maintain their customary lifestyle and honor the commitments to family that this entails, but the foundations of their blue-collar world have collapsed.

Where Have All the Good Jobs Gone?

For American workers in Steve Miller's position—relatively young men with high-school educations who lose jobs in manufacturing—finding a comparable replacement is virtually impossible. Getting another job is no longer just a matter of putting in applications at other factories down the street. High-paying industrial jobs have been drying up all over the region for years. Even if Steve is lucky enough to hire in at another local factory, wage rates there will be in the range of five to seven dollars an hour—half what he was earning at the auto

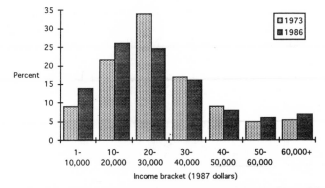

Fig. 4. Earnings distribution of prime-age men (men aged twenty-five to fifty-five who worked at least one hour a year) 1973 and 1986. Data from Frank Levy, "Incomes, Families, and Living Standards," in *American Living Standards*, ed. Robert E. Litan, Robert Z. Lawrence, and Charles L. Schultze (Washington, D.C.: Brookings Institution, 1988), p. 122, Fig. 4-3. Calculations based on CPS microdata files.

plant. If his experience is like that of most dislocated workers in the United States today, he can expect to suffer a 37 percent cut in pay during his first year of unemployment.[5]

For this reason the search for new work often feels like a no-win proposition. The competition seems too fierce, and the pie too small, to generate much hope of success. Steve admits that a lack of optimism makes it difficult for him to pursue all the job leads he knows he should. "I think there's just too many people out there looking for a good job that pays decent wages," he says with a sigh. "We're just afraid there aren't enough good jobs to go around," Connie adds anxiously. "There weren't before [the auto plant] shut down, and now there's even less."

By a "good" job, the Millers mean one that pays a middle-income wage to a person with a high-school education who is willing to work full time at a job in heavy industrial production. Connie's fear that there are fewer and fewer jobs of this type is well justified. Jobs in the middle range of the wage distribution *are* harder to find. As economists Bennett Harrison and Barry Bluestone report in their book *The Great U-Turn*, there has been a dramatic decline in the creation of good-paying jobs since the early 1970s. From 1963 to 1973 almost nine out of every ten new jobs created paid middle-income wages. From 1979 to 1986 that figure shrank to only one in two.[6] The impact of this "job shortage" can be seen in the earnings distribution of men who are twenty-five to fifty-five years old (fig. 4).

The largest drop has been in the percentage of men earning $20,000 to $50,000 a year. This is precisely the income category that Steve and Connie Miller consider "middle class," and indeed, by this reckoning Kenosha's autoworkers were all squarely in the middle class.[7] As they look for work in today's labor market, they are increasingly faced with a choice between high-paying jobs that require a college education or technical degree and "bad" jobs that pay less than they are accustomed to. The economic profile is not simply a picture of the "disappearing" middle class; it also reveals a steady trend toward a *polarization of incomes*. The proportion of workers earning less than $20,000 grew substantially in the 1980s, and the proportion earning over $50,000 also increased in size. Only the group in the middle has shrunk.

There is a marked regional dimension to the current pattern of income polarization. The Midwest, hardest hit by the decline of manufacturing employment, has witnessed the obliteration of virtually all new job creation in the middle-wage category.[8] As good-paying industrial jobs vanish, new employment in the rust belt has been almost entirely in the low-wage service sector of the economy (see table 1). Even for those who remain in the middle class, it has become harder and harder to support a family on one paycheck. In contrast to the rising incomes of the postwar years, most of today's workers have seen their earnings fall over the past twenty-five years. For the 80 percent of the United States population classified as "production and nonsupervisory" workers—for example, factory workers, construction workers, restaurant and clerical workers, nurses, and teachers—average adjusted weekly earnings dropped from $375.73 in 1973 to $335.20 in 1989 (see fig. 5).

In an economy where incomes are not growing, the only way workers can improve their standard of living is by moving into higher-paying jobs. They can no longer stay in the same job and expect to see the real value of their earnings rise over time as they could during the postwar years. For workers dislocated from good manufacturing jobs, this makes prospects in the service sector twice as grim. Not only will their initial wages be lower, but they cannot hope to see their earnings improve over time. The standard of living they lost with a high-paying industrial job will in all likelihood never be recovered.

Harsh realities like these demand an explanation. Why are millions of industrial workers losing their jobs and falling out of the middle class? Because our work is invested with moral meaning, we are not

34

Table 1 Percentage of Net Job Growth by Region, 1963–1986

	1963–1973	1973–1979	1979–1986
Northeast			
Low stratum[a]	(29.6)[d]	38.5	24.7
Middle stratum[b]	88.4	69.9	51.3
High stratum[c]	41.2	(8.4)	23.9
Midwest			
Low stratum	(5.2)	16.5	96.0
Middle stratum	81.4	80.8	(4.8)
High stratum	23.8	2.7	8.8
South			
Low stratum	(13.2)	16.2	33.7
Middle stratum	98.0	76.3	52.8
High stratum	15.2	7.5	13.5
West			
Low stratum	5.1	16.4	29.8
Middle stratum	75.7	71.4	60.1
High stratum	19.2	12.2	10.1
New England			
Low stratum	(70.7)	29.6	16.6
Middle stratum	117.9	66.7	61.8
High stratum	52.8	3.8	21.6

Source: Bennett Harrison and Barry Bluestone, *The Great U-Turn: Corporate Restructuring and the Polarizing of America* (New York: Basic Books, 1988), adapted from appendix table A.2.

[a] Low stratum = earnings of less than $11,104 a year (in 1985 dollars).
[b] Middle stratum = earnings of $11,104 to $44,412 a year.
[c] High stratum = earnings of $44,413 a year or more.
[d] Negative numbers are given in parentheses.

comfortable with the idea that misfortune of this magnitude can befall anyone at any time. We have a pressing need to determine whether this suffering was caused by something people did or is due to forces beyond their control. Are dislocated workers victims in need of emergency aid, or do they in some sense deserve this particular fate? How we interpret this situation will guide our behavior in the marketplace and, even more important, determine how we judge the behavior of others. Social scientists, policymakers, and the residents of factory towns all across the United States are forced to make this moral judgment every time new employment data are released, every time a new bill on industrial policy crosses lawmakers' desks, every time a plant closes.

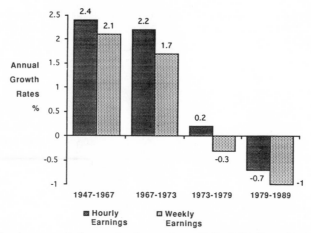

Fig. 5. Earnings growth for production workers, 1947–1989. Data from Lawrence Mishel and David M. Frankel, *The State of Working America, 1990–91 Edition*. Economic Policy Institute (Armonk, N.Y.: M. E. Sharpe, 1991), p. 74, fig. 3B.

Deindustrialization

When the Millers reflect on what has happened to them, they blame the United States government for allowing American corporations to move good jobs out of the country. Connie speaks for many Kenoshans caught in the plant closing:

> What galls me the most about the whole affair was that [Chrysler] shipped that one auto line to Mexico to build them there and put our people *here* out of work. I just don't think that's right. And [American businesses] do that with so many things! In the future, I see you're gonna have a rich class and a poor class and that's gonna be it. And I don't think that's right!

The "export" of manufacturing jobs is certainly an important dimension of the problem American workers face. Over the past twenty-five years, United States companies have built more than 1,800 manufacturing plants in Mexico.[9] These *maquiladora* factories employ more than 500,000 nonunion laborers under a program sponsored by the Mexican government, which guarantees American businesses a low tariff on the goods they ship back into the United States.

Capital flight—the diversion of corporate funds from investment in domestic plants and equipment into speculation, foreign ventures, mergers, and acquisitions—is the primary culprit that economists

Barry Bluestone and Bennett Harrison point to in their definitive account of what is happening to the United States economy, *The Deindustrialization of America*. "Deindustrialization," as they define it, is more than a descriptive term applied to the closing of industrial plants: it the "widespread, systematic disinvestment in the nation's basic productive capacity."[10] During the 1980s, Bluestone and Harrison argue, the overseas investments strategies of United States corporations changed dramatically. Instead of investing in domestic production for foreign markets, major industrial firms began producing goods abroad for import back into the United States market.[11] During the late 1970s and 1980s, disinvestment in domestic operations showed up on corporate balance sheets as "excess production capacity," and thousands of idled factories were closed.[12]

Economists disagree on the exact causes and nature of this trend, but few dispute that manufacturing employment in the industrial Midwest has been in free fall for the past two decades.[13] At no other time since the Great Depression has employment in manufacturing plunged so far so fast. From the 1950s through the end of the 1970s, at least 1.5 million manufacturing jobs were *added* to the economy every decade (see fig. 6). This pattern abruptly reversed itself in the 1980s. Between 1978 and 1982, one out of every four industrial jobs was eliminated in the nation's largest manufacturing companies.[14] As domestic firms continued to slash payrolls and close aging factories at an unprecedented rate during the 1980s, the number of manufacturing jobs lost soared past 850,000 in 1988.[15] If the 1980s rate of plant closures, layoffs, and forced retirements continues unabated, more than one million industrial jobs will be eliminated by the end

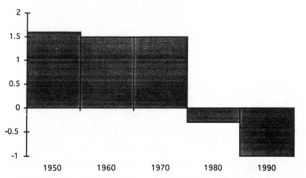

Fig. 6. Creation and destruction of manufacturing jobs (in millions). Projection for the 1990s is based on current trends. Data from Donald L. Barlett and James B. Steele, *America: What Went Wrong?* (Kansas City, Mo.: Andrews and McMeel, 1992), p. 18.

of the century.[16] During the 1950s and 1960s, one-third of all working Americans had jobs in manufacturing. That figure fell to 20 percent in the 1970s, and by the end of the 1980s, only 17 percent of the workforce remained employed in manufacturing.[17] Today fewer people than ever before can earn a living making things with their hands.

What Difference Does Education Make?

Donna Clausen is the wife of a tavern owner and the mother of four. She was among the thousands of autoworkers laid off in 1984. Just before her unemployment compensation ran out, Donna took a job at a local factory that was paying $3.75 an hour—a drastic cut from the $14 an hour she had been earning at American Motors. For much of the next year Donna and her family struggled to make ends meet. To their immense relief, Chrysler stepped in and called Donna back to work during the summer of 1986. It took the Clausens several months to get out from under the pile of bills that had accumulated during this nineteen-month layoff. "Even when the [1988] announcement of the closing came, that was the first week my check was clear, except for groceries," Donna recalls, "I was so happy—until I heard about the closing . . . that didn't make me too happy."

Like so many other Kenosha autoworkers, Donna learned about the plant closing while sitting at the kitchen table with her family, eating supper and listening to the evening news on television:

> It hit me like a rock. It was *terrible*. I waited until my kids were in the front room, and I said something to my husband. Because of going through what I did in '85, and you know, starting with the $3.75, I told him now maybe I can understand these families where the spouse is killing his children and his spouse and committing suicide. I said I can understand that now. He just looked at me really scared and told me I'd never said something so scary before. It's just . . . like my *heart* was ripped out. It's that I had to start all over again.

In the Clausen household, Donna's job at the Motors had enabled her husband, Teddy, to take the risk of buying a tavern and going into business for himself. Even when forced to work for lower wages during her layoff, Donna's steady paycheck saw the family through many bumpy months at the tavern, where cash flow is typically erratic and unreliable. Teddy's Bar and Grill is several blocks from the main plant. Weary autoworkers relaxing after each shift were the mainstay

38

of his business. The Clausens know they cannot rely on tavern receipts alone to get them through this critical time in their lives. With the plant gone, what will become of the bar and Teddy's first stab at entrepreneurial independence? Donna's deepest fear is that she will see everything they have worked for evaporate before their eyes:

> I would rather [kill myself] than have to put [my kids] through not having enough food or a good place to live. I'm not talking no hundred thousand dollar home. I'm just talking about a *nice* home. I don't want my kids to have to play out in the street because I can't afford to keep them out of the street. There's just too many kids that live that way now. Too many kids I see at the school that come half-dressed. And I just couldn't. . . . I would rather not be here than have to put my kids through that.

For a growing number of families, the difference between a precarious place just above the nation's poverty line and middle-class status is the contribution a working wife makes to the household income. This is especially true when women take on the challenge of industrial work, which is still dominated by men. Many women find the challenge more than worth the effort. Their income in durable goods industries is generally three to four times the earnings of "pink-collar" workers in the service sector.[18] Donna and her female coworkers often earn as much as the men they marry, or more; and many are divorced or widowed, struggling to support children on their own.

For families in which both parents are high-school graduates, the second income provided by a working woman is often the only way to maintain a middle-class standard of living. Over the past two decades, the wages of high-school-educated men have fallen significantly (see fig. 7); much of the "vanishing middle class" can be attributed to their reduced earnings.[19] Americans without college degrees constitute about 75 percent of the population, and their average incomes are now about 16 percent lower than they were in 1970.[20]

The earnings of men and women with college educations have not increased since 1971. From 1971 to 1986, however, the wage gap between college- and high-school-educated men doubled to 49 percent, with male college graduates earning, on average, almost twice as much as less highly educated counterparts.[21] The only group to see little or no change in average earnings has been female high-school graduates. Although stagnant wages are clearly preferable to falling wages, if these women are married to men who are also high-school

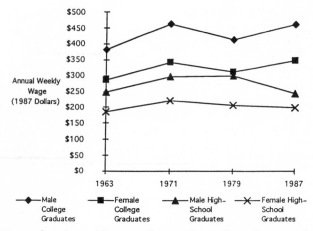

Fig. 7. Wages of workers with one to five years' experience, by sex and education, 1963–1987. Data from Lawrence Mishel and David M. Frankel, *The State of Working America, 1990–91 Edition*, Economic Policy Institute (Armonk, N.Y.: M. E. Sharpe, 1991), p. 98, table 3.21.

graduates, they must deal with the pressure of a declining family income.

Losing a steady income, insurance, and the perquisites of seniority is not all Donna has in mind when she experiences the terror of having to start over. Like many other autoworkers in Kenosha, her life has been shaped from her earliest years by cultural and emotional ties to the world of work in the auto factory. Both of her parents worked at American Motors, bringing home enough on payday to raise six children out in rural Kenosha County. They were by no means rich, but there was always food on the table and a roof over their heads. Donna has special memories of riding into town with her grandparents to pick up her parents at the factory gates. Uncles and cousins who had jobs in the plant would be getting off work too, and it was like an informal family reunion almost every day.

After high school, Donna enrolled in a secretarial course at the community college, but two semesters left her thoroughly discouraged with the tedium of office work and the prospect of low wages. When she got her job in the plant at age twenty, two sisters were already working there, and the fourth joined them a year later. For Donna, as for many others of her generation, automaking was "in the blood," and the plant itself was at the heart of an intricate web of family and community ties.

Changing Demand for Labor

Autoworkers like Steve Miller and Donna Clausen are caught in the crosscurrents of economic and industrial change. On one hand, they are victims of the overall economic slowdown that is affecting every sector of the labor market. College education or not, United States workers in all but the highest income brackets have had difficulty getting ahead or simply trying to make ends meet. On the other hand, Steve and Donna are being edged out of the shrinking manufacturing sector, and this has enormous consequences for their ability to find new jobs at comparable pay. Taken together, these two trends create an uncertain, if not bleak, employment picture for workers of their age, educational background, and region of the country.

In the early 1970s almost 50 percent of the workforce employed in goods-producing industries—manufacturing, mining, and construction—had no more than four years' high-school education. These production workers typically earned 10 percent to 14 percent more per year than similarly educated workers in the service sector.[22] As seniority-based layoffs ravaged the ranks of industrial labor during the 1970s and 1980s, young workers were the hardest hit. Not only were they the first to be laid off, but by the late 1970s jobs had become so scarce they couldn't get hired at most factories in the first place. The age distribution in the Kenosha plant clearly reflected this demographic squeeze.[23] Like a top-heavy tower of blocks, the older workforce teetered over a small number of people in the eighteen- to twenty-nine-year-old range.

The changing demand for labor in manufacturing and services industries has dramatically altered the kinds of job opportunities open to young workers. The proportion of young, high-school-educated men who work in goods-producing industries fell sharply, from about 50 percent in 1973 to 42 percent in 1986 (see fig. 8). Women with high-school diplomas were also less likely to work in goods-producing jobs than in 1973. Industry shifts do not appear to be affecting young men with college educations, however. Although the earnings of these men stagnated during the 1980s, service-sector employment alone cannot account for this slowdown. Indeed, rather than losing ground in manufacturing, college-educated workers were slightly more likely to be employed in goods production at the end of the decade (fig. 9).

These contrasting employment pictures tell us that the experience of industrial decline differs profoundly for people with different educational credentials. College-educated workers have been stung by

41

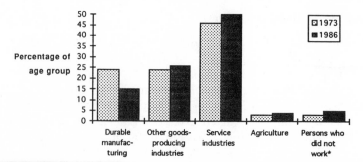

Fig. 8. Distribution of men aged twenty-five to thirty-four with four years of high school across industrial sectors, 1973 and 1986. (*Refers to persons who did not work at all during the year, including the unemployed, the disabled, and those who were out of the labor force voluntarily.) Data from Frank Levy, "Incomes, Families, and Living Standards," in *American Living Standards,* ed. Robert E. Litan, Robert Z. Lawrence, and Charles L. Schultz (Washington, D.C.: Brookings Institution, 1988), p. 152, from table 4-12.

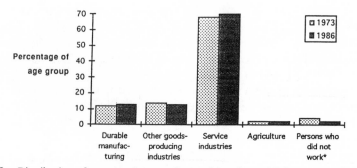

Fig. 9. Distribution of men aged twenty-five to thirty-four with four years of college across industrial sectors, 1973 and 1986. (*Refers to persons who did not work at all during the year, including the unemployed, the disabled, and those who were out of the labor force voluntarily.) Data from Frank Levy, "Incomes, Families, and Living Standards," in *American Living Standards,* ed. Robert E. Litan, Robert Z. Lawrence, and Charles L. Schultz (Washington, D.C.: Brookings Institution, 1988), p. 152, from table 4-12.

economic contraction, but the transition to a postindustrial society has had minimal impact, if any, on their employment opportunities. A starkly different situation confronts those with high-school educations. Not only have they seen their real earning power decline, but their chances of employment in high-paying manufacturing industries have decreased substantially. The way workers interpret this situation is rarely as pragmatic or instrumental as economists and labor market analysts would lead us to believe. More education is not always the best choice.

Luis Ramirez is the thirty-four-year-old son of a Mexican American sharecropper. He and his wife came to Kenosha in the early 1970s when her family, working as migrant laborers, came north to pick crops. Luis's first job at AMC was spot welding car bodies—one of the most strenuous and unpleasant jobs in the plant. Despite his strength and his capacity for hard physical labor, Luis admits ruefully, there were many times when he thought about quitting and going back down South. But eventually he was able to move out of welding and onto that part of the line called the trim department, where most interior and exterior parts—from seat belts to taillights—are installed. He has been in trim every since, for a total of fifteen years at the plant.

Luis heard about the plant closing on the car radio as he was driving to work. His first thought was that he shouldn't have bought the car he was driving, purchased secondhand a month earlier. Then he began to wonder if the news could be believed:

> Can't be. I wasn't officially notified! They've made mistakes before. But that's the only thing on your mind from then on. You want to get the newspaper outa the way. You want to get to a more reliable source, if there can be a reliable source. You want to hear it from someone directly, someone you trust. Who that is, I don't know.

In truth, there is no reliable source where blue-collar workers—or most other workers, for that matter—can get the information they need to anticipate industrial trends and workforce reductions. The management of American corporations is virtually a "black box" to the general public, academic institutions, and the United States government. Data about the linkages between industry, employment, and community upheaval are generally limited to what the industry itself decides to report.[24] Workers faced with a plant closing have little choice but to accept the word of industry spokesmen and assume that the company has good reasons for what it is doing. But as Luis says, representatives of the company are the last people autoworkers are inclined to trust.

Within the next week Luis must decide whether to accept a transfer to Chrysler's transmission plant in Kokomo, Indiana, or to begin a sixteen-week course on air-conditioning and refrigeration at a local technical college, where Chrysler will pick up the tab for tuition. Luis has three more months of unemployment benefits, so at least he can count on that income while he is going to school—but afterward, will there be a job waiting for him in this new field? "I've got two paths before me," Luis says, "and they both are . . . they both look promising. Which is good, I mean, for me. Some people, I guess, don't have that clear of a choice. Some are a lot worse [off] than I am in that sense. But it's just the anxiety—the tension—of having to deal with it, I mean, that's all part of life, true, but . . . I don't know, maybe it didn't have to happen in the first place."

Being forced to make a decision about a career change is quite different from choosing to make a career change. Not only must you deal with anxiety of the unknown, which is "all part of life," you must also come to terms with what you have lost—again, not what you have voluntarily given up, but what has been taken from you. If Luis chooses to go to school—not, I should point out, in a field of his own choosing, but simply in a class where there happened to be an opening during this summer session—he will give up fifteen years' seniority with Chrysler and all the retirement benefits he might accrue with continued employment. "And I hate to throw that away," he says. But deciding to go to Kokomo isn't without drawbacks either. "If I go to Indiana, I don't know if it will be permanent."

Luis runs an anxious hand through his thick black hair and looks at me as if I might provide the answer he is seeking. I encourage him to talk about his concerns in Indiana. "Well," he continues, "will I be laid off again, as this roller coaster thing has been going? Or do I keep chasing Chrysler around? Or do I just drop them and pursue a different career, where hopefully it will be a lot more steady?"

As we talk, I learn that Luis has been through a retraining program before. When he was laid off two years ago from AMC, he took a course in electronic servicing, for which he got a "vocational diploma." He had been told that it would be a course on TV/VCR repair, which looked interesting to him, given the four other courses he had to choose from. Once in the class, however, it became apparent that he was being trained to do electronic servicing for large factory machinery, not the smaller repairs he had envisioned. Luis stuck with the course even so, hoping that at the very least it would help him find a steady job. But once he graduated he quickly discovered that this training was of very little practical use in the labor market. To enter a career in this field, he would have go to school part time for another three years to get an associate's degree; and beyond that, most employees require four years of on-the-job experience. Getting through the whole program seemed like a very slow process. When

Luis was called back to the plant in 1987, he had no difficulty deciding what to do.

I ask him why he went back to the plant. As he reflects on this a moment, he smiles with pleasure at the memory:

> I was *happy* to go. You got that work family, I was telling you about. You've spent years in that plant. That's part of your life. All your buddies are there. The familiar surroundings are there. Your routine is there. The paycheck is there every week. I mean, the money is good. It's something that's sort of like a habit—a habit that's your *life.* Whereas, you're entering a new area, an unknown area, if you stick with school in another field. And it's . . . well, a different area, a whole new start. You don't know what to expect. You don't know how much you're going to be earning. You can't plan anything because you're wondering, Well, what if I make so much and I can do this or that? And there [at the plant], you know what you can do. You know how much you can limit yourself or how far you can step out.

When Luis talks of auto work as "a habit that's my life," he is talking about something much more important than a comfortable routine. Our sense of self—our subjectively experienced identity and feeling of self-worth—is intimately bound up with the kind of work we do. An occupational identity doesn't come from flipping through a college catalog and fantasizing about the person we might become if we take certain courses; it doesn't even come from taking the courses and receiving certificates and diplomas. It comes, Luis explains, from performing the jobs we know how to do and feeling that our actions are valued by others in the marketplace:

> Your identity doesn't depend on the actual [company or person] you're working for. I think it's mostly what you're doing. For fifteen years I've been in the automaking industry. I think there's a pride in being an autoworker. Yeah, you can identify with that field. You can be a carpenter, you can be a plumber, you can be a what-have-you. But I chose that. There's a lot of people involved. I think maybe I'm a people person. I like people, friends. That's got a lot to do, in my life, [with what] satisfies me.

So much for the image of autoworkers as depersonalized automatons. Work has meaning because it is truly one of the few ways in American society that people can demonstrate their moral worth. Every occupation provides a stage on which our moral character can be displayed, and an attentive audience from whom we seek validation and applause. But unlike middle-class professionals, who can transport their educational credentials and job history from place to place, industrial workers demonstrate their ability on the shopfloor and compile a track record that is inseparable from their place of employment. Linking place, culture, and identity, Luis describes how auto work has shaped his life:

> Kenosha has a history of [automaking], and it's the pride of being part of it. You know, it started way before my time, and just belonging to that group—there's a sense of *pride* in it. Like I say, being a part of the autoworker family. I think that's where it's at. You can . . . like I'm going to school and probably'll get into another field maybe, if I choose that. And I don't know, maybe years from now I'll be proud of being in that refrigerator/air-conditioning family. But this will always, I think, be Number One Son. The other will be probably a stepchild. [Auto work] brought me up, from being a kid, let's say, to being an adult. It's been with me all my life . . . you know, a *friend*. It's brought me a lot of good friends, a lot of material things. And I've expanded with it, grown with it.

Luis pauses, and then adds simply, *"It's been me."*

What does the future hold for workers like Luis? For families like the Clausens and the Millers? Much will depend on the choices they make. Much will depend on the state of the economy. And the two, of course, are intertwined. Individual choices and economic trends are linked by cultural systems of meaning that guide people's behavior in the marketplace and invest that behavior with moral significance. Whether or not these autoworkers go back to school or find another factory job, their lives, their sense of self, and their understanding of American society have been irrevocably changed. The American dream has failed them, and they feel betrayed. Hard work—the sweat in your eyes, backbreaking labor of the assembly line—has not brought them the success and economic advancement bestowed upon their parents' generation. How they reconcile their expectations with the realities of today's world is the subject of this book.

Much has changed since Eli Chinoy first posed a question like this to industrial laborers. The autoworkers he spoke with in the early 1950s found meaning in a distinctive version of the success ethic that fit in well with an era of economic expansion and cold war truths. Today Kenosha's autoworkers face an uncertain world and an uncharted future. For them, on one level, the American dream is dead. The optimistic spin of the wheel of fortune has turned treacherous and foreboding. On another level, however, the dream lives. It lives in autoworkers' feisty hope of redemption and interpersonal understanding. Why that hope is so hard to sustain these days is also the subject of this book. Economic change affects far more than our workaday lives. It subtly alters the ways we evaluate hard work and success, and it challenges our sense of community at the deepest level.

— But is this productive hope?

PART TWO

Culture of the Mind

For years the Motors kind of ran the town, and there was
a certain arrogance that people perceived among the
Motors workers. You know, they'd go on strike and they'd
fight it out with the factory, and the town would sit there and
go, "Geez, I hope they settle this," because everybody was
hanging in the balance. There was a jealousy, I think, from a
lot of the workers who couldn't get the same [wages and
benefits] that the autoworkers have. But now it's . . .
when somebody finally falls, there's always a whole bunch
of people to kind of gang up around them and point
the finger. Well, the autoworkers have finally fallen, and now
there's a big rush to say, "Well, no big deal," and to kind of
laugh up your sleeve about it. [People feel like,] "Hey, I went
out and I got a teaching degree, and I was a teacher, and
I'm only getting $18,000 a year and he's getting $25,000 and
he can't even spell 'education' right. Now he's finally getting
what he deserved." You know, the world is right: they're finally
being punished for their noneducation, and I can feel glad
that I'm not like that.

MEMBER OF KENOSHA'S COMMON COUNCIL

49

CHAPTER FOUR

Turning the Tables

By the winter of 1988, when the auto factory's gates clanged shut for the last time, a new breed of politicians presided over city government.[1] Elections in April of that year had brought the defeat of the incumbent mayor, a sheet-metal worker on leave from Chrysler, and the upset victories of six new aldermen. When added to the other "new" faces on the city council—aldermen who had ousted long-term incumbents in the 1986 elections—this group of recently elected politicians represented a complete turnover of the municipal government that had existed in Kenosha before 1986. These stunning upsets involved more than a sudden changing of the guard. The watershed elections of 1986 and 1988 ushered in a totally new kind of local representative. In contrast to the blue-collar workers who were regularly elected to public office during the prosperous decades following World War II, the new politicians are all young white-collar professionals. Coming from private-sector businesses, critical of the status quo, and eager for change, they appeared on the hustings in the mid-1980s with a radical agenda in mind. To the surprise of many, they were elected by landslides unprecedented in local history.

political corollary

New Politicians

Recalling this period, Brendan Woods explains why he and six other young professionals simultaneously decided to break the local "collar" barrier and run for the city council in 1986:

> The city has always been run by the union. After the problems with the [Renault] deal, there were a lot of concerns that

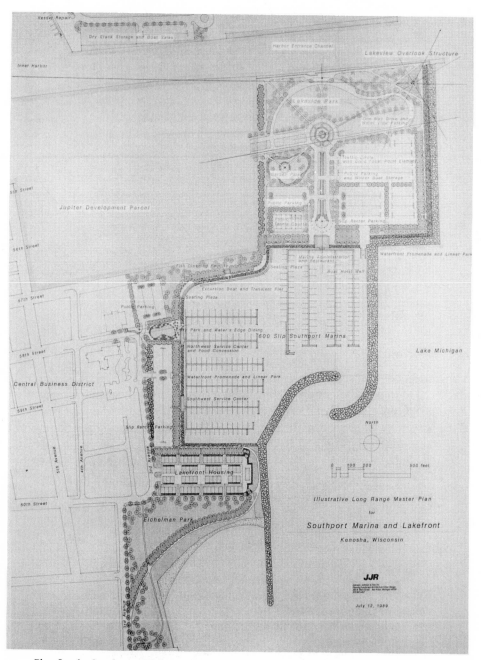

Plan for the Southport Marina and lakefront development. Photo courtesy of the *Kenosha News* archives.

the old guard was not managing things well. Taxes were starting to go up. There were no plans to diversify. There were no real plans for the future. The marina [project] was stuck and wasn't going anywhere. The new industrial park was empty. And people got scared. They said, we can't screw around anymore. And then a bunch of us, really unconnected with each other, all decided in the same year that we couldn't stand it anymore, and we ran for office . . . and they elected us all. They put seven white-collar businessmen on the council. Previously, I think they had one person with a bachelor's degree on the council. All of a sudden they had three people that had masters' and above, and the rest had bachelor's degrees, and those were all elected that year.

In 1988 six more professionals were elected to the common council, filling vacancies left by old guard defeats and retirements. To middle-class professionals like Brendan Woods, these victories represent a bold new era in local politics. Critical decisions about the city's future will now be based on sound economic analysis, regional marketing research, efficient urban planning, and a willingness to try new ideas and innovative procedures. Gone are the bad old days of profligate spending, union graft, and municipal featherbedding. Changing times require a change in leadership, this mode of thought goes, and only the most qualified, growth-oriented professionals can lead the city out of its current predicament. The new leadership could count among its members a panel of experts in the fields of law, medicine, social work, advertising, and marketing. In contrast to the old guard, denigrated as an amorphous band of factory operatives, new politicians consider themselves able to make distinctive contributions to the common good

Bobby Cannara is a new politician who was elected in 1988. As the son of an autoworker and as alderman of a traditionally blue-collar district, even Bobby believes that the declining influence of the local unions is a good thing:

It's probably one of the best things to happen to us, ever. We're getting off our butts and we're going to be doing something, whether it's helping the small businesses or diversifying the economic base. I can't say the unions were all bad, because I've got what I've got today because of how they helped my father and my family in the workplace. Kenosha's just gonna—in my opinion, we're booming. Because now we're worried about everybody, not just one group. So, if anything [the plant closing] made us realize that, Hey, take a look at yourself as a city and start to make your changes. Start to cut

53

away the fat that has to be cut in government, local spending, whatever. So I'm pretty happy with the direction that Kenosha's taking. But I still say you owe a lot of it to labor, and the people who stuck in this town.

In his effort to acknowledge the positive role of labor in local politics, Bobby Cannara is unique among the new politicians and other professionals I have talked with. One of the youngest aldermen elected in Kenosha, Bobby is a college student who still lives at home. For much of my interview with him, we are joined by his elderly father, who follows our conversation with great interest and every now and then interjects some thoughts of his own in broken English and in Italian, which Bobby translates for me. As Bobby attempts to reconcile the outlook of his colleagues in city government with the filial respect he feels for his father, I am aware of how poignantly he embodies the crosscurrents that are tearing Kenoshans apart. Bobby would like to believe in a bolder, brighter future that grows naturally out of the past—a vision of change and progress in which the past is not forgotten, but honored as the nourishing soil out of which all future life springs. Yet this sense of historical continuity has been difficult to sustain in Kenosha. The Chrysler plant closing dramatized a symbolic opposition between the past and the future, and when push came to shove, Bobby Cannara and other local politicians were forced to choose between the two.

Speaking to the people in a *Kenosha News* editorial written in the aftermath of the shutdown, the town's new mayor captures the essence of this symbolic opposition: "As we move into the 1990s Kenosha is going through a dramatic change. Many of the symbols of our past, both economically and politically, are being transformed and the seeds of our future are being planted. The greatest challenge the Kenosha community faces will be the ability to accept this change, and whole-heartedly support the transformation that is taking place."[2]

The symbols of the past the mayor refers to are, of course, the auto plant and the political power of the labor unions. As the wrecking ball swings and blue-collar aldermen are ousted from power, the seeds of the future are being planted in the form of a posh new marina and waterfront, high-tech businesses in the industrial parks, a revitalized downtown, and the character of the city itself. The choice, Kenosha's mayor implies, is absolutely clear. Citizens must let go of the dreary industrial past and embrace a high-tech, college-educated future. In this phoenixlike transformation, there will be no room for blue-collar culture, and no nostalgia for it either. The city has a new juggernaut, and citizens must fall in with the procession or be crushed under the wheels of progress.

New politicians speak of the transformation under way in Kenosha as if it were an evolutionary process so natural and inevitable, that—like the spectacular "rise" of civilization from the Stone Age—it must not be tampered with or impeded. The only role for government in this process, professionals argue, is a proactive one: evolutionary change can be promoted or enhanced, but never restricted or reversed. By defining current economic and industrial trends as natural and inevitable, Kenosha's white-collar minority is able to craft a notion of the common good out of a series of lucrative business investments, engineered by self-interested entrepreneurs and supported by tax dollars. Citizens must accept the challenge of unstoppable social change, new politicians argue, because in the end the speedy transformation of the city into a convention center, a tourist resort, and a bedroom community for Milwaukee's and Chicago's commuters will be good for everyone. Business leaders neglect to mention that the requisite "social changes" are going to fall most heavily on one segment of the population. Only blue-collar workers are expected to sacrifice their cultural traditions for the greater good of the community. No comparable sacrifice is being made on the white-collar side of this transformation. Efforts to explain this admitted inequity are couched in the symbolic logic of cultural evolution, and the blue-collar way of life is itself portrayed as an impediment to progress.

In this sense, criticizing the blue-collar "mentality" serves an important purpose. It is difficult for new politicians to claim a mandate for their vision of Kenosha's future on the grounds of election results alone. Their base of support has generally come from white-collar districts or evenly balanced white- and blue-collar wards. Kenosha's political leaders face the same crisis of legitimation that haunts elected officials at every level of government in the United States. Because a significant portion of the American electorate has simply given up its claim over the political landscape, the very foundations of democracy are in doubt.[3] For political leaders ushered into office by a narrow fraction of the eligible vote, traditional claims of a universal mandate—made possible by a decisive victory over the opposition—necessarily ring hollow.

Most Kenoshans, like their middle-American counterparts across the country, don't vote.[4] In the 1986 elections, only 35 percent of the city's registered voters hit the polls. The 1988 elections, held at the same time as the national presidential elections, drew 54 percent of those registered to vote.[5] In both races, new politicians won easily among the city's well-to-do voters. Quite likely, their new faces and ideas brought out a substantial number of white-collar voters who might otherwise have stayed home. But the undeniable fact remains:

blue-collar disaffection with the political process is always a ballot-box advantage for pro-business politicians.[6]

Voting patterns in Kenosha's pivotal 1988 mayoral election tell us a great deal about how political power is shifting in the nation's deindustrializing cities. Political turnover in Kenosha did not occur simply because autoworkers were misled or apathetic. In this race, Kenosha's blue-collar majority, and the autoworkers in particular, had their own candidate to vote for: Eugene Dorff, the interim mayor.[7] A member of the State Assembly for twelve years and alderman for nine, Dorff became Kenosha's mayor in June 1987 when his predecessor took a position in state government. By trade a skilled worker on leave from the auto plant, Dorff was the mayoral candidate officially endorsed by UAW Local 72.

Figure 10 shows the breakdown by ward for the 1988 mayoral election.[8] Successful in seven out of thirty-four wards, Dorff lost by margins of only five votes or fewer in four wards and by thirty votes or fewer in four others. When the distribution of these election returns is compared with a profile of the occupational composition of residents in these neighborhoods (shown in fig. 11), it is overwhelmingly clear that Mayor Dorff had the backing of voters in predominantly blue-collar, working-class neighborhoods.[9]

By contrast, Dorff's challenger, Alderman Patrick Moran (a new face on the city council as of the 1986 elections), drew his support from neighborhoods in which the occupational composition was either evenly balanced between industrial operators and managerial/technical workers or conspicuously tipped in favor of the latter. In a city where factory operatives outnumbered technical and managerial workers in 1980, this is the political profile of a city divided.[10] A widening chasm between rich and poor underlies this profile, as it does in so many American cities. Neighborhood surveys of the median family income, the number of families living in poverty, rates of homeownership, and median home values all reveal the same configuration. Old factory neighborhoods, clustered around AMC's lakefront plant and main plant at the center of town, have grown increasingly impoverished, while the upscale South Side neighborhoods and suburban perimeters continue to prosper. Mirroring urban areas across the country, this too is a portrait of a city divided.

The voting pattern of the city's neighborhoods highlights an important point about the political participation of blue-collar workers. When they do vote, it is often for the kind of candidate that professional-managerial voters rarely take seriously. When Mayor Dorff stumbled over his words at Jesse Jackson's rally in Kenosha and

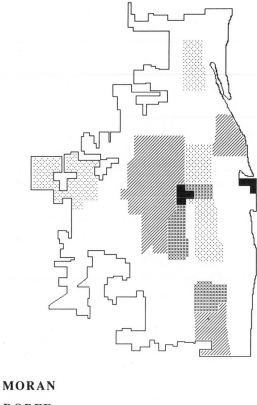

☐ **MORAN**

▨ **DORFF**

▦ **DORFF BY < 5**

▢ **DORFF BY < 30**

Fig. 10. Ward totals for Kenosha mayoral election, 1988. Data from the *Proceedings of the Common Council,* Kenosha, Wis., April 1988.

introduced Jackson as the "spearchucker" the country needs—rather than as the man needed to "spearhead" a movement for change—his political opponents were quick to condemn this slip as a racial slur and lament the "racist" image of Kenosha that Dorff projected to the rest of the country.[11] This despite the fact that Mayor Dorff took time out of his own campaign in February to stump for Jackson on a pre-caucus swing through Iowa.

Such incidents added spice to the blue-collar stereotype that new politicians invoked, to great advantage, in their campaigns against the

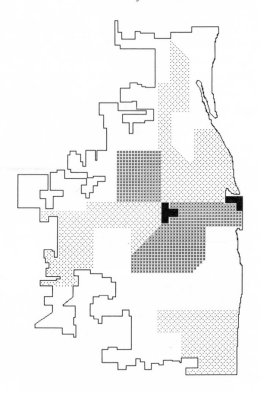

Ratio of Managers to Operators

☐ 0–50%　　▦ 51–175%　　▩ 176–400%

Fig. 11. Neighborhood profiles by occupation, 1986. Occupational ratios based on data from the 1980 U.S. Census of Population and Housing in Kenosha City Plan Division, "1980 Neighborhood Profiles for the City of Kenosha," Department of City Development: Kenosha, Wis., July 1986.

old guard. New politicians were able to draw on the credentialist values of the larger society to impute a whole complex of backward traits to the working-class mentality and the lack of formal education presumed to be at its core. Young professionals tapped into a long history of discontent within Kenosha's educated middle class, which was especially intense among the city's teachers and small business owners. Through the skillful manipulation of old grievances and powerful cultural symbols, politicians managed to turn local elections into something much more than a referendum on whether blue-collar workers were qualified to lead the city into the twenty-first century. A deeper cultural issue was at stake. Not on the ballot, but in the mind of middle-class professionals, these elections resolved a long-standing moral ambiguity. Manual laborers, it was finally decreed, do not—and never did—deserve to be middle class.

Culture of the Mind

The day after the April 1988 elections, the editors of the *Kenosha News* proclaimed: "It would appear that the people of Kenosha see Pat Moran not only as a man for the time, but as the man of the hour. In a city such as ours, devastated by the anticipated loss of 5,500 jobs at Chrysler, it is not surprising that voters want something new. Never has there been such a time for change. The election results seem to indicate that the voters are ready for change—the old ways and the old ties will not do."[12]

Kenosha's professionals—editors of the *News* included—interpret the plant closing as the collapse of past lifeways and the dawn of a new age. For them the plant closing dramatizes something fundamental about the moral order of American society. Change is good and positive if it comes from *within* as a form of self-examination and revitalization. Resistance to change in these circumstances becomes a form of spiritual backsliding, an inability to rise to the occasion. This moralistic language is especially striking in the context of a hotly contested election and the mobilization of a good part of the citizenry against the shutdown. Portraying Mayor Moran's victory as a decisive moral triumph is a way to say "case closed" to others in the community who do not see the proposed changes in a positive light. Significantly, professionals do not speak of the "change" represented by the shutdown as one imposed on the city from the outside. Although the effect of Chrysler's action is sometimes described as "devastating," the event itself, curiously enough, is not judged to be a disaster. Like a rite of passage, the plant closing simply creates the ritual context within which a symbolic transformation of identity can occur. For Kenosha's white-collar community, this transformation is personified by the new politicians: young, ambitious, college-educated professionals.

Political scientist Alan Ehrenhalt would find in the election of Kenosha's new politicians strong evidence for his theory that the kind of people entering politics in America today are much more ambitious, articulate, and professionally oriented than politicians in the past.[13] Ehrenhalt believes the political system at all levels of government has become much more "open" to individuals who nominate themselves for office and run on the strength of their ideas and personality, rather than as the hand-picked candidates of business cronies, party bosses, or political machines. He argues that voters elect more of these bright, independent-minded professionals simply because there are more of them entering politics than ever before. Although supply and demand may indeed play a role in this transformation of the political process, I suspect that a deeper shift in cultural meanings is involved.

The victory of Patrick Moran over the "old ways and ties" represents the triumph of a particular kind of social order. The old order has been rejected and a new order is taking its place—one in which hard work is measured not by physical exertion, but by educational credentials and individual accomplishments. In this new order, people are rewarded for "thinking" not "sweating," for brains not brawn, and for the time they have invested in developing their minds. This cluster of cultural constructs can aptly be called the "culture of the mind," for it is the mind, with its associated properties and functions, that forms the key symbol for this distinctive perception of moral order.

Two features of "mind" make it an especially salient symbol for structuring a sense of morality. In the first place, mind is the private property of an individual. This makes the symbolic boundary between self and other a matter of self-consciousness (knowing your own mind) and voluntary communication (speaking your own mind). Any blurring of this sacred boundary becomes a sign of disorder and danger, which can easily be represented by the specter of a "group mind" or herd mentality. In the second place, mind is an intangible, potentially limitless quality of being. This means that the symbolic boundaries we draw around different kinds or "degrees" of intelligence are critical. Symbolic boundaries must define the source of these abilities as well as legitimate their use.

Cultural attributes like power and prestige, as anthropologist Mary Douglas has pointed out, are generated by a well-bounded social order as well as by behavior that transcends clearly defined roles. Thus, while educational credentials can determine the nature of a person's mental abilities and position in society, intelligence that seems to go beyond institutional instruction or certification has a dangerously ambiguous quality—it is either genius or madness.[14] Qualities of mind provide a potent reservoir of concepts from which culture can craft a wide variety of notions about the power, control, and influence of one individual over another. Belief in the "evil eye," the efficacy of black magic, and the possession of souls by satanic witchcraft are just some of ways cultural systems attempt to conceptualize and control the intangible powers and dangers of human thought or mind. In contemporary American society, manifestations of mental ability may seem somewhat less exotic, but the underlying principle is the same: every cultural system must create symbolic categories that define the proper agent of such powers and their legitimate source.

In the culture of the mind, the proper agent of social power and influence is the individual, and the legitimate source is controlled by the educational system. For middle-class professionals, the moral order dramatized by the plant closing and the upset election of Kenosha's new politicians is the order created by the culture of the mind. But it is never enough in culture wars of this nature just to win, to lie back on one's laurels and enjoy the view from the top. The real gratification, and ultimately the sole proof of a *moral* victory, is to demonstrate that you deserved to win—that it was not a fluke, a mere interlude between traditional blue-collar regimes. This, professionals need to demonstrate, is the one true social order—not just for the moment, but for all time.

After all, you cannot justify a rise to power and a bold new vision for the city's future on a hunch or on ballot box dropouts. Change of this magnitude must be presented with all the knee-trembling fanfare of God's booming command, with clouds parting and a sudden shaft of light. To produce this effect, Kenosha's white-collar community relies on a selective reading of history. Through their reconstruction of the past, professionals claim the right to lead this lost city into the future. In this retelling of history, all roads lead to their door.

History as a Metaphor

New politician Tony DePalma slaps his forehead in exasperation when he contemplates the blue-collar attitude toward change. While the rest of the world has been evolving by leaps and bounds into the high-tech age, local yokels remain stuck in a time warp:

> Their way of thinking is a combination [of] conservatism and resistance to change, fear of the unknown. [People say things like,] "I don't know if we want anything new, we just want to keep Kenosha 1950s, old ethnic neighborhoods." Being from Chicago [myself], you come here and say, "My *God*, this is like a time capsule! I'm going back in time. This is the 1950s!" Kenosha is a very thick and cohesive place, and you have these nice ethnically defined neighborhoods. It's like a political precinct place for Mayor Daley in Chicago in the 1950s. I mean, that is what Kenosha was like in the *1970s!* It was like

a throwback, and even somewhat to this day. It's just starting to change. There's nothing wrong with that—I mean, there's a certain quaintness, and there's something really positive that can be said for the strong sense of community and wanting to maintain this tradition. But by the same token, I think the downside is [the attitude], "Well, it can never happen here, it will never change, and why are you rocking the boat?"

As self-proclaimed boat rockers, new politicians are determined to steer the city out of these primeval swamps. The Chrysler shutdown, far from being seen as a threat to community traditions, is perceived as an opportunity to save the city from those traditions. The way appears clear at last to propel their city into the kind of change that is already taking place in other parts of the country.

A good deal of this revolt against cultural tradition is motivated by a finely tuned sense of moral outrage. Although the old political precincts run by a Daley-like machine might well have been "quaint," they are also held to be a primary reason progressive change never came to Kenosha. With blue-collar politicians hand picked and promoted by cigar-chomping union leaders, local government had become one big back-scratching apparatus. City employees were guaranteed lavish wages and benefits, while dim-witted factory operatives masqueraded as public servants, holding rubber stamps poised to approve the unions' every whim. This den of iniquity is lovingly contrasted to the squeaky-clean intentions of all the local Mr. Smiths who decided to stand up for their principles and "go to Washington" in their own small ways. Unlike the old guard, new politicians say, they did not enter political life for personal gain and—wouldn't you know it— voters sat up and took notice, grateful to be given a choice.

New politicians like to boast that the 1986 elections were decided as soon as the local cable station began to broadcast the council meetings during the early part of the election year. As one alderman dryly observed:

> They just started televising the council meetings, and some of these guys were really bad. One guy came in wearing a jacket with a picture of a naked woman on the back! It left something to be desired. The fact that they had to debate for six hours about whether or not they should wear ties to the meetings. . . . You know, there were some problems with them.

Cultural markers like bar jackets and crewnecks are meaningful to new politicians because they reinforce the symbolic line that separates the old guard from the new. Rarely do city officials portray their differences with the past leadership as ones of political philosophy or ideas. The dominant refrain is that the blue-collar leaders *had no ideas.* Even actions that could have been criticized on ideological grounds are routinely dismissed as indicating a "lack of mind" or inability to think:

> They are self-centered, insulated, blind. They don't have a vision of Kenosha. Their vision is, don't spend any money, things are bad enough already. Our vision is, if you don't do something, you haven't seen nothing [the worst of it] yet! I fully expect that they'll throw us all out of office. Someone's probably going to pay anyway for all the trouble, and it's probably going to be us. But it's a matter of no consequence. By that time the future will be secure. They can't get us out of office in time to stop us. We're going to save them in spite of themselves, and that's it!

Like a team of dedicated surgeons, these noble civil servants will do what needs to be done no matter what odds they encounter. If the recovering patient sits up and spits in their eye, so be it: a professional duty has been performed and the suicidal patient has been saved.[15]

The old guard's refusal to spend public funds on economic development is seen not as "thrifty" or "prudent" but as self-indulgent. From this angle Kenosha's "monoeconomy," built up around the auto industry, begins to look less like an accident of history and more like the result of pork barrel politics. "It was always the notion that you don't invest in a whole bunch of other things because you can always depend on the Motors to be there," Brendan Woods says. "So why invest in a new industrial park? Or this or that? You know, [they thought] these are bad investments." This is not simply a matter of short-sightedness. If the blue-collar leadership had not been so intent on fattening its own purse, it would have been investing in the "common good" all along.

Accounting for Kenosha's evolution as a company town is just one part of the professional-managerial version of history. A second component is equally important. The city's reliance on one major employer is seen as a distortion of "natural" economic development, and this "unnatural" situation has produced a "maladaptive" blue-collar culture. Under these conditions, the whole town is in danger of being dragged to the glue factory. This business manager's remarks are typical:

> Kenosha had an image of being a blue-collar labor town, a one-horse town, in the sense of being tied to AMC. Not really going anyplace unless AMC went someplace. Chugging

along. It was losing population. It wasn't getting much new development. It wasn't retaining the college students. They'd go off to school and not come back. There was a real stifling of other industries because you just couldn't compete. You cannot compete in a community [where] 10 percent to 15 percent of your workforce is making sixteen dollars an hour, [especially when] the skill level is not that high for the sixteen bucks an hour.

The cluster of symbolic elements in white-collar accounts of local history point repeatedly to a sense of being drained, suffocated, sucked dry, and left behind. The ever-present fear, of course, is that of "becoming history." Middle-class professionals are united in the belief that the express line to extinction was the one that formed down at the auto shop on payday. The high wages of industrial workers are the flip side, symbolically, of all the pennies pinched by blue-collar politicians. Both economic strategies are thought to withdraw capital from circulation, capital that could otherwise be used for investment in plants and equipment, research and development, and a "friendly" business environment.

White-collar Kenoshans believe that their understanding of local history explains what went "wrong" in Kenosha morally as well as economically. Quite apart from the question of whether they have arrived at a sound analysis of the city's history, we need to appreciate why this telling of history and not some other one proves compelling for so many. History, in an anthropological sense, is not an objective narrative of actual events but a creative synthesis of memory and desire that enables people to make sense of their place in the order of things.[16] A great deal is missing, after all, from the professional-managerial rendition of industrial decline. Absent are the critiques of corporate America and industrial policy that are so well honed among autoworkers. Invisible are the structural shifts in the national economy that have made white-collar workers' own standing in the middle class increasingly precarious. In place of these possible understandings is a unilateral indictment of the moral turpitude presumed endemic to the blue-collar way of life.

Whose Common Good?

If you go down to the lakefront, you see the plant coming down and you see the marina taking shape. Things are becoming visual. People are seeing the Civic Center II project going up; they see the marina being dug out, the development of WisPark [an industrial park]—these are all physical things now we can see. They're no longer diagrams on a sheet. I mean, all the talk, all the hot air we talk about diversification of the economic base, it's finally starting to take shape. People are able to drive by and look at it. That says a lot.

Bobby Cannara is not your typical city booster. As a twenty-two-year-old college student from a blue-collar family, he is not in a position to capitalize on the real estate bonanza opened up by the demolition of the lakefront plant and the new mood in city hall. In the chrome and glass rising out of the old downtown he sees the embodiment of a vision, the future made manifest. Like a bold idealist drawn from the pages of Ayn Rand's *Fountainhead* or *Atlas Shrugged*, Bobby feels pride in what the new political leadership has accomplished, mixed with a powerful sense of just deserts.

Ground could not have been broken on many of these projects had city officials not been willing to stick their necks out and clip red tape. One issue in particular divided the old ways from the new. Beyond the defeat of the old guard, the true test of the new leadership came on the night when Kenosha's city council and county board convened to decide whether to pursue a breach-of-contract lawsuit against Chrysler. For those aldermen and county supervisors who had no connection to the blue-collar community, the decision was easy: entering into controversial litigation with a major corporation was no way to enhance Kenosha's business climate. For representatives with stalwart blue-collar constituencies, the choice was also clear: Chrysler should not be allowed to abandon America's hardworking auto towns with impunity. Kenosha would fight back. But for Bobby Cannara, a vote was a sign of faith in the new social order.

"They were nuts!" he exclaims, looking back on that night. A large contingent of autoworkers representing Local 72 had packed the auditorium where the town meeting was held. When chairs ran out, standees lined the walls. Placards were smuggled in and banners unfurled. The local cable station provided gavel-to-gavel coverage, and a record number of viewers tuned in. The stage was set for a major showdown.

"I watch them on the news," Bobby's father says, visibly agitated. "They was always hollering and screaming, calling each other this and that. There's no sense, there's no sense!"

"What about the death threats I got?" Bobby demands, talking as much to his father as to me. "The mayor was shot at! The minute the meeting was over, they called up and threatened my mother. That's the kind of garbage!"

Mr. Cannara turns to me and explains earnestly, "I told my wife, don't worry about it, it's just talk. If somebody's going to do anything, they ain't going to call you up and tell you."

Bobby continues his disturbing recollection, saying, "Yeah, they were waving their fists at us." He pauses and looks puzzled, as if to ask, Why me?

I ask how this made him feel.

"My first response was anger," he says defiantly. "I couldn't believe it. We had to be escorted out of Gateway [the local technical college], where they held the meeting that night, by sheriffs, state troopers, and cops—Kenosha cops. That's pathetic! It was on CNN. It was on the Milwaukee and Chicago news. It made Kenosha look so bad! Okay, it was an emotional issue, I understand that. But they were nuts!"

In spite of myself, I have to suppress a smile. I find it curious to see city officials wringing their hands over Kenosha's "image," as if the paramount duty of government is to worry about what the neighbors might think. But obviously there is something more here than a pious concern about airing dirty laundry. By voting to drop the lawsuit, new politicians wanted to make it clear that the city was no longer being run in the interests of organized labor. Presenting their newly unveiled image as a city with a good business climate and a docile labor force was maddeningly difficult when Local 72 kept popping up like a nutty jack-in-the-box.

Bobby and his father give this familiar story an interesting twist. As I listen to the conversation between father and son, I am aware of a careful play of checks and balances that keeps Bobby from saying anything too harsh about the autoworkers and his father from saying anything too extreme about the city council. In truth, I realize with a sudden jolt, this is the only time I have ever seen a new politician and an autoworker sitting down and talking to each other.

"They just throw everything to the city council and the county board," Mr. Cannara offers, as if to explain his son's behavior. "And what are they going to do about it?"

Earlier Bobby told me he felt the city and county had been "set up" by state officials to "take the fall" for Governor Thompson—the man who had originally threatened Chrysler with a lawsuit. Bobby, like many autoworkers, now believes that the governor (a Republican, after all) never intended to go through with his threat. When the moment of truth came, rather than lose political credibility, the governor turned the responsibility for a lawsuit over to local officials, with the private warning that they would receive no support from the state. "We were the bull's-eye," Bobby said, "and we took the hit."

Now Bobby responds to his father's support with a grateful smile and says to me, "And this come from a man who's worked there for over thirty years!"

"I ain't the only one," Mr. Cannara responds. "I got brothers, I got relatives. They got it rough, you know. They lost their jobs. Their jobs are gone. They got a family."

"My family was tougher to answer to than anybody else," Bobby admits. "You know how many times my uncle talked to me? And cornered me in a corner, whenever he'd come over for a cup of coffee or a glass of wine? Those were the people I had to answer to."

I ask him to tell me what that was like.

> If there was an engagement party, or a wedding party . . . you usually run a hundred people for an Italian wedding, and we're a very close-knit family. I got all my uncles there. They corner you and you're sitting at the bar and you're having a drink, talking, just finished with the meal, and there was some hostility there. They sit there and they say, "What's going on? Why ain't you guys doing anything?" And you had to talk to these guys about it. And I come from a family where you *new* respect your elders, no matter what their opinion is! And they *generation* would get hot about it.

Bobby forged his understanding of the larger cultural and political conflict in the heat of these intimate family gatherings. This is why the transformation of architectural drawings into real buildings represents such a vindication for him. Those buildings prove that he wasn't just "talking a lot of hot air" to put people off. What he said would happen is indeed happening.

Bobby knows he risked hard feelings within his family and a break with his blue-collar constituents when he voted against the lawsuit. The official vote at that fateful town hall meeting was fourteen to three on the city council and nineteen to three on the county board. "I'm up for reelection this year in April," he says with a shrug, "and sure, I went to some people's houses and they slammed the door in my face because, 'Oh, you voted not to sue—boom!' But then again, I had many people say, 'Well, it's nice to see Kenosha's taking shape.'" People have lost their way with the closing of the plant, and the future he wants them to see is one of hope: hope through change.

Like other new politicians, Bobby Cannara points to the results of a public opinion survey called *Kenosha Focus 2000* to suggest that there is widespread support for the controversial actions of the new city council. "One of the major goals set by the *Focus 2000* group—where we asked literally thousands of Kenoshans, What do you think we should do, as elected officials?—their main response was, diversify the

economic base, spread it out more evenly. And that's what we did."
Bobby overstates matters with the claim that *Focus 2000* encapsulates
the views of "literally thousands of Kenoshans." The final report
was based on a return of only 904 questionnaires, a rather meager
response rate of 36 percent. Background information on the occupations and residential areas of those who participated in this survey—and those who did not—is not available in the final report. This
makes it extremely difficult to evaluate just how representative of the
community this survey truly is.[17] But the importance of *Focus 2000*
goes beyond issues of accuracy or representativeness. The results of
the survey were made public in October 1987, three months before
Chrysler announced it would close its Kenosha plant. In the local
campaigns of 1988, *Focus 2000* was a tub thumper's dream, providing
new politicians with what seemed to be a scientifically obtained mandate for their vision of the future—or, as the report itself claimed,
with "a grassroots consensus on community goals." Ostensibly com-
missioned to give "citizens a voice" in local government, *Focus 2000* is
now used to demonstrate that new politicians speak for all the people.

The uses this survey has been put to make it a fascinating cultural
artifact. Just what are the goals that Kenoshans purportedly agree
upon? As Bobby insists, *Focus 2000* does present evidence that many
Kenoshans believe "economic diversification is the most important
goal for the city." This finding is based on one survey question. Respondents were asked to select, from a list of nine options, what they
felt was the "most important goal for Kenosha." The most popular
choice—selected by 55 percent of those surveyed—was, "Diversify
our economy by increasing the variety of businesses and industries in
Kenosha." Following this question was one that received no public
attention at all. Respondents were asked to choose from a list of ten
possibilities what "type of community" they would like to see Kenosha
become in the future: 41 percent wanted to see the city remain a
"manufacturing center," while 17 percent chose the option "high-
technology center."

Based on what can kindly be called a selective reading of these survey results, city officials were able to trot out the spurious claim that,
thanks to *Focus 2000,* the city could now "work toward a common
purpose for the common good of Kenosha."[18] And that common
good, invoked by new politicians like a civic mantra, is said to consist
of three goals: diversifying the economic base, improving the city's
image, and developing the lakefront. In the 1988 elections, autoworkers were generally inclined to take this agenda at face value.
Who could argue with progress, especially when the goals in question

seemed so benign? No one ever told them that "lakefront development" and "economic diversification" would involve the demolition the auto plant and the end of automaking in Kenosha. And no one ever said that "improving the city's image" meant abolishing its blue-collar character and way of life.

Some new politicians candidly admit that their plans for the city's future do not include blue-collar workers who cannot change with the times. Brendan Woods says that several of his colleagues on the city council would not be distressed to learn that dislocated autoworkers were being forced to "vote with their feet" and leave town. "Many [council members] are really business kinds of guys, which is fine. They really don't give a damn about a lot of these people. [Blue-collar voters] didn't support them, you know, so it's no big deal to them. They'd like them out of town. They'd like to bring in a lot of people from the suburbs of Chicago, repopulate large parts of the city, and make it a yuppie bedroom community. That's what they would really like to do."

Brendan insists he does not share this attitude, even though he is a staunch proponent of the marina project and the revitalized downtown that will come along with it. The city council was justified in authorizing the use of public funds for the marina project, he argues, because there was no choice. "The only alternative to that is to have a ghost town with empty factory buildings down there! I mean, there is no alternative! Those that are saying the city shouldn't put up the money and should wait for a developer are the same people that waited for the Motors, and [still] wait for somebody to come save Kenosha. Kenosha has got to save itself!"

New politicians believe their vision of Kenosha's future is the only way to go, and they are determined to portray their opposition as a special interest group that has no right to speak for the community as a whole. In an editorial titled "Kenosha's Future," the new mayor informs readers of the *Kenosha News* that "when confronted with a crisis, an individual or a society must make one of two decisions." You can either "externalize" the blame for your misfortune to "outside forces" or you can "proactively carry out a program that will lay the foundation for security for generations to come." Quoting Saint Paul addressing the Romans, the mayor writes, "'Besides this you know what hour it is, how it is full time now for you to wake from sleep. For salvation is nearer to us now than when we first believed; the night is gone, the day is at hand. Let us then cast off the works of darkness and put on the armor of light' (13:11–12). As St. Paul states," the mayor goes on to say, "Kenosha must cast off the political works of darkness and put on the armor of light. If we uphold these profound truths not only economic prosperity, but political equality will prevail for all our citizenry."[19] There can be no doubt about whose "political works of darkness" he is referring to.

New politicians are convinced they know what is best for the city. They are determined to see their plans for social change carried out, even in the face of considerable opposition. In different circumstances, community opposition of such proportions might seriously undermine a local government's sense of its own legitimacy. But city officials base their right to govern on a moral imperative that draws on some of the most powerful themes in American culture. Social change on the order that new politicians advocate will not benefit all Kenoshans equally. Some people are going to win, and some people are going to lose. And this, Kenosha's middle-class professionals agree, is as it should be.

CHAPTER FIVE

Social Darwinism Revisited

Alderman Bobby Cannara realizes that not everyone in Kenosha is as thrilled about the city's new identity as he is. Yet he has trouble understanding this viewpoint as anything other than sour grapes. There were those who fought to keep the plant open, and now that they have been defeated, they seem determined to prove that the death knell has sounded for Kenosha:

> You've got your diehards out there. They're just determined to say, Hey, doom and gloom, no matter what. No matter what! Other people, they're going back to school; they're retraining themselves. I'm sure they appreciate what's going on. You just don't have it as easy as you did before. That's the problem! You just don't have the job [like the one] at Chrysler to go to if you are unskilled. You know, punch the time clock and make thirteen dollars an hour plus your benefits, whatever it was. You just don't have that anymore. It's time to buckle down and pull your way through, I guess.

Bobby's assessment of the situation is a perfect illustration of how the culture of the mind frames the problem of economic dislocation. Bobby doesn't go as far as some professionals do and blame the autoworkers for causing the shutdown—that would hit a little too close to home. But he has lost patience with people who seem unwilling to face facts squarely, to straighten up and fly right. And those facts, as he sees them, are beyond question: "unskilled" (meaning uncredentialed) people cannot expect to earn a middle-class standard of living. Only those who go back to school for retraining can truly "appreciate what's going on" in Kenosha. The new postindustrial society is like

At the September 1988 town hall meeting, a worker reacts to a speaker's opinion that a lawsuit would sour Chrysler's dealings with other local businesses. Photo by Charles S. Vallone and the Racine *Journal Times*.

the New World once was to America's immigrants. You must come to these shores with a dream in your heart and a willingness to work hard, but in the land of high tech that hard work begins in the classroom, not on the shopfloor. In this country of limitless possibilities, you can glimpse the vision and understand the promise only after you have put your hand to the plow—or in this case the personal computer.

Measuring Social Worth

Middle-class professionals do not ask where all the good-paying manufacturing jobs have gone. As far as they are concerned, the very existence of such jobs has always been evidence of the natural order gone awry. The real tragedy is that somewhere along the line blue-collar workers honestly came to believe that their "unnatural" wages were an accurate reflection of their self-worth and value to society. And this is the bitter pill they will now have to swallow. New politician Brendan Woods articulates these ideas bluntly. As the autoworkers try to get back on their feet, he tells me, they are going to have to face the fact that they are simply not "worth" as much as they think they are:

> We're going to see some real serious depression down the line. Because the reality for a lot of these people is there really is no hope. They have made the most they're ever going to make in their life. They don't have the educational wherewithal to get to a job that's going to make that much. So they're going to go from thirteen dollars an hour down to probably about four dollars an hour, and with a lot of luck, they might get up to six dollars an hour sometime in their life again.

Brendan displays a sensitivity to the psychology of unemployment that I generally find only among the social workers I have talked with in Kenosha. The capacity to feel hopeful about the future, these professionals realize, is a critical component of psychological well-being. Yet even as Brendan and the mental health professionals try to imagine themselves in an autoworker's shoes, they look at the world through the lens of their own cultural expectations. No matter how victimized workers feel by the Chrysler shutdown, Brendan argues, they will eventually have to come to grips with the fact that they are responsible for their own fate:

> They're going to lose their home. They're going to lose their car. They're going to lose their self-respect. And they don't know what they're going to do about it yet. I don't know what

they're going to look like [when this happens]. I don't know what I would look like, I honestly don't. If someone took my income and cut it in half and made my wife go to work full time and made me lose my dream of sending my children to college—and I knew that it was *my fault,* sort of, that I'd not educated myself when I thought I had—I don't know what I'd be like. I'd probably be a mess.

Brendan touches upon a point that bears closer examination. What does it mean to say dislocated workers should know they are "at fault" for not educating themselves? Obviously these workers weren't fired from their jobs because they lacked the appropriate education to do the work required of them. The line of cars transferred out of Kenosha went to Mexico, where the workforce cannot be said to boast a particularly high level of education. Self-blame, evidently, is thought to come from discovering that you are not qualified to do anything *other* than factory work. The experience of being shut out of the labor force, Brendan imagines, will lead to the gut-wrenching realization that different life choices in the past would have spared you this pain in the present.[1] The "proper" choice would have entailed several more years of schooling—exactly the route middle-class professionals took.

When professionals argue that only the educated deserve success and upward mobility, they invoke a modern version of the Protestant ethic that anthropologist Katherine Newman aptly calls "meritocratic individualism." This secular doctrine holds that meritorious individuals should rise above the crowd in recognition of their special talents, while the incompetent and slothful should drop to the bottom as they deserve. "Cast in this way," Newman observes, "success is not a matter of luck, good contacts, credentials or technical skill but is a measure of one's moral worth, one's willingness and ability to drive beyond the limitations of self-indulgence and sloth."[2]

Meritocratic individualism invests our position in the social order with a cultural significance that goes far beyond the notion of work as a means of putting a roof over your head and food on the table. Work becomes a way of demonstrating your innermost character, and your place in society becomes a measure of your moral worth. Meritocracy replaces the idea of divine reward for hard work with the idea that an individual's ability to master and overcome the forces of the marketplace—like the immutable laws of nature—should determine who wins and who loses in life. In this updated version of the Protestant ethic, it is not God but the economy that rewards people of good character while punishing the shiftless and improvident. The spur to success in contemporary American society comes not from anxious musings about the heavenly hereafter but from nervous glances down the occupational ladder at those who have failed society's critical tests.

Darwinian imagery lurks behind these calculations of social value. The culture of the mind contains an implicit argument about the naturalness of competing for our place in the social order. Not only do the best and brightest individuals win the struggle for social position, but the whole social group can move forward—in a word, *evolve*—only when competition is allowed to flourish untrammeled. Competition brings out the best not just in each individual, it is believed, but in society as a whole. The quick, the smart, and the strong can adapt to the demands of technological change and in so doing transform mere change into *social progress*. The slow, the weak, and the stupid are unable to adapt, and as a result they must inevitably fall to the back in the human marathon. Just as the notion of progress transforms competition into a noble goal, the Darwinian imperative cautions against charity by putting the onus of survival squarely on the shoulders of the individual. If progress depends on the fleet and strong leading the race, unimpeded by the foot-dragging masses, then society cannot assume the burden of coddling dullards and dropouts. To do so, in this way of thinking, endangers the progress of humanity as a whole. If the strong slow down to let stragglers catch up, the whole society will soon find itself mired in mediocrity.

For many in Kenosha, the decline of America's automobile industry provides a perfect example of what happens when a society tolerates incompetence—and worse yet, interferes with free-market principles to "protect" the noncompetitive. "Okay," says business manager Michael Hoffman, "if I look today at the fact that millions of UAW workers across the country are out of a job, the question is why?" For Michael, the answer is simple:

> The cars aren't selling. So what do you do? You can have all sorts of promises and contracts to keep the people employed, but if the product isn't selling, how do you do that? People aren't buying the cars. For one reason or another, they're buying Japanese cars or German cars or whatever. Now I don't know how the government or how communities or how the union can force a company to continue to produce cars if they aren't selling. Ultimately what that means is that you put them out of business, and then nobody'd have a job.

Michael dismisses import restrictions with a wave of the hand. Protectionism simply throws another wrench into what should be a freely operating market system. Products that do not sell are, by definition, inferior products. Neither the workers who make these products nor the companies responsible for producing them should be protected from the harsh realities of global competition. While sympathetic to the charitable impulse behind the Chrysler "bailout,"[3] Michael firmly believes that America's "syndrome of subsidizing things" actually creates an "individualistic, greed-driven" society. The syndrome begins, Michael explains, when people feel bad about sitting back and letting a business "die" when it can't support itself:

> So we try to prop it up, and then that in turn needs more props! So what we've got, really, is a total life that's not too real, I guess. We subsidize businesses to move into a community. We subsidize businesses to stay in a community. We subsidize car industries; we subsidize dairy farmers, tobacco growers, and on and on and on. And we just create this big thing that makes it so complex that you can never sit down and say, "Hey, wait a minute, is this a good thing or a bad thing or does this make sense?" So now you've got this wretched thing of *greed*, because we don't have a pie big enough to take care of everybody anymore. So there are some that get and some that don't; and when you've got that situation, there's winners and there's losers.

It would be a mistake to interpret this as unmitigated social Darwinism. Michael is not saying—as a character in the movie *Wall Street* does—that "greed is good!" In truth, middle-class professionals in Kenosha are dismayed by what they see as the feeding frenzy created by all the special interest groups that compete for government "handouts." Greed and selfishness, in their view, are the *result* of government efforts to coddle the unfit. Incessant meddling in the free market, not global competition, has reduced the size of the American pie. Squeamishness about letting the noncompetitive die a natural death creates an "artificial" situation in which people are forced to compete for the crumbs. If the free market were allowed to operate as it should, everybody would win. The economic pie would be "big enough to take care of everybody," as presumably it was during the postwar period of expansion.

The Darwinism in this laissez-faire vision of the moral order is not a manifesto for rapacious derring-do. Rather, it is a *mythic* understanding of the natural mechanisms by which society's sacred and immutable order is maintained. The moral order, professionals believe, depends on Darwinian struggle. What kind of world would this be, they ask, if the hardworking were not rewarded for their talents and self-discipline? What kind of economy would you have if every

failing industry were shielded from the rigors of global competition?
What kind of character would people have if they were not motivated
to be the best they can be? Charity is no charity at all if it saps people's
will to succeed on their own.[4] If America is to retain its place in the
world, the artificial props built up over the postwar years need to be
kicked away. People must be forced to realize, if they haven't already,
that survival in the postindustrial age depends on a disciplined mind
and a well-educated workforce. Developing your mind is no longer
optional; it is a social and moral responsibility.

WHEN DO YOU HELP?

In the moral order established by the culture of the mind, people
who refuse to "educate themselves" to meet the demands of industry
in the twenty-first century must be held individually accountable. This
is why Kenosha's middle-class professionals can in good conscience
"blame" the autoworkers for their own misfortune. Workers didn't
take advantage of the educational opportunities offered to them in
high school, and many are turning down the offer of retraining even
now. Professionals feel no cruelty in saying that the uneducated will
have to pay the penalty of falling to their "natural" place in the social
order. Technological change has finally let the air out of autoworkers' "inflated" sense of self-worth. As the United States makes the historic shift from manufacturing to services and high-tech industries,
Michael Hoffman says, there will be fewer and fewer jobs, even at the
low end of the totem pole, for people who don't know how to "think":

> People are going to have to continue to grow, and they're go-
> ing to have to continue to learn. The dangerous part of that
> is they're going to have to learn how to think. That's a tough
> thing. Most educational systems do not require people to
> think. Memorize whatever you need to get out of school;
> memorize whatever you need to get a job—and God forbid
> the job should ever change! I think that's the problem the
> autoworkers had, because they knew a lot about the task they
> had, but it didn't take much *mental* processes, other than con-
> tinue to do this thing, one at a time, as fast as you could, as
> good as you could.
>
> [The autoworkers had] an inflated . . . the whole perception
> of value. We base a tremendous amount of self-respect on all
> the things that we have around us. So if I make $35,000 or
> $40,000 a year, my value and where I live is up here [he raises
> his hand midway in the air]. Well, now, all of a sudden you
> take that person off the automobile line—and he can't read
> or write—you can't even get him a job at the hamburger
> stand. That's saying nothing about whether they could live on
> that money, but they couldn't even *get* the job!

Upward mobility—the grand old American dream—has become a matter of "brain work" geared to an economic order that is calibrated by educational credentials. Professionals see nothing strange in this because it is the system of meritocracy they have believed in all along. But they are not entirely consistent in their thinking about why an autoworker's value has plummeted overnight. To be sure, the white-collar community has always thought autoworkers were grossly over-paid, but as long as the local economy was being fueled in a positive way by the auto industry—during the 1950s and 1960s, for example—the business community accepted these wage rates as a feature of the landscape. In the aftermath of the plant closing, however, managers are eager to extol the virtues of laissez-faire conservatism. They are able to do so with confidence, since the market is currently pulling industrial wages down to a level they consider acceptable. Nevertheless, it remains true that autoworkers were never making more than the market itself once permitted. It's one thing to say that the market has changed and that this has made past wages excessive under present conditions. It's quite another to argue, as professionals do, that blue-collar wages were *always* illegitimate. Logically, union wages were able to rise only in accordance with the same market principles that have now brought them down.

The quick retort to my questions on this fuzzy issue is always an indictment of unions in general, and UAW Local 72 in particular. In the bad old days, business managers argue, the free market wasn't able to operate the way it should have, because you had all these people banding together in unions and driving up wages through collective bargaining. Unionization is considered an "unnatural" interference in market principles, particularly in this company town, where Local 72 threw its weight around like the giant guarding the golden goose. The image of an economy held hostage by a mentally incompetent tyrant resonates well with a basic tenet of the culture of the mind: power is not supposed to come through numbers. No good can come of the moblike use of force to advance partisan demands, and a herd mentality is thought to be especially dangerous when it mobilizes masses of people at the bottom of the income ladder.[5] Legitimate power accrues to intelligence, which bestows upon a select few the right to speak as authorities and make decisions for others. Dialogue among enlightened experts, not mob rule, is the hallmark of civilized society.

Had autoworkers been forced to compete in the market as individuals, not as a group, they would never have been able to get the kind of wages they did. Just look at what's happening now, professionals say: without their union, autoworkers are unable to find work at comparable wages. The plant closing, from the perspective of college-educated Kenoshans, serves as a "status degradation" ritual—a cultural recognition that blue-collar laborers are of a lower social status than they have been pretending to be.[6] The ceremonial unmasking of these impostors confirms what white-collar onlookers have believed all along: autoworkers have always been brash interlopers and undeserving usurpers of middle-class standing and privilege. Moral righteousness, far more than any thoughtful analysis of industrial decline, gives the spectacle of a plant closing its dominant cultural meaning as a justly deserved fall from grace.

Social Darwinism

Critics of the economic policies promulgated by the Reagan and Bush administrations have often compared the "logic" of laissez-faire capitalism to the social Darwinism presumed to be rampant in the late nineteenth century. Typical of this vein of political commentary is a 1982 article featured in the *New Republic* with the cover line, "Social Darwinism, Reagan Style." On the cover of that issue, President Reagan is shown "evolving" from a knuckle-walking ape to an upright human being.[7] The political logic of these critiques is straightforward enough: without proper government controls, a society ruled by the impersonal laws of the market will become a Darwinian jungle in which only the fittest can survive. The power of this imagery is so tantalizing that even a Republican insider like Kevin Phillips discovers significant parallels between the social Darwinism of the Gilded Age and the philosophical underpinnings of Reaganomics. During the expansion following the Civil War, Phillips writes, "Avarice became an achievement—a display, almost, of social fitness. Preeminent were the men who took Charles Darwin's 1859 biological theory of evolution and transformed it into a cultural and economic thesis of the survival of the fittest. Unbridled competition, they proclaimed, was really economic nature at its most productive." Phillips finds the clearest expression of this thesis in the deregulation frenzy of the 1980s, which, in turn, led to the S and L debacle, merger mania, and the decline of basic industries.[8]

At first glance the logic of social Darwinism appears inextricably wedded to a theory of political economy that revels in the "dog eat dog" nature of modern capitalism. Indeed, some historians interpret social Darwinism's fateful combination of biological science and social theory as a case of science following social philosophy, rather than an

CAN THIS APPLY TO NEWSP CLOSINGS?

instance of social thinkers applying new discoveries in science. In this view it is the British philosopher Herbert Spencer, not Charles Darwin, who developed the doctrine of social Darwinism.[9] Spencer was a great champion of the "ethical progress" of humankind. Moral progress, he believed, occurred as the human character became better and better adapted to the conditions of life. The evil inherent in the brutal and predatory life of our ancestors would gradually fade when people developed "a new moral constitution fitted to the needs of civilized life."[10] Spencer wished to protect this "natural" evolutionary process from the meddlesome interference of misguided do-gooders. He opposed state aid to the poor on the grounds that they were socially "unfit" and should, in the natural order of things, be eliminated. People had to learn to adapt to the selective conditions of progress, and this could not happen by promoting "the artificial preservation of those least able to take care of themselves."[11]

Remarks like these notwithstanding, there never was an ideological movement called "social Darwinism." As the historian Richard Bannister has shown, no one in Gilded Age America ever publicly admitted to being a social Darwinist. Few people laced their prose with "buzz words" like struggle for existence, natural selection, and survival of the fittest. On the strength of such evidence, Bannister proposes that social Darwinism functioned as a sort of political pie throwing. It was a great label to stick on your opponents, and difficult to shake if it was stuck on you. By the Progressive Era, social Darwinism had become the perfect straw man that reformers of all stripes could rail against to dramatize the dire consequences of failing to adopt the policies they were promoting.

In short, Bannister concludes, there never were any social Darwinists in America. No one ever actively subscribed to an ideology that said the natural laws of struggle and survival should operate without restriction in human society.[12] Social Darwinism, he argues persuasively, is actually a cultural myth that serves to justify policies that advocate social engineering. Accusations of social Darwinism trigger an alarming image of society as a jungle, red in tooth and claw. Since social life would be impossible in this "state of nature," the argument goes, government intervention is needed to establish moral order. The image of Darwinian struggle in a world without social controls is a rhetorical device most often used to argue *for,* not against, extreme regulatory measures.

It is the opponents of deregulation, not its supporters, who most often invoke the specter of social Darwinism revisited. It is liberal, not conservative, economists who routinely suspect laissez-faire zealots of Darwinian sympathies. And it is concern about the lack of corporate accountability that leads economist Robert Reich to hurl the epithet of social Darwinism at modern-day proponents of industrial consolidation: "Charles Darwin's celebrated theories provided convenient justification for any economic trend of the time by which the rich grew richer and more powerful."[13] No matter that America's giant corporations do not quote the *Origin of Species* chapter and verse to justify their business practices. As long as the policies they advocate produce greater social inequality, Reich suggests, United States industry embodies the logic of social Darwinism.

Like Robert Bannister, I am leery of considering secondhand attributions of social Darwinism—by the opposing political camp, no less—as evidence of the real thing. But if we restrict our concept of social Darwinism to a list of the self-identified champions of ruthless economic competition—individuals who, furthermore, trumpet the demise of "the unfit" as an ineluctable fact of human evolution—surely we are throwing a party no one will come to. A more fruitful avenue of investigation is open to the anthropologist, if not to the historian. Thinking of social Darwinism as a mythic form opens up a whole realm of cultural phenomena that a historian, who is focusing on documented statements of political ideology, might well overlook.

In cultural anthropology, the exploration of myth has a rich and complex tradition, rooted in the structural studies of Claude Lévi-Strauss and the literary analysis of Kenneth Burke.[14] Myth, for the anthropologist, is a vital link between a community's system of symbolic meaning and the order people perceive in their everyday lives. Through myths, we explain our actions to one another and to ourselves. In this process the conceptual order of our society is continually being communicated and reinforced. Myth, as a cultural form, is the symbolic language through which we communicate and comprehend the moral order of our society.

As anthropologist Will Wright observes, myths establish a "principle of order" that organizes cultural categories into a coherent symbolic system:

> The people and things in a social group must be conceptually arranged in a hierarchy of power, prestige, importance, and value, and this conceptual hierarchy [is what] makes communication and social action possible. By appealing to this principle of order—whether addressing a superior as "sir," writing American history, or simply laughing at a joke—an

individual reinforces that order and locates himself in it; if the appeal is successful, and communication takes place, he has shown himself to be a recognizable and acceptable component of a symbolically classified ordered world.[15]

The idea that social advancement occurs through the natural selection of the most well-adapted individuals is a myth. It is a myth, first and foremost, because it is not true. But the notion of progress through selection is also a myth because we believe it is true. As a myth in American culture, social Darwinism provides us with a model of how our society is ordered and how it changes over time. The "principle of order" it conveys tells us why some people succeed and some fail. Survival, we believe, is a matter of adapting to the conditions of our biosocial environment. To the extent that these conditions are constantly changing under the impetus of science and technology, we must adapt to the process of change itself.

But the myth of social Darwinism goes one step further. A lasting legacy of the Darwinian revolution is the idea that social survival depends not merely on adapting to current conditions, but on being at least one step ahead of the times—on anticipating future trends and then growing a long neck or leopardlike spots if need be. In American culture, the Darwinian metaphor is a symbolic lingua franca that we all understand, whether or not we fully agree with its implications.[16] It is our tacit understanding of this myth that enables us to position ourselves vis-à-vis one another in a changing society.

When history teacher Bruce McCloskey reflects on the dramatic changes taking place in his hometown, he views these events from the standpoint of someone who has successfully crossed the glacial tundra to address us from this side of the Ice Age:

> At the time Kenosha became a blue-collar town, that was the thing to be. But all things change, and now the town is going to have to adjust. It is trying to make itself move into a different time where things are much more technical. I think the closing of Chrysler is like the dinosaur finally rolled over and *died,* and let's bury him! They're gonna knock the buildings down, and let's go on from there. It will be a fond memory like a lot of other things are fond memories. We'll get through it, and the town will probably be better for it.

The power of the Darwinian myth lies in its seeming neutrality. We rarely feel the urge to weep over the passing of the dinosaurs. Dwarfed by the majestic remains of *Brontosaurus* or *Tyrannosaurus rex,* as schoolchildren we learn something fundamental about the natural order of things and our own place in it: success is a matter of survival, and the past is a continent to which the unsuccessful are routinely banished.

Conceptualizing Disorder

Most studies of plant closings have focused on the impact of mass unemployment on workers, their families, and their communities. As the social consequences of deindustrialization became increasingly severe during the 1980s, the literature on the human costs of economic dislocation grew substantially. Psychologists, sociologists, and cultural anthropologists are once again addressing the problem of mass unemployment and downward mobility with a sense of mission not seen since the Great Depression.[17] The portrait of America that emerges from these studies is a bleak one indeed. Shattered lives, decaying institutions, and abandoned communities are poignant and important features of the growing ethnography of industrial disorder. Social disintegration and economic crisis are the dominant concerns of this research, and the collapse of moral order is often the deepest fear.

Missing from these discussions, however, are the cheerful, upbeat voices of the middle-class professionals I've come to know in Kenosha. Nothing I'd read before starting my fieldwork on the Chrysler shutdown quite prepared me for the fact that a lot of people in and around Kenosha were *happy* to see the plant close.

The excellent community studies of plant closings I read as I embarked upon my own project—Buss and Redburn's *Shutdown at Youngstown,* Bensman and Lynch's *Rusted Dreams,* and Pappas's *Magic City*—all tend to view plant closings as unmitigated disasters for workers and communities. In these works a plant closing is a disaster because it creates hardships for individuals, and individual hardship, multiplied exponentially, disrupts the social ties that create the structural basis for community cohesion. Social groups can respond to the threat of disorder by consciously strengthening their commitment to the survival of the community. But if this commitment proves impossible to sustain, the social order breaks down and people lose sight of the values that once gave meaning and direction to their lives.

This is the classic sociological model of disaster.[18] A disaster, in this model, is something more than a "freak of nature" or an event with a clear-cut beginning and end. Many traumatic events are caused by social forces, and the people involved may continue to suffer for an indefinite period. To understand a social disaster, sociologist Kai Erickson points out, we need to reverse our usual way of thinking about cause and effect. "Instead of classifying a condition as a trauma because it was introduced by a disaster," he writes, "we would classify an event as a disaster if it had the property of bringing about traumatic reactions." This definition opens the door to a wide range of social phenomena. Growing up in poverty, being forced out of your home by urban renewal, the experience of old age, and modern life itself can all be seen as trauma inducing. "One of the long-term effects of modernization as we know it," Erickson observes, "has been to distance people from the nourishing roots of community, and the costs of this process have been heavy for certain portions of the population."[19] A disaster is ultimately a loss of community.

The difficulty with this concept of disaster is that it focuses almost exclusively on the experiences of *victims*. Many community studies attempt to correct the image of passive victims by emphasizing the strategies people use to cope with their situation, but the focus remains squarely on the people who are traumatized by the event under consideration. This approach implicitly assumes that the source of social disorder comes from *outside* the afflicted community, and that everyone inside that community will experience or perceive the event in essentially the same way.

Sociologists David Bensman and Roberta Lynch take this approach in their study of a steel mill closing. These authors locate the cause of industrial disorder in the operation of impersonal market forces and in the attitudes of policymakers. The fate of the United States steel industry, they observe, has rested in the hands of people who believe it cannot or should not be saved:

> The death of the smokestack industries became a commonplace of public discourse. Some believed that no matter what America did, it could no longer compete as an industrial power against the low wage countries of the third world. Others held that unless the steel industry could stand on its own, it did not deserve to survive. In this Darwinian economic model, the fittest would emerge, trim and tough from the harrowing rigors of economic competition.[20]

Bensman and Lynch argue that these views are based on faulty economic reasoning, and after a cursory critique of this reasoning they call for a vigorous government-led effort to save our basic manufacturing industries. But what, we may ask, would lead them to believe that such an effort can succeed with the public now when it has failed to attract widespread support in the past—especially now that the government's prophecies appear to be coming true? The authors shy away from acknowledging the very real cultural appeal of the "Darwinian model" and are consequently in no position to explain why it has played such a powerful role in guiding our industrial policy.

Belief in free market competition and the survival of the fittest is more than just an economic model. These principles are also part of a meaningful cultural system that allows people to invest their behavior in the marketplace with moral significance. Darwinian thinking is not simply about the beneficial effects of eliminating the unfit. It is also about how success should be measured in a world where resources are limited and the competition is fierce.

CHAPTER SIX

That Haunting Thing

From the window of the mayor's office, you can see a wide stretch of Kenosha's harbor and lakefront. Cerulean vistas draw the eye eastward across the lake to a horizon of water and sky, giving the illusion of an infinite expanse. Demolition crews have already begun to dismantle AMC's lakefront plant, a rambling, two-story structure that occupies several city blocks along the shore. Separate from the main plant at the center of town, these old factory buildings have stood watch over Kenosha's harbor for more than a century. Wrecking cranes, it might seem, would be no match for this fortress. But now, as I look down curiously, gaping holes appear where walls have been stripped away, and the interiors of buildings stand exposed like broken eggs.

As we stand by the window surveying the work in progress below, Alderman Tony DePalma points out where the new multimillion dollar marina will be built. He moves his finger across the glass, tracing out a new city superimposed on the old one. "Here's where the high-rise condominiums will be built," he says proudly, "and there's where the boardwalk and municipal park will be." These developments are expected to attract new investors to the downtown area, who will in turn set the streets astir with entrepreneurial enterprise. When Tony turns from the window with a broad smile, it's clear that in his mind's eye these things are already taking place.

I ask Tony what these changes will mean for Kenosha. "We can no longer cling on to [a] false sense of security," he says decisively, attributing this unfortunate attitude to the way blue-collar politicians ran the city. They treated the public in much the same way the UAW

Wrecking crews began dismantling the lakefront plant during the winter of 1989. Work on the new marina began that summer. Photo by Chuck D'Acquisto and the Racine *Journal Times.*

treated AMC, he asserts, and this led to the gross misuse of public funds:

> A lot of nonproductive things had been negotiated. If you look at compensation levels that had been negotiated for county and city employees, when you had people coming from that particular environment [labor unions] negotiating contracts—the highest compensations per job classification for all the counties in Wisconsin were here in Kenosha. That's because that particular [city official] of that point of view [who] was trying to negotiate for the taxpayers, or "management," was literally giving the store away. That's why these compensation levels were high.

The problem with a blue-collar city council was that the taxpayers were left with no one to represent their interests. A city is headed for certain ruin, Tony believes, when public coffers are controlled by people who identify with the interests of labor—it's like letting the fox set up operations in the chicken coop. And events in city hall were a mirror image of what was going on over at American Motors:

> For a small company, [AMC] had a noncompetitive contract. The wage rates [there] were higher than at other, larger

manufacturers domestically. So to really maintain quality within the manufacturing context was an impossibility. There was a lot of featherbedding. They had a lot of noncompetitive elements within their contract that evolved because [AMC] was a small fish in a big pond. You had management, in the thirties before the Wagner Act, that were insensitive to workers' needs and they abused the rights of workers and consequently [workers] organized. But then the pendulum swung, where this particular local was the largest labor local in the state of Wisconsin, and the union—they became more tyrannical than the tyrant they overcame!—and what they did was really to price themselves out of a job.

Tony speaks for many in Kenosha's white-collar community when he reads the events of the past three decades in this way. "During the 1980s, the leadership [of Local 72] really embraced the tactics and attitudes of a movement," he complains. "They really didn't really foresee the need for change—in terms of inner management-worker relationships." In short, they refused to acknowledge the inevitable:

They just couldn't see that you can't depend on this industry to be here forever! The world around us is changing megatrends, and just look at the reality, Kenosha! I mean, don't be complacent and think this is always going to be here! But you had leadership in that particular union—it was the same litany, the same gospel of confrontationalism: "Oh, [they'd always say,] we've heard *this* before! and they're *never* gonna close! and we've got the big stick and, by golly, we're gonna use it!" So I think there was really something lacking within the union ranks.

What was lacking, Tony is convinced, was a commitment by union leaders to do whatever might have been necessary to save the company from extinction. Even after Chrysler stepped in and bought AMC in 1987, the union continued to stonewall, refusing to make the kinds of concessions Tony thinks might have kept the plant open a little longer. But in the end even Chrysler's decision to transfer assembly work to Kenosha was only "another Band-Aid." The union's stance remained unchanged. "Again," Tony sighs, there were "the attitudes, the posturing politically on the part of the union. 'You know, [they'd say,] we've got three to five years and we're going to tell [Chrysler] what to do.' We told AMC what to do, and the tail is still wagging the dog. But it was a new, a new . . ." He gropes for words.

"A new dog?" I offer.

"A new dog!" he laughs with obvious pleasure. "Literally, it was."

After a thoughtful pause, he says, "When I first came to Kenosha, I had kids in my classes—I was a schoolteacher then—that said, Mr. DePalma, you're making a lousy sixteen Gs as a teacher. My old man and his dad have always worked at American Motors, and do you know something? They make 95 percent of their pay even if they're laid off! I don't need this high-school diploma. I don't need this written competency or this math competency. I'm going into the automobile industry and I'll live happily ever after."

Tony gives me an emphatic look. "And this at a time when this change [in the auto industry] was occurring! But this cultural malaise, or this behavior that had been developed generation to generation to generation. . . ." His voice trails off, and he just shakes his head. He looks out the window and adds, "I really do think [the plant closing] is to the benefit of the people and their children. That kid, when I was teaching in class, who said, 'Mr. DePalma, why do I have to have this high-school diploma?' And it goes back to that. It's almost a haunting thing . . ."

A Lost Generation

"The mentality of many people in this community was that American Motors or Chrysler was going to be the salvation," says Ron Carleson, a business administrator in the Kenosha school district. Ron grew up in Kenosha, and as the son of an optician who served many clients in the blue-collar community, he feels he has a special understanding of the day-to-day realities factory workers must deal with. When auto sales were down, people were laid off, and eyeglasses and vision tests went by the way. When sales picked up and people were called back to work, the town breathed a collective sigh of relief, and squads of squinting kids trooped back into Doc Carleson's Spec Shop. Ron shakes his head and chuckles. The whole town was on a "crazy roller coaster ride," going up and down with every cough and sneeze over at AMC. To his amazement, the wild swings in employment that began with AMC's death throes in the late 1970s didn't snap people out of this way of thinking. "With more extremes of the roller coaster ride," he says, "the mentality grew to an even greater extent. We still had that one-industry mentality that drove this town."

People were so "dependent" on the auto industry, Ron believes, that like people addicted to drugs they eventually lost touch with reality:

> They continued to think [the auto industry] was going to save us and we were going to maintain jobs at $15.75 an hour—assembly line types of jobs, unskilled labor types of jobs, me-

nial types of jobs. Those things were still going to be around
and everything was going to be fine. Little did they know that
[the shutdown] was going to happen. They still believe that
there's going to be another employer coming in with jobs at
$15.75 an hour. I'm of the firm opinion—just knowing and
reading enough about the way our society is going—that
those types of jobs are gone, and they're gone forever. People
of the twenty-first century are going to have to have skills
and they're going to have to have an education. I guess I see
that transition happening in kids' minds a lot quicker than in
adults' minds. I think kids understand that those jobs aren't
going to be there and that they'd best get as good an education as they possibly can. . . . I only wish all of them felt
that way.

School professionals like Ron see in the Chrysler plant closing a
morality play about the virtues of education. As they see it, the blue-
collar mentality always prompted people to forgo an education in favor of a quick buck at the auto plant. Today that system of values
stands revealed as the irresponsible way of life educators always knew
it was. Moral vindication, long denied, is finally at hand: let all those
who dodged math drills to take joyrides down Main Street contem-
plate these sins while standing in the unemployment line! In this twist
of fate, teachers see a golden opportunity to hammer home lessons
that have hitherto fallen on deaf ears. They look back on AMC's glory
days and recall a time when students would respond to a homework
assignment, a counselor's advice, or a principal's reprimand with the
impertinent retort that school was nothing but a boring interlude between childhood and a good-paying job at the Motors. Until now blue-
collar students have had no incentive to work hard in school and no
examples of academic success to emulate at home. The plant closing,
educators feel, at long last removes the single greatest obstacle to a
cultural conversion experience in the classroom.

This high-school principal conveys a sentiment shared by many of
his colleagues:

In the past students would say—to teachers, to counselors, to
principals—"hey, I don't need an education. I can work on
the line like my dad, uncle, grandfather, and I'll make more
money than *you* the first year I'm on the job. And they were
right. The wages and salaries for starters at AMC and Chrysler were in the neighborhood of $30,000. A starting teacher
gets $18,000 to $19,000. That's a big difference. Why should
a kid who has no support from home to get an education, to
be a professional, go on to become a teacher, doctor, or law-

yer? They've got their parents at home telling them, "So what if the school hassles you? You can always get a job on the line. I'll get you into American Motors." So, absolutely, that's been a problem. Many of us in education are very happy to see the auto industry go, for that reason alone.

Educators hope that the shutdown will finally make reality sink in and dramatize to everyone in the community how important education is. Perhaps now they will have half a chance of drawing students out of their adolescent stupor and talking to them about the social and economic changes that are affecting their lives. Something that hits this close to home for so many of their students might just be the kind of dynamite needed to blast students out of their Walkman headphones. Yet there is a bleak undertone to the missionary zeal with which teachers speak of saving lost souls. Grave misgivings surface about their chances of success with the generation of students currently occupying their classrooms.

Larry Cramer has been teaching history and economics in a Kenosha high school for over twenty years. When Larry talks about the frustration he feels with his current crop of students, he suggests that—with this generation, at least—his hands are tied. These kids seem to be beyond help: the blue-collar mentality is too deeply ingrained to disappear overnight. I ask Larry to describe the attitudes of his students, and he has this to say:

> There's no reality in [the idea that] "First, I get my high-school diploma, then I get myself a job, or then I go on for additional training, or so on." It's "*Now!* I've got my new car *now!* I've got a job that requires me to work thirty-some hours a week to support that car. If I'm too tired to go to school, that's all right, but God help me if I'm too tired to go to work." And that is very, very prevalent. It's not only the question of "Why do we study U.S. history, this is all *old* stuff?" It's "Why should I go to school if I can get a job that pays me X number of dollars an hour without it?" The reality hasn't sunk in yet that that's just not possible.

Larry isn't surprised when his students say that they prefer work to school because they don't get paid for going to school. But he links this critical life choice to a moral failing: the inability to delay gratification. In a mad rush to indulge consumer passions in the present, his students are missing the main chance they will have to secure good jobs in the future. Like the generations of blue-collar workers before them, these kids are giving school short shrift in pursuit of faster, easier pleasures. But now, Larry points out, when they dash out of

91

school into the only jobs available to them, they will have a rude awakening. The jobs that once offered the kind of money they expect to earn are no longer there. Like the comic-strip characters who run over the edge of a cliff, they can tread air for a while, but they can't prevent the inevitable.

Teachers suggest that blue-collar kids have been bequeathed an "obsolete" mind-set—that they are part of an entire generation that is "lost in space" with no place to go in the social structure but down. Calling the problem a "cultural lag," history teacher Bruce McCloskey explains how this situation arose:

> What I see happening is that the jobs that required very little skill, but made an awful lot of money, are being eliminated. These smokestack industries are either having to change and become more technical or go out of business. People who are the old generation, who were working in these jobs, I see them slowly but surely being phased out—or they're retiring, or they're dying, or whatever. And I don't see their kids moving into these jobs, because [those jobs] have become automated. So we've got kind of a void here, where you had these lowly educated people who made quite a bit of money, and now we've got a void because no one can go into these jobs, they're being eliminated. Now all of a sudden their kids are here, and these kids are not educated enough to move into the new technical jobs, and yet there are none of the jobs that they used to have, with the strong back and the weak mind. They're not there any more, so you've got this void, and you got a bunch of people here who don't really know what they're going to do.

The idea of a culturally transmitted mentality is appealing to many middle-class professionals because it seems to resolve the issue of who is to blame for the social disorder that accompanies technological change. Teachers do not blame the school system for failing to prepare the children of factory workers for the industrial transition that lay ahead. On the contrary, they stress how hard they try to do their best by these students, but all to minimal avail. In their mind the blame lies with a particular way of thinking about moral obligations to self and others—a "deviant" culture that gets passed down from one generation to the next.[1]

The main problem with the present generation of students, Bruce says, is that "they have all the protections of adults, and yet they don't have to take on the responsibilities of adults." Students today can tell you what their rights are in this society, Bruce feels, but they do not understand that rights and responsibilities are intertwined or that they owe something to society in return for the freedoms they enjoy. Their culture, in short, does not provide them with an adequate morality:

> This breakdown [in values] is not something that happened overnight. This has been a long-term deterioration. This has gone on probably since the fifties, and now we see the ramifications of all these so-called freedoms. Our kids do not have what we used to call *respect,* a healthy respect. You take a look at our desks: they're completely written on. "You wouldn't do that at home, would'ja?" "Ah, no [students say]." "Well, then why do you do it here?" "This is a public school [they say]: I'm free to do what I want in a public school."

At first glance, graffiti on desktops would hardly seem to portend the downfall of American democracy. In the eyes of Kenosha's teachers, however, these cryptic etchings represent much more than a flagrant disregard for the rules of civilized society.[2] Teachers see in these tattooed surfaces a loss of moral order, a threat to the system of rights and responsibilities that at one time allowed a person in their profession to feel worthy of respect. Blue-collar culture is deviant, in this sense, because it fails to maintain what teachers consider to be the proper balance between people's rights as individuals and their obligations to others as members of a community.

"Kids today know that they are completely protected, not only by the laws, but even by their parents," Bruce complains. "There is very little responsibility that they have to take on, because no matter what happens, they're gonna have somebody on their side. And they seem to really abuse that. It seems like there's an abuse of rights."

I ask Bruce if he can give me some examples of the kinds of abuses he has in mind. He throws up his hands and laughs as if to say "Where do I begin?" As it turns out, Bruce is thinking of all the seemingly minor insults and challenges to school authority that teachers must let slide, day after day, with clenched teeth. It's the kids who slouch in their seats wearing hats and coats in the classroom. It's the kids who skip classes and fail to turn in homework assignments—and when warning notes of failing grades are sent home, there is no concerned reply from parents: there is no response at all. It's the kids who wear offensive, outrageous clothes: slashed-up punk outfits that look like they've just been through a knife fight, sweatshirts and gym shorts appropriate for a basketball court or—and Bruce's eyes smolder on this one—T-shirts emblazoned with profanities. In his day, Bruce points out angrily, you would *never* have been allowed to wear something like that:

> There wasn't any question, the T-shirt was taken from you, and you were sent home. Well, today, not only would you have to send the student home, but then you'd have to write a letter explaining why. Then you'd have to go through a due process hearing, and the kid would have to be given due process, and you'd have to follow all of those rules. Where in the past, that was an automatic, that was not what society accepted and you were gone! And you wouldn't have a parent come to school saying, "My son has *the right* to wear that." Today you would find that.

There is more to this story of professional harassment than meets the eye. As Bruce talks about the legal protections his students have gained and now appear to be abusing, I am reminded of Tony DePalma's indictment of Kenosha's labor unions. In the past, Tony believes, employers were taking advantage of workers, so unions justifiably fought for more rights. But then, in his words, "the tyrant became greater than the tyrant it overcame," and unions began to abuse the rights they had won. Like Tony, Bruce invokes the image of a pendulum swinging from one extreme to the other when he talks about the balance of power between teachers and students. At one time, Bruce asserts, teachers could take advantage of their position and treat students unfairly. So there was just cause for the reforms demanded by students in the 1960s—a movement that Bruce, as a college student, fully supported. But now the pendulum has swung to the opposite extreme, he says, "to the side of the *student* is always right, and the *teacher* is probably wrong."

Middle-class professionals like Tony DePalma and Bruce McCloskey suspect that the scales of justice were knocked out of kilter sometime between the civil rights movement and the Vietnam War. There was an unhealthy tilt toward individual rights at the expense of responsibility to community, an imbalance that has only grown more disproportionate over the years. With the demise of the auto plant, business leaders and educators feel, the scales of justice will begin to right themselves. People will be forced to see that they have an obligation to the community, if not to themselves, to become educated, productive members of society. Economic advancement and membership in the middle class will come to depend on credentials and individual merit, not on seniority and collective bargaining.

A Matter of Self-Respect

Corporate America can lament the state of our educational system and its lack of a well-trained workforce; it can even bolster the nebulous resolve of our government to do something about it. But, when all is said and done, education comes down to teachers and teaching: real people engaged in efforts that are, for the vast majority, more than just a job. Teachers, like most of us in this market economy, make a moral commitment to the work they do. They espouse deeply cherished goals; and whether they define these goals as helping others, nurturing children, or making a contribution to the community or to the future of human endeavor, they look to their teaching experience for a confirmation of their moral character and self-worth. This is why Bruce McCloskey's discussion of rights and responsibilities is more than just a grouchy jeremiad about obnoxious students. When the scales of justice are askew, he is saying—when individual rights are celebrated and social obligations ignored—then the work of people who are looking out for society's best interests is bound to be devalued.

"What has happened," Bruce reiterates, "is it used to be that the teacher was 100 percent right . . . the perception is now that the teacher is all wrong. I think that's probably why a lot of people in education feel very bad. They tried their best, and yet it appears that no matter what they do, they're always condemned for it. And a lot of teachers have a hard time with that."

Indeed, virtually all the teachers I speak with at high schools in and around Kenosha express this disheartening sense of being devalued. Like their counterparts across the country, they have been faced with budget cuts, crowded classrooms, and a public grown hostile toward tax increases of all kinds.[3] Yet it is not so much a lack of support from the government—from the top down, so to speak—that creates feelings of self-doubt and burnout, but a lack of support, or at least respect, from the bottom up. Kenosha's teachers would love to see dozens of rapt young faces turned toward them in hushed admiration. Yet in this traditional manufacturing town, that is precisely the moral reward they have been denied.

History teacher Molly Brown responds with peals of good-natured laughter when I ask about her students' knowledge of current events. "They are not aware of what's going on around them, beyond their own immediate realm and peer group," she says. Molly looks at me with an exasperated smile, as if to say I cannot possibly comprehend the full import of what she's saying. "They are *not* aware! It is really,

really sad! My group of regulars is fighting me tooth and nail simply because I'm insisting they know the fifty states and where they're at! And they are fighting me on that because they think that is the dumbest thing for anybody to be required to learn!" Molly has no doubt that a firm grasp of national geography is a vital component of a good education, and she exhibits no sign of bending to student pressure on this point. Yet her laughter belies a genuine anguish. Like so many of her fellow teachers, Molly is deeply aware that her efforts to "reach" kids who fall to the bottom two-thirds of their high-school class—those in the "basic" or "regular" academic tracks—are often in vain, and she is sincerely troubled by this. After all, being able to enrich and uplift the lives of gangly teenagers is at the heart of why she became a teacher in the first place.

Carol Jencks, an American history teacher for thirty-five years, just shakes her head and sighs. "I feel sad very often when I look at them. I think, oh, your world is so limited! There's so much out there," she insists. Carol runs her hand through her hair, a woman at wit's end. Here she is, day after day, laying out all the riches that education has to offer, and students just turn up their noses. "I liked school, so I have a different perception, probably," she supposes. "Today [the kids seem to feel], 'This is what we have to do by law. I can't wait till I get out! Set me free!' It's almost like a prison. I don't mean everyone, but I have an awful lot of regular kids that fall in that category."

Beneath their real concerns about what, or even whether, their students are learning, teachers are searching for a way to validate their identities as professional people deserving of special respect. What is a teacher worth in the scheme of things if kids can get along in life without knowing the fifty states? Is it possible to maintain a sense of professional dignity when the social function of a teacher seems uncomfortably like that of a jail warden? Without the recognition and respect of the community they are dedicated to serve, many experience a gnawing sense of doubt about their effectiveness as teachers and about the goals of contemporary education. Carol Jencks realizes that her frustration is due, in some measure, to social factors beyond her control; yet this thought does not comfort her. Taking part in an educational system that fails to educate its students can drive you crazy:

> A lot of my students today are not capable of carrying on a conversation beyond what's going on in their immediate world, which might be drugs or problems at home, alcoholism. *That's* their world. I almost feel crazy sometimes when I'm talking to them. Are we really reaching these kids? Are

we going to have to change our philosophy of education with them? I don't know where our educational system is headed. I have students who just absolutely do not know the skill of *listening*. I can tell by the questions that get asked, immediately after I give directions for something. It's like they never even heard me.

For some teachers like Stanley Davidson, the gray-haired chairman of a social studies department, the bad eventually outweighs the good, and dignity is sought in admitting defeat:

> Most of [my students] don't know anything about what's going on, and *they don't care.* I'm really discouraged. I'm just happy this is my last year. I just can't handle this anymore. The apathy of the students . . . in terms of learning, homework, doing a good job. They just want to get a D and pass the course. This is different in the college prep courses—they're generally the nice kids. Oh, but you get down to the bottom two-thirds, they try to get away with not doing the homework. Oh, they lie, and they lie with such a straight face. There's no feeling of guilt. Oh, I'm just so . . . this is called burnout. But it's not something really within me, it's been *caused* by these kids.

White-collar work, despite its presumed superiority to blue-collar labor, is clearly not without its dissatisfactions. In *The Hidden Injuries of Class,* sociologists Richard Sennett and Jonathan Cobb argue that Americans of all classes view their place in the occupational structure as the result of individual effort and as a reflection of self-worth. Entry into white-collar occupations promises special fulfillment because it is supposed to require the extra effort it takes to acquire educational credentials—the "certification of mind" that deems you a worthy person of special talents. Academic credentials—"badges of ability" as Sennett and Cobb call them—create "moral symbols" around white-collar work that induce people in these prestigious jobs to feel they have risen to a place in the social order where they will be valued as intelligent individuals who have a special contribution to make to society.[4] Because entry into white-collar occupations is thought to be a matter of self-improvement, success, and upward mobility, Sennett and Cobb argue, people tend to believe that the boredom and frustration they experience in white-collar jobs is the result of some personal failing, some inability to find in this privileged position the self-fulfillment that was promised.

Teachers experience the dissatisfactions of white-collar work in a particularly acute way. Not only are they bound by the moral symbols of work that requires mental rather than physical labor, they are also responsible, in large part, for inculcating this morality in their students. The satisfactions of high-school teaching are usually found in teaching the honors or college prep classes. Not surprisingly, these are the assignments that teachers mention with the greatest pride, and in the informal pecking order of the faculty lounge, they carry the greatest prestige. Only with students who are genuinely interested and engaged in what's happening in the classroom, teachers imply, can they really use their *own* minds to the fullest and, in so doing, fulfill their moral commitment to education. When students come into their classrooms with no inclination to see education as a social obligation, teachers confront the uphill task of instilling a sense of responsibility into refractory minds.

Teachers always emphasize that the tracking system they use—one that sorts students into basic, regular, or honors courses—is meant to reflect a student's classroom "performance," not innate intellectual ability. But there is little doubt in the minds of most teachers about what these designations really mean. School performance is less a matter of IQ points hard-wired in a student's brain, teachers unanimously agree, than it is a measure of the "values" they learn at home. Molly Brown explains the difference between students in her basic and regular classes and those in her honors class:

> [It's] the value systems in education, for one—from a teacher's standpoint. [How students answer questions like,] Where am I going? What am I going to do with the rest of my life? Is there anything in the future? What's the point of it all? I think it manifests itself just in terms of the lack of motivation. I can compare some of the students I have in my regular class versus my college prep classes. They just don't read. I've got some in there, they can read, but they're not understanding a word that they're reading. I may as well be talking Greek! I think it starts in terms of exposure at home. Maybe it starts with cultural exposure or the lack of cultural exposure, and then from there, through the learning process, it [comes to the point where students say], "Hey, this is of no use to me. I don't see that it's going to benefit my future." And it works its way into the value system.

Students will be excited about learning, Molly believes, if they have been brought up to believe that doing well in school and having educational credentials will matter to them in the long run, in terms of the future they are able to envision for themselves. Boredom and apathy, by contrast, spring from a lack of "exposure" to the values that would enable them to imagine a place for themselves in a postindustrial economy. If, as teachers contend, students are handicapped by the "culture" they learn at home, what is it, exactly, that this culture lacks?

Teachers like Molly see the problem as a "lack of imagination" or a limited sense of the possibilities in life. Students who can't imagine themselves going into a professional line of work are the ones who express little interest in cracking the books now. Most teachers interpret this dearth of interest as the absence of certain values that they readily identify with their personal value system. The notion of a "cultural deficit" makes intuitive sense to Kenosha's teachers. Much like the nation's budget deficit, it is a sign that people have gone into the red because they borrow from the future to pay for a lack of common sense and self-discipline in the present. Blue-collar culture, teachers believe, likewise encourages young people to leverage their futures. Students have forgone the necessary preparations for life in the twenty-first century in order to support a profligate and ultimately untenable lifestyle in the present.

The economic metaphor is not coincidental. Teachers are acutely conscious of the purported link between America's economic decline and the slipping test scores of our children. Yet as sociologist Fred Block points out in his analysis of economic discourse in the United States, the "hidden metaphors" we use to understand the functioning of capitalist markets say more about how we would like to believe the economy works than about the forces that actually govern its operation. One such metaphor, in Block's view, is the notion that economic recovery and well-being can best be brought about through sacrifice and redemption. In this metaphor the national economy is portrayed as "an individual who has succumbed to temptation" by overindulging in laziness or sensual pleasures. Only a sustained period of asceticism will "atone for past sins and allow the nation to return to the path of righteousness."[5]

Just as the American people are being urged to tighten their belts and increase personal savings, students are being implored to stay in school and improve their grades. The fate of the nation is said to rest on these twin acts of sacrifice and studiousness. Metaphors are used to simplify complex and abstract social relations, and that is their beauty. But just as increased savings rates will not automatically turn the economy around, holding more students captive for longer periods of their lives is not the magic secret to national recovery.

Metaphors of redemption through sacrifice are dubious precisely because they focus on individual behavior in circumstances where the critical problems exist on a societal level. Public policies are needed to alter the context within which individuals make the choices that pattern their lives in one way or another. When Kenosha teachers use the metaphor of cultural deficit to explain the behavior of low achievers, they feel they have put their finger on the source of a societal problem. In truth, however, they have focused on only one dimension of the problem, the one that impinges directly on their sense of self-worth: the issue of individual motivation and responsibility. Few teachers are prepared to examine the other part of the problem. Few seriously ask if society has fulfilled its obligations to these under-achieving students.

PART THREE

Culture of the Hands

Kenosha is a very divided city. You do not have people
that stick together. I figured our city council, the way they
reacted at first, they were going to try to come up with a
lawsuit to keep [Chrysler] here. Then all of a sudden [they
decided], "No, we don't want [the autoworkers]." We had no
backing from them at all. You know, we were no-good, rotten
people. You have the people that work [in the plant]. You have
those that don't. Two totally different . . . it's like nationalities.
It's . . . we're hated. We're really a hated breed of people.

Assembler, thirty-five years old

CHAPTER SEVEN

Shopfloor Culture

The meaning of work for Kenosha autoworkers is shaped by the structure of social relations formed on the assembly line. In most assembly plants, about three out of every four blue-collar workers have a job of one kind or another on the line. People working off the line include those in the skilled trades, maintenance workers, material handlers, inspectors, repairmen, machine operators, and so forth. Yet even for these workers, the line structures the nature of their tasks in such a way that they are drawn into a plantwide network of blue-collar ties.

As a distinctive labor process, the assembly line has been the hallmark of auto manufacturing and other mass production industries since the early 1900s.[1] This organization of work continues to be of special interest to students of labor organization because of the considerable control it gives management over the rate of production and the intensity of labor workers are subjected to. For autoworkers, however, the line is more than a production process. They frequently use the imagery of the line to talk about the nexus of social relations within which their work is performed. For those both on and off the line, the meaning of work—its satisfactions as well as its frustrations—springs from this informal network of social interactions. The line is a symbol of the common bond that all workers share, the collective experience that ties them together as a special group with its own code of conduct. The line is the key feature of the shopfloor culture into which workers are initiated by "proving themselves" on the line.

A group of autoworkers contribute background vocals to the anti-Iacocca song, "Hey Lee." Photo by Bill Siel and the *Kenosha News.*

On the Line

In the Kenosha plant, as in all modern auto assembly operations, the line is composed of many different assembly and subassembly lines. These continuously running lines snake through a maze of production departments in factory buildings the size of football stadiums. Shop traffic runs through these buildings much as through a small city. Full-sized streets run down the length of each production complex, allowing forklifts to bring stock to the lines and maintenance trucks to tote refuse away. As finished cars roll off the line, workers jump in and drive them to final test stations and inspection points. Overhead are multiple conveyor belts bringing down engines and other "subassemblies" from peripheral lines on other floors. Lines are constantly moving in every part of the plant. "It's just all over," Connie Miller says, describing her impression of the production pro-

104

cess. "You look, and it's like alive, you know?" This confluence of work streams was especially exciting in the final assembly department, where Connie worked with her husband Steve. Called "I-94" after Kenosha's nearest interstate highway, the final assembly line was where the production lines from all other departments fed into each other as motors, transmissions, rear ends, front ends, and car bodies were brought together into one unit.

The line, as workers experienced it, truly did seem "alive," possessing a life of its own. Control over the line's speed, and hence the pace of work that management demanded, was entirely out of workers' hands. As we will see, workers usually found ways to take back a measure of control over the speed at which they did their jobs, but such efforts rarely altered the absolute rates set by management. The line's implacable demands for more work, faster work, and ceaseless work remained an ever-present reality. Some people found this lack of autonomy utterly unbearable. Almost always, they were the ones who quit on their very first day of work, walking off the line in disgust, never to return. Others persevered. Some made peace with this harsh taskmaster while others aspired to jobs off the line, which could be achieved by accumulating seniority or completing an apprenticeship in the skilled trades.

Bill Sorensen, a tool and die maker in his late thirties, compares his first few years on the line to "Chinese water torture":

> On the assembly line, you cannot speed up, you cannot slow down. The line determines your speed. It's totally out of your hands. If you wanted to really get cracking and do a bang-up job, if you're really feeling energetic on a particular day, you can't do twice as many cars as you've every done before. It's impossible: the line determines the pace. And if you're feeling like death warmed over, it doesn't matter . . . you still have to do the same number of cars.

The "torture" of the line is that it circumscribes the expression of any individual feeling or action. The imperative to perform at a preordained rate imposes upon all line workers a stultifying uniformity, which crushes individual initiative even as it compels an individual response. With every movement of their hands and bodies coordinated for maximum efficiency, and distinctly personal decisions about when to eat or when to take a break regularly made from above, line workers can easily come to feel at the mercy of forces larger than themselves. Like wooden puppets dangling from strings, autoworkers may feel like "death warmed over," yet still go through the motions of their job, much as though the will to do so were not their own.

This separation of action and volition is often thought to be the sine qua non of work on an assembly line. Popular American culture is replete with images of the dehumanizing nature of industrial work. So antithetical to the virtues of individualism is line work that factory workers are often portrayed as being in danger of becoming machines themselves. The Hollywood classic *Modern Times* is a silent-movie version of this theme, showing Charlie Chaplin as a hapless tramp working on an assembly line, who becomes so automatic in his reflexes that he gradually becomes a robot. Among scholarly writers, the auto assembly line has been dubbed "the classic symbol of the subjugation of man to the machine in our industrial age."[2] Auto assemblers are described as "the prototype of the mass man [who] is relatively powerless, atomized, depersonalized, and anonymous."[3] Life in an auto factory is said to be "dull, brutish, weary, and stuporous."[4] And the United States Department of Health, Education, and Welfare has characterized the automobile industry as "the *locus classicus* of dissatisfying work; the assembly-line, its quintessential embodiment."[5]

Given such negative images of factory work, it becomes easy to conclude that the only people who feel alienated and dissatisfied on the job are those who work in mass production industries.[6] When auto work—and assembly line work in particular—is held up as the symbol of dehumanizing labor, every other form of work becomes more prestigious by comparison. The cultural symbol of "mindless" auto work, I should note, does not express concern about the job satisfaction of autoworkers. Quite the contrary, a belief in the unsatisfying nature of auto work effectively reinforces the notion that only people with an education do satisfying work. Subhuman stereotypes of blue-collar labor convey a moral judgment about the way skill and ability should be measured and rewarded in modern society.

Behind the banter about "grease monkeys" and "line rats" lurks the concept of a Darwinian struggle for existence in which severely routinized work is assumed to require little or no human capacity. Manual laborers fall to a lowly place on this evolutionary scale of occupational types while more "capable" people—those with certified skills and intellectual abilities—rise to higher, more developed states of human worth. When industrial labor is seen as the occupation of last resort for the mentally incompetent, factory workers are marked as a "deviant" cultural category: like animals, they appear to put up with conditions that "normal" human beings would find intolerable.

Kenosha autoworkers challenge the dominant culture's image of factory labor by honoring a different notion of human capacity and an alternative way of measuring skill and ability. Workers believe that a person's intrinsic moral worth has nothing to do with one's position in society or how much education one has had. Instead, individual ability is demonstrated by what people do—by their actions rather than their words, by deeds rather than fancy degrees, and most important, by the tangible results of their labor. Building a car every minute, autoworkers like to boast, is no mean feat. Not everybody has what it takes to keep up with the demanding pace of the line, and those who do consider themselves special people with a unique capacity.

In later chapters I will take up the question whether autoworkers can maintain their distinctive system of values in the world outside the factory gates. My focus here is on the nexus of blue-collar ties on the shopfloor, and on how this social structure gives rise to a system of cultural meanings that recognizes the dignity of work done with the hands. The autoworkers' shopfloor culture is shared by all who get paid by the hour, and this includes assemblers as well as those in the skilled trades. It crosses the boundaries of sex, race, and ethnicity and bridges divided loyalties to the several unions represented in the plant. Perhaps most surprising, shopfloor culture crosses the barriers of educational credentials—the very barriers that create such a gulf between autoworkers and middle-class professionals. In the words of journeyman Bill Sorensen, himself a college graduate, "We were cheek to jowl in that plant, with people who had master's degrees and complete illiterates side by side—in production [on the line], at any rate."

As the specter of unemployment loomed in the wake of the plant closing, there could be little doubt that educated workers—those with degrees and those in the skilled trades—faced fewer obstacles to reemployment than their uncredentialed coworkers. Not surprisingly, these men and women think of themselves as belonging to a labor elite, a class of people in a fundamentally different predicament than other autoworkers. Objectively speaking, they are quite right. The external society is far more willing and likely to confer dignity (and jobs) on workers with proven track records outside the plant than on the unknown quantity of an "unskilled" assembler. Yet not all in-house positions had direct counterparts on the outside. Not all trades could be practiced outside the factory without first surmounting the cost and difficulty of meeting outside licensing requirements and standards. Moreover, college degrees and teaching certificates earned long ago but set aside do not have the same currency they might have had fifteen years earlier. The sense of individual worth that many in the skilled trades feel came as much from the prestigious position they occupied on the shopfloor as from any credentials they might possess.

The cultural solidarity that exists between the credentialed and un-credentialed segments of the blue-collar workforce derives from the shared experience of a labor process that encourages collective effort and an egalitarian ethos. Of all the ties between diverse groups in the plant, the bond between workers with a college education or some advanced training and those with no more than a high-school di-ploma was the most fragile, and it was the first to disintegrate in the aftermath of the shutdown. But this eventual unraveling should not mislead us. Educated autoworkers occupied an uncertain "border-land" between the culture of the mind and the culture of the hands. Degree of allegiance to one system of meaning or the other varies with the circumstances and with the individual. These workers offer eloquent testimony to the painful dilemmas about ability that Ameri-can culture can generate. For as their experience shows, to fully em-brace one of these value systems is to turn your back on the other.

Whatever direction credentialed workers go in the aftermath of the plant closing—whether they go back into the ranks of manual labor or out into the white-collar world—they express an abiding respect for the integrity of industrial labor. My discussions with them reveal an acceptance of "cultural diversity" (in this case, different ways of measuring human ability and moral worth) that is far more nuanced than the thinking of most in the credentialed mainstream. Bill Sor-ensen, for example, toys with the idea of pursuing a master's degree in business. Yet to his mind factory work is inherently more stressful than the work done by a corporate executive. If American society were consistent in its values and truly honored people whose work involved great stress, Bill argues, industrial workers would be at the top, not the bottom, of the pecking order:

> The common concept in our society is that the head of a cor-poration is in a very stressful job. That is the wonderful myth in America. You work your way up, and that's the most stress-ful thing you can do. But people who have more control, more decision making in what they're going to do, have the *least* amount of stress. The people who have no decision-making capabilities and no control over their work environ-ment have the *most* stress. Decisions are made for them,

whether they're good decisions or bad decisions. The person that's telling you what to do, how to do it, and when to do it, oftentimes isn't as bright as the person doing the job. So there's a lot of built-in stress.

In his irreverence toward people in decision-making positions, Bill has both feet squarely on the shopfloor. Kenosha autoworkers, no matter what their educational background, are unanimous in the belief that simply having power and position doesn't mean you are intelligent, and being intelligent doesn't necessarily lead you to pursue power and social position. Credentials mean very little in their calculation of individual worth. Indeed, workers who flaunt such accomplishments find not greater respect among their fellows, but mocking derision and more than a few cold shoulders.

Turning society's scale of ability on its head has an important function on the shopfloor: it provides workers with a way of asserting their common humanity and personal dignity. It offers a framework for thinking about work in the auto plant that allows people to reclaim a sense of their individual efficacy against enormous cultural pressures to the contrary. To say that workers are dehumanized by the production system assumes that they have no way to cope with this system and thus automatically succumb to feelings of blind obedience, apathy, and lack of personal agency. Undoubtedly some production workers do come to experience the labor process in this way—and they suffer grave psychological distress as a result. Shopfloor lore in the Kenosha plant was spiced with stories about coworkers who had really "lost it" or "gone off the deep end." But as the constant retelling of these tales suggests, autoworkers are keenly aware of the need to safeguard their psychological health and emotional well-being. When speaking of frustrations on the job—such as unavoidable reasons for falling behind the line, the arbitrary directives of foremen, and so forth—workers almost always shrug off these irritations with remarks like "you can't let it get to you" or "it was just [the boss's] game—I didn't let it affect me."

If workers don't literally become dehumanized, they often feel that management treats them like interchangeable mechanical parts, or robots expected to obey mechanical laws.[7] This treatment naturally sparks anger, resentment, and defensiveness—but these feelings are not those of "dehumanized" individuals. On the contrary, autoworkers have these feelings because they are human beings struggling with issues of freedom and dignity in a highly regimented social institution that actively suppresses individuality. In the Kenosha plant, the struggle to assert individual worth found expression in the social ties they established among fellow blue-collar workers. The satisfactions of this remarkably rich and enduring shopfloor culture enabled autoworkers both on and off the line to resist the demoralizing effects of the labor process to which they were subjected.

Collective Reliance

The line, as autoworkers experience and construe it, is a social project or group game in which everyone in the plant takes part. Work on the line is rarely conceived of as a job done in isolation, and few workers—even those on punch presses and other piecework jobs—speak of feeling locked into solitary relationships with machines or mechanical parts.[8] Rather, autoworkers participated in a distinctive system of informal group norms that encouraged them to think of their work as a team effort in which the collective strength of the group is a critical resource that individual members can rely on. Taking part in this teamwork transformed routine operations into a spirited game of looking for quicker, more efficient ways of doing things.[9] And being part of a team—especially one as closely tied to hometown traditions as "Team AMC"—made work itself seem like a high-stakes contest in which the Kenosha workforce took on global competition to produce the best cars in the world.

The idea that factory workers engage in "games" on the shopfloor is a concept developed by sociologist Michael Burawoy to explain why workers essentially "agree" to their own exploitation by working as hard as they do. In his classic study *Manufacturing Consent*, Burawoy shows how the organization of work in a piecework machine shop leads to conflict not between management and workers, as one might expect, but among workers themselves as machine operators compete with one another to "make out" or achieve individual levels of production that earn incentive pay. The hierarchical domination of workers by management is effectively dispersed into lateral antagonisms mediated by the informal rules or game of making out. Workers enter this game to increase individual production levels and hence to enhance their material rewards. By playing games like these, Burawoy argues, workers are ultimately satisfying the company's need to exploit them in pursuit of greater profits. In this way the labor process generates a form of "voluntary servitude" that induces workers to reproduce the relations of capitalist production. Burawoy calls this reaction "manufacturing consent."[10]

On the assembly line, consent is also manufactured through shopfloor games. But here, unlike a competitive piecework system, the labor process serves to reinforce, not undermine, lateral ties and group solidarity. Autoworkers must pull together, not apart, to meet the production quotas and quality standards that ultimately enhance Detroit's bottom line. Their shopfloor culture is stamped with an ethos of cooperation and esprit de corps.

Assembler Connie Miller invokes this sense of contributing to a group effort, when she explains why she took care to do her job well. Burdening or irritating her coworkers was of greater concern to her than the possible reprisals of management. "You really have to try and do each car perfectly right, otherwise it ends up in the hands of a repairman down here and he's got to fix it. Or if you've got some one person that misses [their operations], that can't quite do the job right, maybe the next ten guys can't quite do their job right. I mean, it doesn't take but one guy."

Agreeing with his wife's view of the interdependent nature of work on the line, Steve Miller chimes in, "Exactly. One person'll put a certain part on, the next person will put a part on top of that, the next person on top of that, on top of that, on top of that. So if this person misses their part, all the rest of them can't do their work."

I ask if coworkers ever got angry at people who missed their operations.

"No," Steve says, "they pretty much understand. Once in a while, you never know . . . a lot of times you'd reach in a box of bolts and you pull out a handful of bolts that you gotta put in the car, and you load them in the gun and you start screwing them in, but one won't go in. You look at it and it doesn't have any threads on it, you know? And just a coupla seconds, and you're behind already. Just something like that puts you behind. If you're not really good, you're not going to catch up. So sooner or later you have to let something go."

Letting something go down the line with an operation unfinished was, for the autoworkers, a versatile symbolic gesture. Sometimes it was the equivalent of a beleaguered shrug, at other times it expressed the defiance of a lone middle finger. The shared meaning of this symbolic action was vividly demonstrated the day the Kenosha plant closing was announced. As word of the shutdown spread through the plant, workers on every line simply refused to do their jobs, stuck a repair tag on the car, and let it go. After several minutes of this silent protest, autoworkers pulled together and soldiered on as usual, but the sight of that string of cars, fluttering with repair tags as they moved down the line, was a moment of powerful communion that few workers will ever forget.

In more routine and commonplace ways, however, "letting something go" represents a moment—and there may be many during the day—when autoworkers have to step back from the relentless demands of the production process and realistically define the limits of their mental and physical endurance.[11] At such times a random bolt without threads simply doesn't justify the exasperation and stress of trying to make up for the lost time it causes. Everyone on the line understands that there will be pressured situations like these when coworkers must say to themselves, "you can't let it get to you, you just gotta let it go." How often and in what circumstances workers opt for this way out, relying on friends or repairmen to pick up the tab, becomes a critical measure of individual character and collective reliance.

Within the system of cultural meanings on the shopfloor, letting something go is more than an instrumental behavior that allows a worker to catch up with the line. Being able to rely on others in this way is also the single most important sign that you are an accepted member of the shopfloor culture. Members of this culture know they are not under the gun alone, that others are there and willing to chip in and support them at critical moments. Every act of reliance upon the collectivity, however, puts the strength of the social system to the test. Workers know there is only so much elasticity in the line: beyond a certain point, other people will be stretched too far, and the system will break down. Developing a critical awareness of where this breaking point exists, and how to avoid it, is an essential aspect of a worker's initiation into shopfloor culture.

Understanding the limits and value of collective reliance makes it possible for coworkers to see one another as real people who have needs and interests beyond doing a job to make money. Out of the experience of collective reliance comes an appreciation of coworkers as individuals who can have good days and bad days, a concept of work as a set of enduring social relationships that transcend the bad days, and a strong feeling of loyalty toward others like you who must be defended against the arbitrary orders of foremen and the shriveling gaze of outsiders. Within autoworker culture, letting something go is a form of symbolic action that communicates to the group something about an individual's predicament or state of mind. Fellow workers are able to determine at a glance what someone's problem might be—whether it is due to defective parts, a foul mood, something farther up the line, a personal problem, laziness, or inexperience. How the group decides to interpret the situation will trigger a range of possible responses, all of which stem from the organization of work on the line and the unique structure of social relations it creates.

In extreme cases, missed operations—if they are due to tardiness or leaving the line without permission—can bring disciplinary action. Industrial engineers ("IE men") set guidelines for the number of seconds required to complete each operation, and foremen are allocated manpower based on these calculations of optimal performance rates. A worker's failure to meet IE standards could result in various penalties, such as being sent home, being given days off without pay, or ultimately being discharged.[12] In other instances a snag in the line is readily identified as unavoidable—such as when parts are defective or cannot be properly installed—and the repair people at the end of the line will pick up the problems as a matter of course. In still other situations a different set of responses reveals the shopfloor culture in full swing. Workers who are having trouble keeping up with the line will discover that there are coworkers ahead of them working a little faster to give them more time, and perhaps others speeding up behind them, trying to lend a hand.[13] These bonds of mutual support and collective reliance have been built up and reinforced over time, as sooner or later every worker participates in and benefits from this generalized cooperation.

In each of these situations informal cultural rules are at work, giving participants a sense of how the situation should be defined and what behavior is appropriate to the matter at hand. Even in the most externally defined of circumstances—where there are formal rules governing the company's response to missed operations—shopfloor culture is mobilized to support the workers involved. Disciplinary action is usually initiated by the foreman against a worker whose unfinished work begins showing up with some frequency on the repair bay's roster. By the time a problem has developed this far, the worker in question will usually counter with the claim of being overworked, and a union steward is called in. The steward's task is to determine whether the job is being done correctly or if the worker is, in shopfloor parlance, just "stroking" the company. When I ask Wendy Miles, a union steward since 1978, what stroking is, she says with a sparkling smile, "Oh, it's maybe goofing off, wasting time in between operations. You can tell. Kind of not wanting to do their whole job duties, maybe I should say. Which you run into, I would say maybe about once a week. It was understandable, because there was quick-paced work."

The steward is responsible for trying to resolve the problem in a way that both the foreman and the worker can live with. IE men might be called in to retime the job and to establish new standards if need be. About 85 percent of the time, in Wendy's estimation, a job change does result. The installation of a screw or a piece of tape might be eliminated from the job description, giving the aggrieved line worker a little more flexibility in performing the job. When no job change is indicated, disciplinary action might very well proceed. But just as often, the intervention and empathic support of the steward can turn the situation around. For Wendy, making this happen was the most rewarding aspect of her job:

> I liked seeing people happy, being treated right. Fairness. Just plain humanity, dignity for the people. I loved the people contact, you know, working with the people continually. Sometimes it was absentee[ism], sometimes it was tardiness, sometimes it was work-related. Sometimes it was the wife didn't cook their eggs enough before they came to work, you know, and they were just crabby. You just had to know the people. You had to get to know them, their actions, their attitudes and that. Sometimes treating them like they were your own kids . . . just a pat on the back.

Wendy's conviction that "you just had to know the people" finds expression not just in the work of shop stewards, but in the way people all up and down the line treat one another. Patting a grown man or women on the back not only eases frustrations and derails possible disciplinary action, it acknowledges the individuality of that worker, the very individuality that is denied by the labor process. This underscores a central point about autoworker culture. In a work environment where we might expect to find the recognition of individual idiosyncrasies as firmly suppressed by the culture as by the labor process, in fact just the opposite is true. To the extent that work on the assembly line may produce feelings of estrangement, meaninglessness, and powerlessness, the shopfloor culture intervenes to recreate a sense of community, purposiveness, and efficacy. Instead of finding themselves submerged in a depersonalized, collective labor process, autoworkers emerge as individuals against the backdrop of this organization of work, precisely because it encourages people to create and sustain a strong system of collective reliance.

Ties of collective reliance establish a distinctive social structure within the blue-collar workforce as a whole. As new workers eventually come to discover, others on the line are generally willing to come to their aid when they must, perforce, let something go. A coworker's gesture of support in these instances constitutes a form of exchange— not of goods, but of services. This system of exchange links workers into a network of informal obligations that compel future reciprocity of action and collective responsibility. For although group assistance is more or less freely given, it is always extended with the vague but implicit expectation that the favor will be returned someday, whenever the recipient is able to do so. The development of plantwide social ties characterized by this sort of generalized reciprocity creates a factory culture that is remarkably egalitarian.[14]

Bonds of solidarity among factory workers are most often noted when labor conflicts erupt and workers band together to express their collective opposition to a disputed management action or policy. In his sociological study of the walkout, or wildcat strike, Rick Fantasia refers to these spontaneous expressions of an oppositional orientation as "cultures of solidarity."[15] Collective actions like these affirm, in an extremely powerful way, a group's awareness of itself as a "microsociety" forged in conflict and constituted in opposition to the dominant social structure. Labor struggles are always marked by workers' heightened consciousness of "us against them," where "them" can include anyone outside their embattled workforce. Far more common, I suggest, is the day-to-day experience of cultural solidarity that workers experience in the work process. In the Kenosha factory, work groups would often pitch in, quite spontaneously, to help a struggling coworker catch up with the line, long before their unfinished work ever reached the repair bay. Knowledge of a coworker's bereavement or personal crisis almost always inspired cooperative efforts. More generally, however, the need for an extra hand was simply chalked up to the hair of the dog and the wisdom that they would all have their day.

CHAPTER EIGHT

Badges of Ability

Autoworker culture is a distinctive collage of themes about individual and collective experience. Being on the line, as we have seen, virtually mandates collective work. Popular conceptions of the nature of collective work might lead us to expect that the expression of individual values would be antithetical to this form of work and largely submerged. With a labor procedure demanding so much conformity and a work group evincing such a solid ethos of collective integrity, we might imagine that there would be strong sanctions against standing out from the crowd or trying to distinguish oneself in any tangible way. What we find, however, is something quite different. Despite an oppositional stance toward the outside world, the culture of the shop-floor is not isolated from that of the encompassing society: strains of American individualism percolate through this worldview.

A central tenet of our highly individualistic culture is the idea that "skill" is a personal attribute. We think of skill or ability as a quality that is possessed by individuals, not by a group, and we assume that it can be quantified and measured in some way, with certain people having more or less than others. In short, skill is a cultural construct that enables society to make often invidious distinctions among people. Some people have "the right stuff" and some don't; and some people have more of it than others. Most workers in the Kenosha plant are routinely categorized as "unskilled labor." The status system in American culture and society makes it clear that jobs that require no special qualifications other than a willingness to work are by definition not very skilled.

Many autoworkers, however, take exception to this characterization

One worker's private lament is transformed during Jesse Jackson's rally into an expression of collective solidarity. Photo by Paul Roberts and the Racine *Journal Times*.

of what they do. On the shopfloor they find countless opportunities to stand out in the eyes of their coworkers as individuals with special skill and ability. Even on the assembly line, where a collective attitude toward work might seem natural, or more closely fitted to the labor process, people continue to look for ways of demonstrating individual skill. The skills that autoworkers recognize have nothing to do with schooling or impressive certificates. But skill for the autoworker, like skill for the wider society, is still thought to be an innate human capacity—something that distinguishes one person from another. Even in a factory where the collective sense is so strong, industrial workers never escape the idea that ability is an individual attribute. The mainstream status system continually bubbles up into shopfloor culture, challenging workers to justify to themselves and to others the intrinsic value of what they do and the moral worth of who they are.

Shop Secrets and Shortcuts

In autoworker culture, one's "skill" is measured in terms of personal control over the labor process. The more discretion workers exercise over how their jobs are done, or how their time on the job is spent, the greater their level of skill. In this calculation, skill rises in direct proportion to the degree of power an individual can wrest from the company. Management has the power to determine the rate of production, and in an auto assembly plant this power translates, quite literally, into direct control over the pace of the line and the amount of physical effort required of each worker. Finding ways to subvert management's domination—by keeping shop secrets or devising shortcuts in the work process—is recognized as a special ability and honored as a skill on the shopfloor.

The dynamics of the factory's internal status system are most apparent at the interface between the skilled trades and line workers in the plant. Those in the blue-collar workforce who practice a trade have completed a four-year apprenticeship, which generally involves classroom training as well as hands-on work under the supervision of an experienced journeyman. By external standards, tradespeople are thought to be more skilled than line workers, and hence we might also expect them to be considered more powerful by others in the plant. In fact, this is not the case. Although it is true that those in the trades often exude a "prima donna cockiness" about their position in the plant, their sense of superior ability derives from the same shopfloor dynamic that gives line workers a similar sense of individual worth. Tradespeople have a special status in factory culture because, and only because, they enjoy greater autonomy from management than their fellow workers on the line. But they acquire a reputation for skill in exactly the same way line workers do: by exercising control over the production process, in allegiance with the oppositional culture of the shopfloor.

Tradespeople know that their ability to demonstrate a special skill depends on close cooperation with others in the blue-collar workforce. John Henschel, a plant electrician for fifteen years, offers a delightful example of how the informal rules of the factory culture play out in the game he often encountered on the line. When a machine breaks down, John says, the first person to know about it will be the "set-up man." An hourly worker like the rest of the blue-collar workforce, this person is responsible for the operation of a particular machine, its tool changes and tolerance settings. If the set-up worker determines that an electrician is needed to solve a problem, she tells her foreman, and John is called out to fix the machine. Solving a technical problem, however, is only a small part of the challenge John faces:

> There were days you went out there and sometimes you ran into a set-up man that didn't want the machine to run, you know, for one reason or another. Maybe he had a fight with his foreman, so he's gonna show his foreman. "Hey, you're not going to treat me like that, I'll fix you." So then his machine would go down. So he'd send for an electrician . . . and lot of times, I just played the game too. Cuz these are people, set-up men, you don't want to get them mad at you, because they can make or break you, as far as an electrician is concerned.
>
> You can walk on the job and say "What's it doing or what's it not doing?" And he might shrug his shoulders and say, "It doesn't work." Well, you don't know *where* to start. You got a machine that's a half a block long. There's maybe thousands of wires in the panel upstairs. You have no place to start if you can't communicate and establish a good rapport with that set-up man. Because he's the one that can say, "Well, head twenty-two won't return." Well, now you know where to go. You can look it up on the print and track down that circuit, and you can fix the machine. But if he shrugs his shoulders and says, "It doesn't work," you might as well go back to the [on call] area, because you'll never fix it.

Having a good relationship with set-up personnel involves a willingness to play the straight man in a highly ritualized and sometimes amusing social interaction. Learning to finesse these little dramas and gain the lasting trust of set-up workers initiates journeymen into the shopfloor culture, signaling their loyalty to the unwritten rules of the line.[1] In exchange for supporting the set-up worker's effort to control the production process, John Henschel could feel assured of future assistance in solving technical problems that were otherwise of nightmare proportions. Failure to honor the code of collective reliance, he knew, was likely to result in endless frustration:

> You'd [find yourself] up in the panel going through the blueprints, and maybe you'll find the problem and you solve the first problem, and then instantly another problem crops up just as fast as you solved the first problem. You happen to

peek around your shoulder and you see the set-up man down there, and maybe he's pushing buttons or maybe he's flipping switches, because he doesn't want the machine to run. So you'd be up there pulling your hair out trying to get this machine to run, and you're running into a stone wall: it's not gonna run. Because that set-up man knows the machine one hundred times better than the electrician that goes out there once a week, because he's with it eight hours a day.

For reasons like these, journeymen are generally eager to take part in the oppositional culture shared by the plant's blue-collar workers. So well understood are the informal rules governing shopfloor reciprocity that an experienced tradesman like John could often skip ritual denials of subterfuge and get right to the point. "A lot of times," he says, "I'd go out there and I'd confront [the set-up man] right out. If it looked like that was the case, I'd say, 'If you want the machine down, how long do you want it down? I'll keep it down as long as you want; just don't make me work any harder than I have to. If you want it down for an hour, I'll keep it down for an hour.'"

Collaboration in these little dramas and ritual interactions is based on each worker's ability to carve out of the production process a small area of personal competence or expertise. Having "secrets" or special knowledge about a piece of machinery allows blue-collar workers a modicum of control over their work and some leverage against what often seem like the arbitrary directives of management. Moreover, by demonstrating a special skill or preserving an individual locus of control, shop secrets operate to balance out the status inequalities that exist between the skilled trades and other workers in the plant. In this sense the power that flows from a journeyman's technical knowledge is, to a greater or lesser extent, counterbalanced by the line worker's long-standing experience with a particular machine or a certain aspect of the production process.[2]

Shopfloor games are small battles in a quiet war of domination and insubordination. Possessing shop secrets allows workers to set their own pace within the narrow limits established by the company's industrial engineers. Line workers also strive to develop areas of personal expertise by devising novel shortcuts that will garner them a stretch of coveted leisure time. By accumulating extra seconds on every repetition of an operation, experienced assemblers can work "up the line," that is, faster than the momentum of the line requires. Eventually these workers may gain as much as ten minutes of leisure time to use as they wish. Luis Ramirez, an assembler for fourteen years, explains how this works:

The idea would be that if you had to . . . let's take a taillight, for example. If you had to install a taillight, but prior to that you had to install the lightbulbs in the wiring harness, it could be that you would walk ahead of the line, and let's say you'd do three cars. You'd install lightbulbs in those three cars, and then you'd walk back to your station, and that part of the job would be done. So then for the next three cars, you'd have it easy, just to install the taillights, instead of having to do the taillight and the lightbulb in the same unit. So you save yourself a little bit of time. Or let's say they issue you two air guns to use. You got those two hoses to deal with. But if you say, Well, I'll just take two tips and interchange them with one gun, now I don't have to deal with that extra hose. So you eliminate that one hose, that one gun. And one gun and two tips is lighter than two guns and two tips. Just stuff like that. You're always figuring something out, or trying to.

Time saved on the job becomes a kind of currency that workers can "spend" as they wish—having a snack, glancing through a magazine, shooting the breeze with a buddy, or helping others catch up with the line. Leisure time used to help others, as we have seen, is an exchange of services that offers the security of knowing others can be relied on in the future. Leisure time also brings less tangible rewards, not the least of which is the prestige that comes from being known by coworkers as someone who is particularly adept at finding quicker ways of doing things. By making a job look effortless and flaunting the time left on their hands, workers gain a reputation for being especially clever people—more intelligent, certainly, than the IE men who designed the job. On the factory floor, the ability to find shortcuts and accumulate leisure will set you apart as someone with special skills.

The status system internal to the factory culture is an interesting counterpoint to the culture of the mind's ideas about skill and ability. In our "credential society," as sociologist Randall Collins observes, people are increasingly rewarded with prestige and social status not for their productive labor, but for their "political labor."[3] Political labor involves establishing the social networks and strategic alliances that enable you to enter occupations that have more to do with communication and administration than with hands-on productive work. In Collins's view, your chances of entering powerful social networks and communicating effectively with people outside your immediate sphere of experience will depend on the "cultural resources" you gained by virtue of your access to special channels of information, other social networks, and educational institutions. Cultural resources generated and acquired in schools are represented in a formal manner by grades and certificates. Educational credentials are, Collins argues, a moneylike system of "cultural capital" that can be exchanged in the labor market as evidence of the cultural goods you have amassed, and hence as a certification of the political labor you are able to perform.

When thinking about social stratification as a barometer of cultural capital, there is a tendency to assume that the only "badges of ability" that matter in the world are educational credentials. Sociologists Richard Sennett and Jonathan Cobb write with great insight about the ways ability becomes "the badge of an individual" in our society.[4] In American culture, Sennett and Cobb point out, we generally assume that ability is a fixed commodity, best represented by a bell-shaped IQ curve. We take it for granted that this curve depicts the "natural" allotment and distribution of intelligence in the population as a whole. People who stand out as individuals at either end of this curve are thought to be either very smart or very stupid. When ability is conceptualized as an innate quality possessed only by those select few who are distinguished from the mass at the center, grades and educational credentials become badges of individual worth. Badges of ability ultimately serve the interests of a class society by presenting social stratification as the inevitable result of "natural" inequalities among people.

On the shopfloor, however, individual demonstrations of ability and intelligence do not promote separation among people or lead to harsh evaluations by others. On the contrary, standing out as a particularly clever and skillful worker strengthens the solidarity of the group. This is an important difference between autoworker culture and the credential society outside the plant. Being recognized as an individual with skill in the factory does not threaten the group's collective orientation toward work and the outside world. Autoworkers participate in a social system that allows them to honor badges of ability that enhance rather than diminish their loyalty to the collective goals of the blue-collar workforce. This arresting revision of American individualism does not suppress individuality, but neither does the shopfloor recognition of individual ability disrupt an egalitarian system of collective reliance and group strength.

Feeling valued as an individual in the factory goes hand in hand with recognizing the importance of each person's contribution to the well-being of the whole. Like credentials in the outside world, leisure time in the auto plant marks people as having special ability. But unlike credentials, which have a widely recognized social value, leisure time represents a form of "cultural capital" that has currency only within the local culture of the plant's blue-collar workforce.[5] Because this moneylike currency has value only inside the factory, it cannot be used to gain status or prestige outside and hence does not result in radical separation between people. Leisure time has social value in the plant, I suggest, because it generates the kinds of experiences that bind the group together as a cultural system in its own right. Finding quicker ways of doing things gives workers the opportunity to socialize with one another. The conversational resources people exchange during these periods of prized time—details about personal experiences or information about the job at hand, gossip about coworkers, standing jokes, and styles of clowning around—are the stuff of an indigenously produced culture. And time wrested from management is the medium through which this local culture is reproduced.

Tom Sheppard, an assembler in his early forties, captures the feel of this cultural reproduction nicely as he describes the rewards of finding "little tricks" on the job:

> When I'm on a job, I can usually find out little tricks to get it done a little sooner than you have to. And the guys—the guys and the gals there—we could talk, joke around, make the day real good. I enjoyed just coming to work. I knew I had these people I could talk to, you know, we could horse around. Lots of people'd come in and say, "Look at that, that guy belongs in a mental institution!" But that was our way of making the day go by faster. I enjoyed it. I looked forward to going to work.

For many autoworkers like Tom, the rewards of knowing little tricks are almost entirely collective and social. These workers take pleasure in the individuality that comes from being recognized as a team player, a good sport, or a very funny fellow. Other autoworkers explicitly emphasize the ability and intelligence that discovering shortcuts displays. These workers take pride in doing the job better than they believe it can be done by anybody else. Yet even their forceful assertions of individuality are tempered by a consciousness of collective purpose. Those who think of themselves as the smartest ones in the bunch are almost always the same workers who speak proudly of sharing their expertise with others and teaching the "less skilled" easier ways of doing things.

Alan Sadowski, a Vietnam veteran with over fifteen years on the line, takes this view of his work:

> I don't do it the way the foremans tell me to do it. I do it my own way, which makes the job easier. Lots of people will sit

there and fight a job, because somebody tells them you have
to do it this way. Whenever I taught a person how to do a job,
I always showed them easy ways of doing it. I'd break the job
down for them and I'd stick with them until they got it. A lot
of [management] people there, they didn't want you to learn
the jobs, all's they wanted was to see you bust your back. I
never did that while I was in there. I always wanted to see a
good product. If you got a good product: job security.

The meaning of having a special talent for "breaking a job down"
is intimately connected to the autoworkers' collective goal of product
quality and job security. Sharing shop secrets—the very information
that makes people stand out—does not make Alan feel any less of an
individual. If he can bestow on others the power to take back some
control over the work process, not only does he feel that his own
status is enhanced, he believes that the vital interests of the group are
being served as well. Autoworkers see their attempts to assert individual know-how on the job as contributing to the quality of the cars
they are making. Shortcuts are thought of not as ways to avoid work,
but as ways of performing a job more efficiently and with greater
expertise.

The pride assemblers take in their work is firmly tied to their belief
in a broader tradition of craftsmanship. They share a conviction that
the quality of the product they make depends on the amount of control each worker has over how the job is done. Like many blue-collar
workers faced with the uncertainties of modern industry, Kenosha
autoworkers believed that craftsmanship and quality work would be
rewarded with job security.[6] Shop secrets most often were shared between more experienced workers and those new on the job. In this
way the tradition of craftsmanship was passed along from one generation to the next. As Alan Sadowski observes, harsh economic realities
and the consciousness of a collective fate underscored the pride and
solidarity workers felt:

It was a close group. You get to know people in the plant. You
push one another once and a while, you know. If somebody's
slacking or something, you might get on his case. But everybody, they pulled together a lot. Because with all these layoffs, everybody's in the same type of boat all the time. You
start sticking together, I guess. We had a point to prove
when Chrysler bought us out: The only way we're gonna keep
our jobs is if we show them quality, give them quality. Which
we did.

Within autoworker culture, developing shop secrets and devising
shortcuts are clearly not the same thing as taking a break or "slacking

off." The fight for job security—and quite literally, the fate of the whole workforce—is seen as a collective effort that calls upon the individual expertise and contribution of everyone in the plant. That a lazy coworker is as likely to be censured by other workers as by the boss tells us that, beyond a certain point, the group will come down on those who are motivated solely by an individual desire to enjoy a smoke at the company's expense. Donna Clausen is moved to tears as she explains how she always tried to make each day a little easier for her coworkers:

> Every day I went in, I worked hard. I even went in early to get jobs set up for people, so it was easier for them when the line started, when they didn't have to stock from second shift, and . . . a lot of people told me I was stupid for doing it, for giving up my free time. But it was my job and I enjoyed it. And it . . . it's just that I worked so hard to try to make it go, and I kept thinking . . . you know, I'd go home with cuts and bruises and everything, and my husband would get mad at me, and I'd say, Yeah, but maybe if there was more like me, we can keep the place open. But it didn't work.

The idea that quality work would "save the plant" gave Kenosha autoworkers—first under AMC and then under Chrysler—a firm sense of collective purpose on the job. Yet, ironically and sadly, their commitment to craftsmanship and quality acquires a totally different face when viewed from the outside. Efforts to find "free time" are perceived as laziness, and the decline of the domestic auto industry is attributed to the shoddy workmanship of American workers. Workers who demonstrate individual talents on the shopfloor know that the external status system does not measure intelligence and ability in the same way their internal culture does. A collective sense of integrity therefore depends on drawing clear distinctions between shopfloor culture and the value system of the external society.

The group's consciousness of maintaining cultural boundaries is evident in the way new hires are initiated into work on the line. As they are gradually eased into the quick pace of production work by more experienced assemblers, their stereotypic perceptions of line work are debunked and their loyalty put to the test. Through this rite of passage, outsiders soon become insiders. Donna Clausen describes the fun to be had during this "breaking in" process:

> Some of the new hires that I had to break in on jobs, they would just look at me like, "You're kidding me?" And I said, "Well, this is the job, take it easy, a little at a time." I'd get them broke in and I'd look at them, I says, "Well, were you

one of those people [in Kenosha] that said we were *bad?* We were *lazy?* We got our pay for *nothing?*" Or I would tell one, "Congratulations, you're part of us now." And they'd go, "What?" [Laughing] "Part of us that don't like to work!" I said, "You're part of the *bad* people now," and they'd always get a big kick outa that.

Claiming and asserting an identity as an autoworker in Kenosha is fraught with tension. Getting a high-paying job at the factory, being able to perform routine tasks at a demanding pace, and deciding to cast your fate with the auto industry makes you a member of a group that has long been stigmatized by various segments of the local population. At the root of this notoriety is the set of cultural images that those in the community drew upon to explain why people might work in a factory and what doing this type of work revealed about the kind of people they must be. Most autoworkers are keenly aware of the ways their identities are discredited by outsiders. In her welcome to new hires, Donna acknowledges the group's stigma but attempts to reassure new coworkers that this is the group to which they naturally belong. "You're part of the *bad* people now," she tells them, gently reminding them that they can no longer think of themselves as part of the outside group or share its condescending view of insiders. Through sharing jokes and shop secrets, new workers are encouraged to align themselves with others of their own "kind," recognizing that only those who suffer from the same identity stigma can genuinely accept them for who they are.[7]

Culture of the Hands

In American culture, an individual's place in the class structure is held to be the outcome of innate ability, moral discipline, and hard work. Kenosha autoworkers claim that their place in the middle class is, in fact, the result of all three. It takes a special kind of person, they say, to do auto work, and this in itself demonstrates an intrinsic human capacity. And let there be no doubt about it, they insist, auto work requires moral discipline and hard work. The staggering physical demands, high risk of disabling injury, relentless stress, and constant exposure to hazardous substances and conditions more than justify the middle-income wages they receive. Autoworkers realize that the world outside their plant does not view industrial work in the same light. They know that people in the community think they're overpaid, and greedy, and lazy, and stupid, and a bunch of alcoholics. They know this because they sometimes overhear remarks at the checkout counter, the bowling lanes, or the beauty shop. Sometimes they read outright denunciations of their character and their union in the local paper, in letters to the editor or in the statements of community leaders. But mostly they know it because they have been through the great culture mill of American society: our school system. They are no strangers to the fuss people with credentials make over good grades and college degrees.

Autoworkers, like all of us, have been steeped in the culture of the mind all their lives. They know that people are encouraged to get ahead by choosing a profession, going through advanced schooling, and developing special intellectual abilities. Upward mobility, they realize, involves striving to make something of yourself, going beyond what is ordinarily expected, and standing out from the crowd as an individual who has done better than average. But most autoworkers say they never aspired to be anything out of the ordinary or to have more money than they need to live comfortably. And what's wrong with being average? To be average, after all, is to be in the majority. And the majority of Americans, they feel, naturally belong in the "middle" class.

Autoworkers believe that there are basically two paths in life. One leads to more schooling, and most workers think of that path as reserved for the talented few—kids who have been encouraged by their families and teachers to excel; kids who don't need the money or who "don't want to work." The other path leads to work in the local factories, and it is the one most traveled by. Kenosha autoworkers grew up believing, with reason, that industrial jobs were plentiful and that a middle-class lifestyle was within the reach of anyone willing to work hard enough. Like Tom Sheppard, they saw their chosen path as the natural one:

> I didn't think I needed schooling, there was no need. I could survive without being a brain surgeon, you know what I'm saying? Jobs are a dime a dozen and you can get one anywhere, that's the feeling I had. I didn't have to have any extra school. I didn't need no college degree. I was never motivated to be anything in particular. Maybe it was because of the . . . I consider I had a good upbringing . . . but maybe it was because I just wasn't pushed for that. I don't know how much people were [pushed] back then.

Do workers like Tom truly believe, deep in their hearts, that their choice is a socially legitimate one? Much of the literature on American subcultures and the "deviant" value systems of various minority groups tends to focus on the extent to which these groups do or do not assimilate the values of the dominant culture.[8] Is it really possible, these studies ask, for people to sustain a subjective version of the status system that is genuinely different from the normative view? Or are their claims always an inadequate cover-up for their failure to succeed on society's terms? Most of the existing research has asked these questions of the nation's disadvantaged and chronically poor social groups. When we probe the life choices of blue-collar Americans, however, the conceptual problem is evident: by economic standards, industrial workers have been successful middle Americans for generations. Only recently, in the wake of a changing economy and nationwide deindustrialization, has the white-collar middle class begun to openly dispute the social value of industrial labor.

Kenosha autoworkers have been able to sustain an alternative version of the status system because for the past forty years a middle-class standard of living has been within the reach of non-college-bound men and women. When describing their class position, autoworkers usually say they are in the middle or even "upper middle" class. They view their class position largely as a matter of income, and their subjective scale of social value is for the most part reinforced by the level of their earnings.[9] Most workers would heartily agree with Clarence Jones, who says that income is the "dipstick" by which a person's place in the world is measured. Clarence is the son of an impoverished sharecropper in Mississippi who moved north and began working at the Kenosha plant—Nash Motors at the time—when he was seventeen. After thirty years on the line, he became one of the first black supervisors in the plant. Today, as we sit in his lovely ranch-style home in the suburbs, Clarence describes himself as upper middle class:

> In my interpretation of upper middle class, from what I've experienced in coming to this level, I know that if you make $50,000 a year [in 1988], you're doin' all right. I think we're measured by money. We have people who can do things, they're talented in various forms, but they don't have any money. So how can you measure it? That's the dipstick.

Simply having a talent or some form of special schooling does not, in Clarence's view, give you a place in the social structure. Intelligence or ability that does not produce anything of value cannot readily be measured by any practical standards. In the moral order established by the culture of the hands, the value of what you produce—not the number of years you spend in school—is the ultimate barometer of your social worth. This is one reason blue-collar workers are so skeptical of the idea that education is the surest route to success. Simply going to school, getting a degree, and becoming a professional doesn't guarantee a steady income or a decent standard of living. English professors can wind up driving taxicabs, workers like to say, implying that people who embark on a risky "paper chase" can end up sliding down the economic ladder instead of climbing it.[10]

Interestingly enough, the idea that credentials can turn out to be "worthless" is shared even by those autoworkers who have some educational background. Journeyman Bill Sorensen, the college graduate we met earlier, is quick to defend line workers against the frequent charge that they are overpaid. Assemblers deserve their good pay, Bill argues, precisely because their work lacks the intrinsic rewards and satisfactions of skilled labor:

> A lot of people in this community think that those people who worked in production were overpaid in their work. Over the last ten years I worked there [as a machine tool technician], I could easily have been [considered] overpaid and underworked because I like what I did. But I would say that the people who worked on the assembly line earned every penny. I'm coming from the perspective of having worked it long ago and saying I can't handle it, never again.

Credentialed workers shared with their uncredentialed fellows a "dipstick" view of human worth. In this scale of social value, people should be rewarded for the kind of work they are able to do. Not all of the labor required to keep America going strong is stress-free, intellectually demanding, or intrinsically rewarding. The people who are willing to do the kind of work that others are not willing or able to do—physical labor that provides vital goods and services that the society as a whole depends on—are entitled to a middle-class standard of living. Who, after all, would want to become a garbage collector if the economic compensation offered didn't make it worth their while? There are certain kinds of jobs, autoworkers say, that society needs people to do—and making cars is among them. Society, whether as private business or the public sector, is therefore responsible for seeing to it that the people who do indispensable physical labor are rewarded accordingly.

In this calculation of social value, credentials are largely superfluous. As Bill observes, people with college degrees often set these credentials aside because the economic rewards of working in the plant were greater than the starting salary many professionals earned out in the community.

> You do have instant financial reward working [in the plant]. If you have a master's degree or want to work in a responsible

position, or a bachelor's degree or whatever, you'll start out someplace making very little money. Oftentimes people went in there with the intention of quitting after a year or two. You'd make good money for a while and then quit. But then looking at what they would have to start with, economically, after they quit, and going to literally half the wages . . . it's kinda hard to say, "Well, okay, I quit." You get used to that amount.

In such cases, educational credentials meant very little when held up to the prevailing structure of rewards. For educated workers, the income and benefits of factory work offered a greater feeling of doing something worthwhile than did the less tangible benefits of putting their education to some worldly use. "[We were] willing to put up with the unsavory aspects of the job just for the money," Bill Sorensen says. "That's why we called [the auto plant] 'the great honey tit' in this town: it was the only place in the world where somebody who was quite genuinely illiterate could work for fifteen dollars an hour." Even more to the point, it was one of the few workplaces in the country where you did not have to be illiterate to choose the hardships of physical labor over the dubious satisfactions of white-collar work.

Tom Sheppard speaks for many of his fellow workers on the assembly line when he describes why he felt good about the work he did:

> I felt that, hey, I've accomplished something. Other than making the good money, hey, we got out some good engines today, you know, this and that. This company's growing. We're selling cars because of the work we're doing. That made you feel good. Made me feel good, knowing I could do something, you know? It didn't take a whole lot of . . . *brains* to work in a factory. But it's obvious a whole lot of people can't work in a factory. They can't take the repetitive nature of it. I guess I was one of the ones that could. Me and five thousand others. It's like a *skill* to be able to do that. I know most employers don't look at it like that, but basically it is. A lot of people can't do the same thing over and over.

By calling attention to the fact that auto work requires a certain ability that not everyone has, autoworkers challenge a basic premise of the credential society: the idea that assembly work is "unskilled" because anybody can do it. The culture of the mind is based on the assumption that certain human capacities can be taken for granted and expected of everyone. Hence, learning how to walk or speak your native language is not usually considered a "skill."[11]

If we accept the perspective of the dominant culture and think of auto work as something anyone can do, it might seem like a contradiction in terms—or an outright falsehood—to say that something done simultaneously by five thousand people is any sort of skill at all. But ideas about skill, we must remember, are cultural constructs and open to alternative interpretations. As Tom Sheppard attests, American culture tends to equate the idea of "having a lot of brains" with having skills or educational credentials, when in fact there is no necessary correlation between the two.

Because notions of ability in this culture are so closely associated with something like a college degree, we tend to assume that having a degree means having brains, which, ipso facto, adds up to having a skill. But these are dichotomous things. A skill, in autoworker culture, is something that distinguishes you from other people. Thus it is possible to have skills without having credentials—even without having "brains." On the shopfloor, as we have seen, finding faster ways of doing things marks people as especially talented and sets them apart in much the same way that credentials confer status upon individuals within American society at large. And certainly the ability to do line work in the first place sets autoworkers apart from many other workers as having a special skill—building a car—one that can be demonstrated only in the company of five thousand people.

This brings us to what is perhaps one of the most important contrasts between the prevailing status system in American society and the autoworkers' culture of the hands. Being skilled at industrial labor, workers believe, sets them apart from the rest of society not only as individuals, but as a special group of people. Factory culture transforms the idea of individual ability—in effect, "standing out from the crowd"—into one of collective ability—"standing apart from the crowd." The ability to do manual labor is qualitatively different from the ability to do mental labor, and therefore it cannot be judged by the same standards. Manual laborers, workers believe, are in a category by themselves.

When you come right down to it, autoworkers are basically laborers, says Ellie Kaufman, a paint sprayer in her mid-forties. Laborers make up a distinctive group of people, she asserts, because in no other occupation do people put their whole body into what they do:

> We're called laborers. Whether it's spraying, sanding, bending, lifting, pushing, pulling—whatever it is, your whole body is in it and does it. Because it's physical labor, and if you're not up to it, you don't last. You go in there with your *whole body*. You don't go in with just fingers because you're gonna

type. Because you got nail polish on and you got lipstick on
and you're dressed nice, and people are going to like you because you're whatever you are. At your job you can do this,
you can be whatever you wanted to be, because you went to
school and got it.

If the certification of mind makes other occupations distinctive, it is
mortification of the body that makes a person a laborer. Mental ability
may be demonstrated by acquiring a degree; physical ability is demonstrated by doing work that is exhausting, dirty, and dangerous.
People who don't have physical ability simply don't last very long on
the job. Not possessing the credentials that allow people to do genteel
mental labor in the external society, autoworkers speak of the earthy,
physical nature of their work as though it places them outside "civilization" altogether.[12] Laborers, their imagery suggests, occupy a place
in the "wilderness," a cultural outpost where strength, stamina, and
independence of character are the telling virtues. Civilized society, as
Ellie Kaufman describes it, is a world only the educated may enter.
Only those who go to school can choose to be something other than a
laborer, and they may express this carefully cultivated self on the job.
In work environments where women wear lipstick and nice clothes
and men wear suits and ties, it is possible to be the kind of person that
civilized society values and accepts as one of its own.[13]

From the standpoint of shopfloor culture, however, the civilized
world is also felt to be artificial, contrived and confining, and ultimately not very desirable. When autoworkers agree that education
gives people choices in life, they do not necessarily mean that they
desire these choices. Indeed, workers make a point of saying that they
had the chance to go to school and decided against it. By making this
choice, they believe, they have freed themselves from the insufferable
attitudes and stifling conventions of polite society. The shopfloor is a
place where people can act naturally, be themselves, and be accepted
for who they genuinely are. Workers often speak of the plant as their
"home away from home" and their coworkers as their "family away
from home." With these people there is no need to put on airs, force
a smile for the public, or be preoccupied with personal appearance.[14]
Freedom from social artifice, in this subculture, bestows its own brand
of human dignity.

In exchange for the freedom to be true to oneself, Ellie Kaufman
points out, autoworkers do the kind of work civilized people would
never consider doing:

Okay, we didn't go to school, so we're laborers, and that's what
they call us, and that's why we work at American Motors or

Chrysler. But we do the labor that you would not even *think* of. Because if you went in your backyard and shoveled your whole backyard and turned it over, okay? Consider that one day at Chrysler. And most people wouldn't do that. You either got to have the education to be what you want to be and that's what you chose, [or] if you want to be a laborer, then you're gonna have to put your whole body and soul into it, and do that too, because that's what it takes.

Ellie's image of "turning over the earth" is wonderfully evocative of the farming heritage she shares with many other workers in the plant. As one of eleven children growing up on a farm in Minnesota, she knows how the hardships of poverty, physical labor, and an unforgiving earth can take their toll. Landing a job at American Motors brought financial and emotional stability to her life for the first time. Even though there is little about her early experience that would draw her back to the land today, her ideas about the nature of productive labor are closely tied to images of working the land and bending the natural environment to human purposes. Work on the line is like shoveling earth, she says, a constant test of human strength and endurance, the point of which may seem absurd to educated people. But there is dignity to be found in facing down the hazards of this natural world. Breathing in paint fumes day after day, despite her protective mask, once resulted in throat polyps so severe that Ellie was unable to speak until they were surgically removed. In her mind such risks are part of what it means to put your "body and soul" into what you do. She had her operation on a Friday and was back in the paint booth that Monday, doing work that is remarkably meaningful to her.

In the culture of the hands, productive work is also profoundly creative. A strong feeling for the transformative power of manual labor is evident in the way Ellie describes the aesthetic satisfactions she derives from being a sprayer. She compares her work to that of a creative artist who transforms a plain object into a thing of beauty. "A painter that paints on canvas, they're looking at something and they have it in their eyes," she explains. "All we had was these cars, but they were dull cars." With great concentration and precision, she sprayed on her favorite shades of paint, finding deep pleasure in seeing the raw car bodies take on the bright gleam of a sensuously lacquered sculpture, moving along under the lights of the paint booth. "I could just lay them colors on and just be artistic with it, and not even have to have a canvas, just a doorframe, you know?" Although this attitude toward line work might seem odd to people, she declares, it was work close to her heart. "I loved it," she says quietly: "I thought it was the best thing there was."

When a doorframe can become an artist's canvas, society's culture of the mind is held in abeyance. The internal dynamics of the factory culture generate an alternative conception of ability, one that allows workers to sustain deep pride and individual dignity in the work they do. Because ideas about ability are socially constructed, autoworkers are able to sustain a sense of their own legitimacy within the context of their work culture, even though shopfloor definitions of skill and ability stand in contrast to the status system of the external society. But precisely because ideas about ability—how it is demonstrated and who has it—are a matter of social agreement, they cannot be sustained by the individual alone. When Kenosha autoworkers faced the prospect of their plant's closing, they were threatened with the loss of much more than their jobs. They stood to lose the social structure their collective integrity depends on.[15]

This, I think, is why losing a job in a plant closing is so devastating. Not only must workers cope with the economic hardship incurred by unemployment, they must also leave behind a distinctive way of demonstrating individual capacities and skills. When a plant closes, workers lose a social structure in which they have felt valued and validated by their fellows. When they are stripped of their workplace identities, dislocated workers face an external culture that no longer seems to value, or grant social legitimacy to, the kind of work they do. The culture of the mind simply does not recognize the kinds of skill and ability that are tied up in industrial labor. Skills honed on the factory floor are nontransferable capacities in our postindustrial age. Professionals may move from job to job or company to company on the strength of the cultural capital represented by their college degrees. But industrial workers cannot transfer their shopfloor badges of ability. They cannot move into the fast-growing service sector simply by demonstrating their special aptitude for finding shortcuts and putting body and soul into what they do. These marks of distinction are bequeathed to them by the structure of social relationships in the factory; and when their plant closes this accumulated cultural capital is lost. Long and respectable work histories are suddenly worthless, and workers are faced with the prospect of starting all over again, from scratch.

CHAPTER NINE

Broken Promises

Ninety-nine percent of the people, I would say, thought we had security for quite a while. Even though [Chrysler] had committed five years, there's always the chance, you know, build good cars, and something else is gonna happen. [Buying the house] was not a bad risk, no. You figure, no. Ever since I've been here, sixteen and a half years, always you heard from American Motors and the union, boy, this place is gonna close, they're gonna do this. You always heard that. Now when Chrysler took over you said, hey, security. A big company, Top Three, and we got it made. Dumb.

ASSEMBLER, THIRTY-EIGHT YEARS OLD

The present generation of industrial workers came into the factory expecting as much from their jobs as their parents did, if not more.[1] Many of today's autoworkers entered the plant at the urging of depression-era parents who had worked at American Motors all their lives, determined to build a solid company that would offer their children a secure place of employment. Fred Shultz, a self-described "union man" in his early forties, recounts a family history shared by many Kenoshans of his generation:

There was a pride in AMC. The workforce was basically built on generations of the same families. A lot of the people who worked there were depression babies, and they came to the plant wanting jobs, and I think that tradition was carried through the generations. My dad, he never had any indoor plumbing facilities until he came here to work. He was work-

135

Autoworkers picket the Milwaukee hotel where Iacocca held a news conference to announce Chrysler's $20 million trust fund. Photo by Charles S. Vallone and the Racine *Journal Times*.

ing for a dollar-something an hour, and that was good money for him. He appreciated the ability to work here, and if there was something wrong on his job he would tell somebody, because he wanted to make the very best so that he would have a job for me. Back then [just out of high school], if I wanted to go to college, that's fine. But if I didn't, then [my father] wanted me to go to work [at AMC] rather than some other factory. Either you went to college or you went to work someplace. It wasn't like today, where if you don't go to college you ain't got nothing. And he wanted me to work in a place that had a future, not a place that didn't have one.

American Motors certainly seemed to be the place with a future during the prosperous 1960s. Job security could be taken for granted back then, and just about everyone who was willing to work could expect to find a job, college or no college. The feeling of job security that Fred describes is not simply a pragmatic assessment of economic conditions. It is also, and perhaps more important, a complex set of attitudes and expectations about the value of industrial labor to society as a whole. American Motors could be counted upon to have "a future" because the products it manufactured were a vital part of the national economy and the American way of life. Could anyone imagine that a day might come when people wouldn't need automobiles?

Who dared to suggest that the plant that had once been converted for critical wartime production could not be retooled to meet any threat the world dished out? What company could hope for a better work-force than one built upon the values of loyalty and quality workmanship handed down through generations of the same families?

The Nation as Family

For Kenosha autoworkers, the concept of job security is firmly embedded in a set of cultural assumptions about what American society owes them in return for their productive labor. Theirs is the type of vocation to which people commit a lifetime, through good times and bad. In exchange, workers are given the comfort of knowing that the more years they put in, the freer they will be of economic insecurity in the future. Freedom from financial uncertainty is also a legacy workers hope to pass on to their children—not as a family inheritance of any great size, but in the form of a successful company built by the sweat of their brows: a community institution that has a future. Workers feel entitled to this sense of confidence. The goods they manufacture are essential, they say, to the survival of the nation.

Victor Russo Jr., a third-generation Italian American, feels that a nation's first priority, like that of a family, should be to "take care of its own." In his way of thinking, the family, the community, and the nation are all linked by military strength. Industrial communities like Kenosha were among the first to respond to the war call, he points out. Their plants were converted to military production, and they sent their wives and daughters into the factories to work. How, Vic asks, can the country now forsake those who have served it so well? And not only that, what sense is there in trying to depend on foreign trade for automobiles? That is as crazy as trying to build up military strength by depending on the enemy for ammunition:

> Umpteen times, American Motors wanted to move out of Kenosha. Why has Local 72 fought so hard to keep it here? Because of the *people*? That's part of it. But the rest of it is: why should we throw our business out and depend on *foreign* trade? Which is stupid! Look back when your dad went to war, did we depend on foreign trade? No! We produced the bombs right here in Kenosha! We produced the bullets. We produced the tanks. We produced the planes. Right here in them plants they're gonna tear down! I know that for a fact. My grandmother was an inspector for the government during those four years. She *saw* those bombs; she *saw* those bullets!

Industrial production, in this scenario, is connected to war production, and both are considered patriotic endeavors, vital to national security and strength.[2] There is a tendency among middle-class professionals—social scientists included—to take blue-collar claims of peacetime patriotism with a grain of salt. Although we find it easy to imagine that a legitimate love of country galvanized those of "Rosie the Riveter" fame, such boasts on the part of balding autoworkers in the 1980s are usually chalked up to jingoistic bluster. Workers who celebrate the heroic in the humdrum are strongly suspected of overcompensating for a life of trivial pursuits.

In *Automobile Workers and the American Dream*, Eli Chinoy observes that autoworkers often lamented the loss of the national purpose they felt on the job during World War II. That was a time, workers told Chinoy, when "you knew what you were working for: to bring the boys back home." Chinoy concludes that the war effort allowed workers to overcome the monotony of their jobs by making them feel they were doing something more important than auto work. They were contributing to a national cause that was recognized as supremely worthwhile by the society at large, and this approval gave value to what was otherwise meaningless or "dead-end" work.[3] Only under such extraordinary conditions, Chinoy suggests, do workers find a genuine sense of self-respect in a mass production industry where individual initiative is discouraged and opportunities for advancement are few.

When the larger society decides that industrial production is contributing to a national cause, Chinoy seems to be saying, then it is legitimate for workers to feel patriotic and take pride in their work. If society as a whole does not attach national importance to industrial work, however, the work itself will cease to carry that cultural meaning. To be sure, the national *devaluation* of factory work forms the crux of the cultural dilemma in which Kenosha autoworkers now find themselves. They are well aware that hundreds of thousands of United States industrial workers are out of work and considered irrelevant to the expansion of global industry. But Kenosha's autoworkers are not acquiescing to the attitudes that promote the dismantling of basic industries. Instead, they question the judgment and integrity of political and business leaders. They refuse to accept the idea that manufacturing has died of natural causes.

If goods-producing industries are going the way of dinosaurs, workers say, it is because the rich and powerful have conspired to pull the evolutionary plug. They have done so, autoworkers like Al Tirpak believe, by failing to honor the moral commitments that once made this nation strong:

They don't articulate this, at least publicly, but what corporations are looking for is the disposable workforce. "Hey, let's go somewhere, have a floating crap game! We'll put up a shack, we'll do our business, and when it gets expedient for us to go elsewhere, we'll go." No commitment to community; no commitment to country. These people have no commitment to the state of Wisconsin. They have no commitment to America.

The notion of "national purpose" has the power to infuse collective work efforts with cultural meaning whether or not those efforts are officially sanctioned. The rest of the country may not see industrial work as contributing to a national cause, but workers certainly do, and they believe the rest of the country is simply wrong, or misled, about the importance of what they do. In contrast to Chinoy's autoworkers, whose sense of patriotism was reinforced by the larger society, Kenosha's autoworkers invoke this proud tradition in *opposition to* the prevailing uncertainty about America's place in the world and the competitiveness of its basic manufacturing industries. Workers are able to maintain this oppositional stand, in large part, because it resonates deeply with the populist convictions that have always formed a subtext to democracy in the United States. Populism, as a political creed, divides the nation into a handful of ultrarich conspirators and a majority of honest "plain folk," and its principled opposition to the abuse of power is a defining feature of the American character.[4]

Autoworkers like Vic Russo insist that the leadership of the country has to be restored to "the American people." His understanding of moral order harks back, in true populist fashion, to the notion that freedom from political tyranny can be won only by popular revolution:

> I got a feeling there is gonna be a war [in this country] between the rich and the poor. There are too many people who are being stepped on, and they're getting tired of it. There's gonna be a civil war. It's gonna be just like the North against the South. It's gonna be just like America against Britain. When you cut the cancer out, it can't come back—unless you let it. Our forefathers didn't let it, and I don't think we have the right to let it. Because this is *our country*—not Taiwan's, not Britain's, not Mexico's. It's the United States, this belongs to us. How many millions of our people *died* for this freedom that we have? If somebody goes out there and puts their life on the line for something, you don't treat it like trash!

There is going to be a populist uprising in America, Vic argues, because "the people" are being stepped on by the rich and powerful, and they're not going to take it anymore. The American people cannot stand by helplessly while major corporations ship good jobs to Third World countries, flood the market with products made by foreigners, and sell off vast chunks of America as though it were worthless swampland. Treating American workers like trash is a crime against the country, for these are the people who made the country what it is. Vic's language may be extreme, but his desire to fight back is widely shared.

Swept up in this call to arms is a heady dose of nativism—the idea that America belongs to the people who were born here. But the anger autoworkers feel about foreign imports is more complex in origin than the doctrines of nativism or isolationism alone suggest. It is not just that imported products are made in Japan by the Japanese; it is that they are brought into this country at the expense of American jobs. There is no difference in principle, workers would say, between smashing a Toyota in their parking lot and throwing crates of tea into Boston Harbor. The ugly side of these democratic sentiments shows its face when workers equate the import of foreign goods with actions of foreign-looking people.

Charlie Stein, a wiry assembler of thirty-nine, thinks there is no reason why Kenosha couldn't have gone on building cars far into the next century. Why, then, did Kenosha close? Charlie points the finger at the kind of people who run this country:

> They have the big bucks. They have *greed*—a lot of greed. They want to make the fast money. If they can take our work out of the United States and send it back over on boats, all built, they'll do that. That's exactly what Chrysler's doing, too. They got plants down in Mexico. [Workers there are] making $1.25 a day. Where would you want to build a car, in Mexico or here? My motto is "Build in America, Buy in America." If it comes from a boat, don't touch it. Support your unions. That keeps my brothers and sisters working. But that's not the way it is anymore. All the property that's being sold to the Japanese, the Chinese! They own millions and millions of acres in this United States! We're damn near exhausted, because they got all the money. They can buy half the United States with what they make. I look for the next president to be a *Chinaman* or something!

In Charlie's account, "the Chinese" can at times be the ultimate elite. At one moment they are the ones with all the money and the political clout. At the next, however, it is the United States government that is handing them this gold mine on a silver platter, all so a few Washington insiders can get rich quick:

The thing is the United States gives away too much. They help too many people. They bring them over here by the *ship-load*. Is that fair? We have millions of people starving to death every day. And those ones that come over here with the slant eyes, they're living in better homes than I am. I don't own a home cuz I can't afford [to] with this up and down thing all the time, but that's the auto industry. It's because we let them import to us, bring it in here. We're fattening up their bellies over there and ruining our own country. All because some big guy wants to get fat fast.

Millions of people are "starving" in the United States because foreigners, or companies with foreign subsidiaries, don't give a damn about the American people. And the United States government appears unable, or unwilling, to do anything about it. "We're getting screwed every day by the government," agrees Ralph Harding, a forty-seven-year-old assembler. "[The government] is supposed to be there to serve and protect, but who are they protecting and serving? Their ass and their buddy who's got all the money!" Government officials have cast their lot, workers believe, not with the people who elected them, but with the big business leaders who pay them off. And if the interests of multinational firms and the American government have become inseparable, then who is representing the will of the people?

Autoworkers' brand of populism aims to speak for the whole nation, not just a small group of disgruntled industrial workers. If the country belongs to the people who have made it strong—all the "real" Americans—then everyone who works for a living is victimized when jobs are sent out of the country. If the United States government were truly "of the people, by the people, and for the people," workers say, it would not allow big corporations to close plants, abandon communities, and dump hardworking people like themselves out onto the streets. Workers like Ralph Harding see in this plant closing the betrayal of the American people writ large. Workers are to the company what "the little people" are to the nation:

> There's a lot of people that got twenty years invested in that goddamn place and all they're getting is screwed. Why? Because one guy wants to make a bunch of money for himself and a couple of his buddies. Those people are not the *company*. They are the company as to the say into money, but they are not the company. The people that make the cars are the *company*. Where the hell would [the rich] be, what would they sell, without the people that make [the cars]? They wouldn't be anywhere, would they? They wouldn't have a goddamn

141

thing to sell or a job to talk about! They sit up there and col-
lect money and talk on TV! But as long as people let them do
it, they're gonna do it.

Only by uniting people behind the common cause of economic justice for the average worker will it be possible to "kick the rascals out"
and restore the leadership of the country to the people. Ralph is
keenly aware, however, that the path toward the restoration of the
nation is strewn with major obstacles:

> Unless you can get everybody together—all your common
> Joes, shall we say—together, on one thing to do something
> about it, you can never get anything done about it. [The rich]
> got too much power. And you can't unite . . . it's just that too
> many people have too many different opinions which puts
> you in too many different groups—which I think the govern-
> ment likes. You know, I mean they manipulate a lot of shit
> like that too.

Ralph suspects that the shattering of the social contract is engineered by elites to break up all hope of universal solidarity. Bonds like
those forged on the shopfloor are threatened by the efforts of a small
but influential minority to sow dissension within the rank and file.
Membership in a labor union has schooled workers in the strategies a
company can use to "divide and conquer" its workforce, and the logic
of worker resistance is extrapolated to national politics. By encour-
aging diverse interest groups, a government can keep people from
uniting to overthrow the rule of elite conspirators.

Autoworkers are suspicious of political movements that rally under
the banner of "special interests." Although they have strongly held
and often diverse views on issues such as abortion, affirmative action,
and gay rights, they find much of the contemporary "culture wars"
downright confusing.[5] Workers find it difficult to believe that "all the
common Joes" can seriously disagree about the fundamental issues in
life, and they tacitly assume that everyone shares their sense of moral
justice. This "universalizing" aspect of populism stems from the belief
that truly moral people should agree on ultimate questions of right
and wrong, no matter what their cultural upbringing or social background.[6] Common Joes should be in spontaneous agreement on important issues, workers reason, because all people are created equal.
No one is better than anyone else, and people should be "treated the
same." There should be no special interests (read "special favors") and
no free rides. "Protect our shores and deliver our mail," workers say.
But beyond that, government should stay out of people's lives.

Their greatest expectation of government is so basic that few think of it as a special interest at all. Above all, workers insist, the government exists to safeguard the economic well-being of its citizens.[7] It must do this by seeing to it that people have good jobs and that they are adequately compensated during unavoidable periods of unemployment. More than any other consideration, I think, it was this notion that people have a "right" to job security that attracted many of Kenosha's autoworkers to the 1988 presidential campaign of the Reverend Jesse Jackson.

An Uneasy Coalition

In many respects the political marriage between Local 72 and Jesse Jackson was a bizarre one indeed. Apart from the autoworkers' overriding concern with job security, there was little else to capture their interest in the spectrum of social issues embraced by Jackson's Rainbow Coalition—and much to dislike. The diversity of lifestyles and opinions that workers shrink from in their private lives was precisely what the Jackson campaign attempted to celebrate. Pushing populist ideology as far to the left as possible, Jesse Jackson called on the American people to move beyond their differences and find "common ground" across racial, religious, rural and urban, sexual preference, and even class divisions. Jackson pushed people toward a more collective, communal approach to solving their problems. Rather than seeing minorities, labor, women, environmentalists, and gays and lesbians as separate political groups with competing interests, he tried to bring these groups together around the idea that they can't get along without each other. He tried to form a coalition that says, in effect, "You are all victims of a common enemy, and that enemy is the capitalist, the 'corporate barracuda.'"

In one sense, of course, Jesse Jackson's populist call for unity against a common enemy is exactly what autoworkers wanted to hear. And they had no doubt that Jesse Jackson had identified the right enemy. "Iacocca, to say the least, is just another greedy beast!" exclaimed a verse of the "poem" given to Jackson at the February rally outside the main plant. "Our Jesse's not a man to cross, or he'll show Chrysler just who's boss."[8] Many workers believe that Jesse Jackson was not only a national spokesman who drew public attention to their problem, but someone who was also willing to condemn Chrysler in no uncertain terms. In another sense, of course, Jackson's Rainbow Coalition was not the coming together of "all your common Joes" most workers had in mind. Their brand of populism is not about celebrating diversity, but about reinforcing the values of their shop-floor culture, a microsocial world in which conformity is the over-riding norm. Few workers are inclined to look with much favor or sympathy on the demands of welfare mothers, undocumented immigrants, pro-choice feminists, or gays and lesbians. When asked about the prospect of a black man becoming president of the United States, most workers reply, "I really liked what he was saying, but I never thought he could win."[9]

From this perspective it might be possible to write off Local 72's alliance with Jesse Jackson as a marriage of convenience. Workers wanted to turn public opinion against Chrysler, and the Jackson campaign was a means toward that end. But there is reason to believe that the cataclysmic impact of the plant closing prompted a significant number of workers to rethink some of their old assumptions. As sociologist Rick Fantasia shows in his ethnographic study of a labor strike, people's conceptions are more fluid and subject to change during periods of crisis than at any other time.[10] The experience of economic dislocation and the realization that a totally unanticipated event could plunge them into poverty caused some autoworkers to see themselves and their place in American society in a different light.

This worker's comments are typical:

> I don't get upset when I see someone standing in front of me at the grocery store with food stamps like some people do. I've been able to earn a living wage, and I think everyone in this country is entitled to a living wage. I recognize that there are some bums—that just are lazy and don't want to work—I'm not so foolish to believe that isn't the case. But I don't think that in order to get them, you should try to get a bunch of helpless victims that would like to have a job and would like to earn a living wage but just can't because the system has been stacked against them.

The experience of economic uncertainty and the arbitrary twists of fate have also made an impression on this forty-year-old assembler:

> There's no way that any of this is my fault. Whether it's the closing, whether it's the money I was making. I had no say in that. How can people look down on us? I mean, your so-called brothers and sisters—how can they look down on us? I can't believe that! None of this was my choice! But I feel like it. It's like you go to welfare—right away you're a little shit. I don't like that. It's *not my fault*. My thoughts about welfare changed a while back. I used to be one of these types that [said], "Oh, [they're] just a bunch of lazy slobs that don't want to go out

144

and make the money or take care of their kids." Which I'm sure there's a lot of them like that, but there's also a lot of them that just can't do anything else, can't find anything else.

Assembler Mary Cleveland, with over twenty years' seniority, was able to keep her job in the Motor Division when the Kenosha plant closed, and she feels a certain amount of survivor's guilt when she thinks about the hardships her coworkers are facing. Reflecting on what happened in Kenosha, Mary has come to believe that dislocated workers are becoming more and more "like minorities" in this society. In her view, the growing income gap between the rich and the poor is making everybody a minority in one way or another. This way of thinking about economic dislocation made it possible for Mary to support Jesse Jackson, even though she knows race remained an insurmountable barrier for many of her friends:

> [Jesse Jackson] talked about what's happening to our lives. I feel if I didn't have a job, I would be a minority. And that's what is happening in our country. We're losing that middle class, and we're gonna be either rich or poor. And I admired him. When you talked to him, it was all types of things for everybody, not just one group. But the people say they aren't prejudiced, but they are. It's something that's probably been put into your head, and it's gonna take generations to change.

In Mary's way of thinking about the American economy, "everybody" is no longer white and middle class but includes an increasingly heterogeneous collection of people who are looking for "all types of things." What she admires in Jackson is his universalizing vision—something for everyone, not just special interest groups. Not all workers experienced the same shift in perspective Mary did, but many were shocked to discover that of all the candidates there were to choose from, Jesse Jackson was the only one who seemed to be talking about "what was happening in their lives."

Support for Jackson in 1988 welled up out of middle America's growing frustration with politics as usual. Rather than go along with the UAW international's endorsement of Michael Dukakis, Kenosha autoworkers opted to go outside the Democratic mainstream. Coming from workers we typically think of as constituting the heart and soul of the Democratic party, this swing to the left signals a profound sense of alienation from traditional party politics. To what extent workers trusted Jackson and how enduring their support for him might be is hard to gauge, given the intensity of the shutdown situation. It may well be that passions will cool with the passage of time. But that they turned to Jackson—rather than to a conservative demagogue like David Duke—is remarkable in itself. Blue-collar populism has always been extremely volatile, sometimes swinging to the left and sometimes to the right. As a cultural response to deindustrialization, however, autoworkers' willingness to embrace an unmistakably liberal candidate provides an interesting counterpoint to the rightward drift of the so-called Reagan Democrats.[11]

The Kenosha case suggests that a realignment of middle American populism may well be under way. In the 1960s and 1970s, symbolic links between "national strength" and military spending tended to divide politicians as far to the right as George Wallace and as far to the left as George McGovern. In this sense Jesse Jackson has been able to do something unprecedented in the history of American populism. By linking the idea of national strength to economic justice and the idea of military spending to the globalization of production, Jackson was able to find common ground between the African American community and white industrial workers. "When the plant lights go out, we all look the same in the dark," he liked to say, vowing that his administration would promote a "workers' bill of rights" and a "corporate code of conduct." "Moving American jobs abroad and abandoning American communities is not in the national interest," Jackson argued in virtually every speech to labor groups. "Merger mania, leveraged buy-outs and CEO-subsidizing golden parachutes are not in the *national* interest. Fighting worker democracy is not in the *national* interest" (italics added).[12] Instead of dividing workers by race, as the Bush campaign was doing with its notorious "Willie Horton" ad, Jackson was dividing workers from the political, business, and military elites who were not acting in the national interest.

The affinity between Jesse Jackson's notion of economic justice and the autoworkers' sense of national purpose is clear. But workers take the idea of national interest one step further. They believe that the rich have been able to intimidate unions and send United States manufacturing jobs abroad only because American *military force* has been used to keep the wages of foreign workers artificially low. The nativistic strain in the way workers think about economic competition is tempered by a growing consciousness of how protecting workers' rights internationally will benefit labor at home. A trilateral conspiracy between government, business, and the military, they believe, enables multinational corporations to close domestic factories in favor of cheap—and repressed—labor abroad. Autoworkers like Al Tirpak, who severed party ties in 1972 to support Richard Nixon, are now in the curious position of arguing that high levels of military spending are *not* in the "national interest":

What you've really got going on in the world today is an un-
holy, tripartite joint venture between the big corporations, the
American government, and Third World right-wing dictators. The United States supplies the military might and the
support for the right-wing dictators, the right-wing dictators
suppress the workers, and corporations move the jobs there.
Now, American workers cannot compete against people who
are being paid seventy-five cents an hour. But *that* is what the
world is coming to.

Kenosha autoworkers believe that it is *industrial* production that
makes the country strong, economically and militarily. Deindustrialization, it appears, has dramatically altered the way blue-collar workers
evaluate the actions of the United States military abroad, even as their
nationalistic sentiments have intensified. Ironically, this transformation in the symbolism of military might—from the use of force to the
abuse of power—made it possible for workers to turn to a political
figure like Jesse Jackson who is so different from them in many respects. Autoworkers agree with a major portion of what Jesse Jackson
is all about, and if his campaign came with a lot of unwanted baggage,
that was conveniently blocked out.

The Social Contract

A central tenet of American populism is the idea that government is
the result of a "contract" in which people give up some of their individual freedom in exchange for the social security that all parties to
the contract desire.[13] Populists reject paternalistic justifications for authority—the aristocratic notion that some people are "born" to lead
or that the masses require "natural" superiors to rule them. Authority,
the populist argues, derives from the will of the people, as expressed
in the social contract. Should the government fail to serve the ends for
which the people have ordained it, this "contract theory" opens the
door to popular revolt—which in modern times usually takes the form
of reform through constitutional amendment, direct election, initiative, or referendum. The populists' enduring belief in consensual
rule—embodied in the credo "let the people decide"—is based on an
idealized myth of the nation's origins. Society, according to this myth,
is created by *voluntary* consent: individuals choose to "join" American
society of their own free will—hence the phrase "love it or leave it."[14]

In language that rings true for Kenosha's autoworkers, Vic Russo
captures the essence of populist contract theory:

You don't fuck with the general public. Because there's gonna
be a man like me out there that's gonna say, "Hey, wait a min-

ute. You're taxing us for this, you're taxing us for that, and
for that, and for that . . . that's *tax upon tax,* Jack, and I ain't
gonna take it! I'm gonna pull my musket out and I'm gonna
blow some motherfucker's head off! Like 1718, remember? If
you went to school . . . between the British and the United
States? They ain't gonna *take* this shit, so they pulled a musket
out and they blew somebody's head off.

Government gains its right to exist as the result of popular consensus and social contract. And its primary duty is to ensure that the
average citizen will not be victimized or exploited by ruthless villains,
thieves, and lawbreakers. A government that fails to protect the "little
people" from the tyrannies of taxes and trusts forfeits its legitimacy.
Events in Kenosha signaled to autoworkers that the social contract was
unraveling before their very eyes. The United States government, by
taking no action to prevent the destruction of American jobs, appears
to be abetting the major corporations in their crimes against the
people. Autoworkers like Mary Cleveland are appalled to realize that
corporations are not held to the same laws that govern everyone else:

> Corporations should have rules like you and I have: "You can
> do this, and you can't do that." They got money to close the
> plant! They get *paid* to close plants the way it's set up now!
> And they get money for one thing, and they use it for some-
> thing else, and that shouldn't be. If we did it, we would be in
> jail. We have to pay our taxes, we have to do this, we have to
> play by the same type of guidelines, and they don't [just be-
> cause] they're the big guys at the top. You got a handful of
> people that actually run the whole show, and they can break
> the rules and get away with it.

Just because corporate executives are higher up the social ladder,
or "bigger," than the average worker doesn't mean they are exempt
from the laws of the land or that these laws can be selectively applied.
The social contract represents the spontaneous consensus of individuals, not business corporations, and all individuals should have to play
by the same rules. Donna Clausen articulates this egalitarian principle
quite clearly in her description of Lee Iacocca:

> I think that he's a man that they let have too much—or let
> him *think* that he has too much—power. He should be put
> down to the level that he is. I feel no human being should
> have as much power as he has. He controls so many people's
> lives, and it doesn't bother him. His comments about [the
> shutdown], during the interviews after the closing came, is
> what really made me hate him: "Well, I'm getting rather good

at closing plants; I've done it before and I'll do it again." And that is what he *said*, in *interviews!* [He should] just stop with the smart mouth [and trying] to look like a big man! I think he needs to be knocked down. Does he remember when he was having problems years ago, and he was bailed out and helped out? It's like he's never been there. He needs to remember that.

Plant closings, in Donna's parental imagery, are caused by a handful of rich and powerful individuals who have gotten "too big for their britches." The function of government, and the mandate embodied in the social contract that legitimizes it, is to prevent big bullies like these from terrorizing the entire schoolyard. Corporate executives like Lee Iacocca need to be "knocked down to size" and forced to honor the rules and values that govern middle American social life. In essence, it was the utter disregard for these blue-collar understandings that made Chrysler's "broken promises" so demoralizing. After appealing to American taxpayers for help in the Chrysler bailout, Lee Iacocca appeared to turn his back on the very people who had made his success possible.

Assembler Luis Ramirez dropped out of a retraining program in industrial electronics when he was called back to the plant. The promise of at least five years of work made this seem like the right choice at the time, and Luis, like so many others, took Chrysler at its word. If you couldn't trust Lee Iacocca, who could you trust? But as Luis sees it now, the man never had any intention of keeping his word:

> [Iacocca] sold us out. For his own personal pride or gain. He wanted that Jeep plant so bad, [and he got it] under the pretense of saying, "We're gonna bring a car over here to Kenosha and we're gonna keep what used to be AMC going strong"—and then to just pick off the frosting of the cake and leave the rest to crumble, I think that's what he was after. But he wasn't *man* enough or straightforward enough to have the guts to say, "This is what I'm going to do, I'm not going to paint you a beautiful picture and then all of a sudden tear it in half." So I think that's what being dealt a low blow here is all about. Why didn't he just come out and say it?

In retrospect, autoworkers are convinced that all Chrysler ever wanted when it acquired American Motors was its Jeep line, the four-wheel-drive technology and the popular Jeep name. Kenosha, long the mainstay of AMC, must have looked like pretty boring fare to this greedy CEO. But as Luis points out, greed alone is not the issue here. At issue is a profound betrayal of trust.

Living up to one's word is a decisive measure of moral character. Within the microsocial realm of the family, promises and commitments derive their social force and cultural meaning from the idea that love or biology binds people together in an absolute way.[15] Obligations incurred among coworkers on the shopfloor are also assumed to be binding because the social solidarity of the collective is largely an extension of the same symbolic precepts. Within both social realms, autoworkers trust that obligations will hold, largely because family and friends have a long memory and powerful sanctions at their disposal to bring wayward sheep back into the fold. But outside this world, in the larger society, the only thing binding people together is a sense that there is a social contract, a set of common obligations held collectively by society as a whole. But today, workers say, no one seems to care whether these promises are kept.

As Kenosha autoworkers reflect on what happened to them, they feel there is much more at stake in their plant closing than a broken promise on the part of Lee Iacocca. They see his deception and "lie" as indicative of a thoroughgoing breakdown in the system of rights and obligations that bind people together in American society. If Lee Iacocca breaks his promise, they ask, whose word can you rely on? If you can't rely on anybody's word, what kind of society do we have? Assembler Ralph Harding sees a society so shattered by lies and unenforced obligations that it has become two separate societies:

> [The government and the corporations] use, like, psychology—anything from schooling to TV—to try to make you see things the way they want you to see them, not how they really are. They're painting a picture, and they want you to accept that picture. We were told that we would be [working] for a minimum of three years, maybe five, and that wasn't true. It's just like our EIP money, the employee investment program. We weren't gonna get that money back. What could we do about it? *Nothing.* What could the union do about it? *Nothing.* That's straight-out robbery! How the *fuck* can they take your money and keep it? If I did that to them, I'd be in jail, wouldn't I? But they can do it. They don't only do it, they *notify* you of it! They put it in the paper! Doesn't this sort of show that there's a law for a rich person and a law for a poor person? Isn't there?

The false picture being painted by corrupt politicians and businessmen, workers argue, makes it impossible for the average citizen to live a life free of demoralizing uncertainty. Society has become a dangerous maze of fun-house mirrors and trick doors. The cultural norms and obligations that once guided American social life now seem like a deadly set of booby traps. For Kenosha autoworkers, the Chrysler plant closing catalyzed a sense of having witnessed the true reality of things for the very first time. The false picture was peeled away, and in its place they see a world beset by social disorder on a magnitude never before imagined. This ghastly new world is one in which few can be trusted and nothing is ever what people say it is. A small conspiracy of Washington insiders, military brass, and multinational conglomerates are playing a cruel joke on the American people. But the cruelest irony, autoworker Al Tirpak says, is that the victims of the conspiracy are the ones judged most harshly:

> They've taxed the American taxpayer to death to support this machine that Eisenhower characterized as the military-industrial complex to provide an umbrella of protection for right-wing dictators, so that they can export their jobs over there and have the people in these Third World countries work like slaves. When they do that, they throw millions of people out of work here. And then those people—who are really the victims of what is going on—become the enemy to the taxpayers, who say, "We don't want to pay to support that bum because he's too lazy to work." And that's wrong. But that's the depth of political demagoguery that we've gone to.

To blue-collar workers who have long considered themselves the backbone of industrial America and the epitome of the Protestant work ethic, being castigated as "too lazy to work" is the lowest blow imaginable.

Tom Sheppard says he would never have bought a house if he hadn't been given assurances by Chrysler management that his job was secure. When he looks back on the events of the year, what stands out for him is the audacity of Lee Iacocca's lies. The false expectations created by the promise of more work did more than make a mockery of his efforts at homeownership. The company's misleading promises have also taken a toll on his sense of self-worth:

> They keep saying this bullshit about the plant being too old. Maybe the plant's so many years old, but who cares? What does that mean, "too old," when we're still getting the quality out? What's that mean? I don't buy that story at all, it's bullshit from the word go. They just basically wrote us off. And I can't believe people who can intentionally deceive people like that. "You did good work," [the company said]. "You got the best quality out, [but] well, we've got to shut the plant down, it's a business decision." It builds your self-esteem up real good.

> You do your best work and where's it get you? You do your
> best and you get rewarded? Not in this case.

The idea that good work will be rewarded formed the central article of faith in the Puritans' pact with an inscrutable God, and it has
long informed the paternalistic practices of American industry. Like
other workers rendered redundant by deindustrialization, Kenosha
autoworkers believe that the decline of American industry can be
traced to the abrogation of this tradition.[16] But for workers like Tom
Sheppard, the breakdown of the work ethic signals a world without
rhyme or reason. When good work is no longer rewarded, how do
you know you are doing good work?

Assembler Jim Taylor recalls how eager Kenosha autoworkers were
to prove themselves worthy of the security Chrysler appeared to
promise. Lee Iacocca "had people bustin' their rear ends for him,"
Jim says. Workers were led to believe that extra effort on their part
might lead the company to bring in a new line of cars and work beyond the initial five years. "When we did break them records, we
thought, well, we're going to stand a real good chance." Echoing the
disbelief and bewilderment of so many others, Jim fights back tears as
he recalls the cruel duplicity of the corporation:

> Right up until the announcement of the closing [Chrysler]
> kept saying, "Do a good job and you'll be rewarded for it."
> Right up to the end, you'd walk through Motor Division and
> they have a sign: Quality—Your Job Depends on It. Well,
> you've got five thousand people out of a job now and they still
> had the quality, you know? I mean it's kind of ironic. [His
> voice breaks, and he wipes a hand across his eyes.] I mean, it
> gets you mad. It really does. It gets under your skin to an
> extent. Now when I see that [sign], I kinda laugh, you know,
> what a joke. Big deal. With no future, you're not going to put
> your heart and soul into it. And we *were* putting our heart
> and soul into it for a long time.

When we talk about the changing nature of work in America, we
are talking about more than the shift from manufacturing to services.
We are also talking about the kind of emotional investment people
make in their jobs and what it means to lose this investment. Very few
of the workers who lost their jobs in the Kenosha shutdown will ever
be autoworkers again. Fewer than half will ever earn as much money
or be able to maintain the same standard of living they achieved while
working in the plant. The plant closing has altered the way people
feel about the cultural meaning of their work and the value of their
contribution to society.

Jim Taylor says it is surprising that even after the closing was announced, the craftsmanship of the Kenosha workforce never really
declined. Was pride in quality work still worth something, I ask him,
even if the company failed to acknowledge it?

"Is it *worth* something?" he replies, giving me an impatient look.
"Yeah, a sharp stick in the eye."

CHAPTER TEN

Mapping the Moral Terrain

The union hall is a modern single-story building, similar in style to the countless suburban schools, shopping centers, and corporate headquarters built in the early 1960s. Laid out like sprawling chicken farms, with parking lots as large as small municipal airports, such buildings mark the transition from the city's industrial center to the outlying farmlands. In Kenosha the transition is a quick one. A fifteen-minute drive due west from the center of town will bring you face to face with the unperturbed countenances of grazing dairy cows. At the entrance to Local 72's parking lot there is a sign that reads NO FOREIGN CARS ALLOWED. Then, in an afterthought typical of the 1960s, smaller letters temporize: Except Volkswagens. As I drive my father's British-made sports car into the lot, a vague sense of guilt pricks my conscience.

A clutch of cars, a few pickup trucks, and a lone motorcycle are already parked near the back entrance at 8:00 this morning. The orientation workshops for the UAW-JDTC Dislocated Workers Assistance Center take place here every Monday through Thursday, from 8:30 to 12:00, with a new session beginning each week. Participation in the program is voluntary, but if workers wish to avail themselves of the other relocation services offered by the union and state job service agencies, they are expected to attend these workshops. Sessions are led by fellow dislocated autoworkers who have been hired as peer counselors or "job search assistants" (JSAs).[1] Sometimes JSAs team-teach a session, and some counselors regularly lead classes on days when the subject is one they handle particularly well. The four-day session covers a fixed set of units: skills inventory; budget manage-

Local 72 workers respond to the city-county vote not to sue Chrysler. Photo by Bill Siel and the *Kenosha News*.

ment; stress awareness; résumé writing; job hunting, and interviewing skills. Today is the third day of this week's session.

The eight autoworkers here this morning have already been through Monday and Tuesday's workshops together, so you would expect them to be at ease with one another by now. But as I look around the room, that doesn't seem to be the case. Four or five men slouch in chairs randomly scattered around the cavernous conference room. The ceiling lights are dimmed, like intermission lights in a movie theater, and the air-conditioning is on full blast. A few of the men wear their blue silk UAW jackets. All are in blue jeans and heavy work boots and to my amazement, most manage to sit diagonally in these hard metal chairs as though they were recliners. The man sitting near me flips through a notebook; three others stare at the floor, their hands in their pockets; another dozes under the lowered visor of his baseball cap. Cigarette smoke and an occasional burst of laughter drift in from the hallway, where the rest of the group has congregated. Yet when these men enter the room, it is one at a time.

From end to end, the union hall is about the size of two contiguous basketball courts. Floor-to-ceiling folding walls have been extended to divide the interior of the building into four large sections. In two sections, office cubicles have been created with cloth-covered portable walls. This is where the JSAs meet with workers for individual counseling sessions, and where I have also been given space to conduct interviews while I am here. In the section at the far end of the hall, a classroom has been set up where workers can do guided individual study toward their high-school equivalency exams. The conference room where the orientation classes are held is in the center, and its doors open out into the hallway by the main entrance. The wall here is lined with framed photographs of Local 72's past presidents. In these slices of time and fashion, there is a legacy of militant leadership that dates back to the 1930s. Not far from this wall of pictures is a table where, ever since the plant closing, volunteers from the Interfaith Council of Churches set up a coffee urn, towers of Styrofoam cups, and Tupperware containers full of assorted cookies.

Wendy Miles enters the conference room, sweeping hallway stragglers along in her wake. She turns up the lights a bit, illuminating the T-shaped formation of tables at the front of the room. Wendy spots me and gives a friendly wave. I was introduced to the group on the first day, so she says nothing now. We both understand that the less attention called to my presence, the better. In these groups, at least, I try to keep as low a profile as possible, not wanting to make people feel any more self-conscious than they already do. The men scoot closer to the T-shaped tables, and Wendy sits on a separate table that faces the top of the T. Her shoulder-length blond hair is gathered into a ponytail, and her dress and manner are casual. Wendy was a shop steward for many years. She is on a first-name basis with some of the men, and the others have warmed to her quickly. A few guffaws greet her announcement of today's subject: "stress awareness."

The springboard for the group's discussion is a multi-item checklist that helps them identify the different ways emotional stress can show up in their lives. The list is included in a loose-leaf notebook that everyone was given at the beginning of the week, so the men are able to follow along as Wendy talks about each symptom of stress. The assignment is to check off whichever symptoms they feel apply to them. But Wendy doesn't start the day's discussion with the first item on the list ("Are you tired all the time?"). Instead, she begins with a dramatic pause. Looking around the table at each man individually, and then directing her question to no one in particular, she asks, "Why are you out of work?"

There is some uneasy shifting of feet, and many downcast eyes. Remarkably, no one ventures an answer. Wendy prolongs this silence until it seems almost unbearable. "That's the million dollar question, isn't it?" she says finally. "But no matter what your answers are, and no matter how good they are in theory, the bottom line is you're out of a job and you've got to get on with your life. All the reasons in the world won't bring us our jobs back, and we've just got to accept that."

It's hard to tell how the men are reacting to this. Wendy is obviously aiming to push them beyond denial, but do tactics like this work? The faces I can see are dispassionate—but thoughtful. As Wendy begins to go over the itemized signs of stress, the men begin to rouse themselves from various states of social isolation as first one, then another, offers the group anecdotal evidence of the hydra-headed stress now popping up in his life.

Wendy's question, "Are you more irritable?" gets the first big response. One worker says, "A lot of people who have jobs just don't understand what I'm going through." Heads nod, and murmurs of agreement ripple across the table. Another worker says, "I see my kids more often than I usually do. When I didn't see them as often, they didn't get on my nerves as much." Another worker adds, "I can't give my kids the things I used to. So sometimes I snap at them when they ask me for things."

Wendy supports these men by assuring them that their feelings are normal symptoms of stress, emphasizing that these are the *symptoms*, not the sources of stress. The best way to reduce the stress, she tells them, is to find a new job, and that's what the Assistance Center is there to help them do. Already the level of tension in the room seems to have fallen a few notches. The men are making more eye contact, and some hazard smiles or offer brief asides to the person sitting next to them. Some jackets have come off, and everyone is sitting up straight, intently following the discussion. By the time the group has worked its way through the checklist, the groundwork has been laid for the free-flowing exchange that follows.

"Now let's talk about the *causes* of stress," Wendy says, smiling slightly. "Any ideas?"

"We were screwed," blurts out the fellow in the Cubs baseball cap. "Plain and simple."

"I used to feel pride, working for Chrysler," a man called Jeeter says. "Now when I see Iacocca on TV, I just laugh."

The guy across the table agrees, deadpan: "I notice he doesn't seem to smile so much anymore."

"Yeah," another snorts. "Did you see him on 'Donahue'? 'I'll answer questions about anything,' he says . . . 'anything *except* my marriage—*or* Kenosha!'"

There is a round of good, raucous laughter, and a fist or two pounds the table. Wendy is visibly pleased with these proceedings, and she suggests we take a fifteen-minute break before returning to view a video on "the job hunt." In my mind's eye I can't help seeing

157

this squad of autoworkers in camouflage fatigues, crawling up a hill and descending with a battle cry upon some unsuspecting employer.

Getting Angry

"Well, I'll tell you what," Wendy Miles says, as we sit in her office after the workshop. "Ninety-seven percent of all the people who come in [to the Dislocated Workers Center] are *mad*. They're angry, and they're gonna sit there and tell you, "*No, I'm not.*" And until you get that out of their gut—that feeling of hate, mistrusting, disbelieving—until you get that out of them, you might as well not even send them out on a job search, because they're gonna betray that. Because deep down inside them, something that they say or their actions is gonna show [their feelings]. So you have to work on that area first and get them feelings out in the open and deal with things."

Better that people who know and care about you discover what's "deep down inside" than some employer who will only reject you for it. But getting down to this human core, as Wendy points out, means peeling away everyday social conventions and overcoming barriers of personal privacy that you would normally respect. "People usually don't want to show anybody that 'yeah, there's a fault here,' or 'Yes, I have a problem.' People aren't like that. We're not taught to be like that," she says. "We're taught to be humble and you keep your problems to yourself and you don't toot your own horn and that's just the way society is. So if you sit down with somebody and, 'How are you today?' The first reaction is, 'Fine.' Either they're gonna go, 'Why should I bother to tell *you*? You don't really care.' Or I'm not supposed to show my most inner feelings to you, the way I was taught."

Wendy's commonsense approach to the psychology of unemployment was not learned in school or from reading books. Like all the JSAs at the Center, she has been through a few training seminars, but largely her wisdom is born of experience—other people's experience of job loss as well as her own. In the time I've spent here at the Center, I've come to realize that this peer counseling program offers its participants much more than the hope of a new job. These workers know that the chances of finding high-paying factory jobs like the ones they've lost are slim. Job loss in this context, Wendy explains, is not simply a matter of losing one job and trying to find another. "It's devastating," she sighs. "It's like . . . 'Okay,' you tell somebody, 'now you have got to get a two-year education to make half the money you were making before.'" Faced with the prospect of retraining for a new line of work in a job market that appears to be operating according to new rules, autoworkers must rethink lifelong goals and moral commitments. This occupational derailment is an unanticipated twist in what once seemed like a fairly straightforward life course. Working together, through improvisation and experimentation, through intuition and faith, Kenosha's autoworkers are charting a moral course for themselves across new and unfamiliar terrain.

The first step in this process, Wendy suggests, involves recognizing the common bond they all share—not so much as autoworkers, but as human beings. Before any of them can leave factory life and coworkers behind, they must reaffirm *as a group* a sense of what really matters in life. Before workers can cast themselves to the wind like a plume of dandelion seeds seeking their individual places in the social structure, they must reaffirm the worth of where they have been and construct a new sense of where it is morally worthwhile to go. Letting your guard down, fessing up to deep self-doubts, anxiety, uncertainty, and anger, contributes to a feeling of "oneness" that is common to people who go through some trial by fire together. The experience of a shared ordeal makes social differences seem insignificant. Pecking orders dissolve, and participants come to share a sense of unity and equality. Anthropologist Victor Turner calls this special form of human bonding "communitas," the Latin term for community.[2] There is a touch of the sacred in communitas, a sense of communion and moral purpose that is often carried over into the life one returns to at the end of the ritual process. You feel you have been in touch with something greater than yourself and perhaps have glimpsed some truer, deeper understanding of the world you live in. Only in the crucible of these sacred "moments in and out of time," we might expect, can new moral commitments be forged.

"Sometimes," Wendy says, pausing to light a cigarette, "you get a real particular tough case, which might be one out of twenty-five, that just won't . . . you know, 'I'm Mr. Macho and you're not going to get to me, no matter what.'" She leans back in her chair and smiles at me. "That's when I usually kick off my shoes in the workshop. I've got a different style than a lot of people. I kick off my shoes and—I don't usually dress up for a workshop. I mean, if I can get away with it in here: T-shirts and sweatshirts. Because then you get down to where they feel comfortable. You're at their level, you know. I usually kick off my shoes and say, 'Okay Tom, what're you feeling?' Nothing. 'Aren't you mad, Tom?' Won't say anything. 'Well, I am,' [I say]. 'I'm damn mad, and I'll tell you what, I'd like to stand up here and *scream!*' Sometimes I will do that," she laughs lightly. "And then—*boom!*— they'll break. It's something you have to build gradually. I always feel a gut instinct, an indication between two people. And as long as I follow that, so far it hasn't steered me wrong."

Anger, in the experience of most Americans, is exactly as Wendy describes it. It feels like a powerful force that builds up inside us until something "triggers it," forcing us to "let it all out." Images of loaded guns ready to go off or volcanoes about to erupt capture our sense that angry feelings—and hence angry people—are powerful, unpredictable, and dangerous. Anger is assumed to be the psychological counterpart of what is at base a physiological disturbance of some kind. Something poisonous is "inside" us, and until we get whatever this is "out" of our system, we will be walking time bombs. This is why Wendy and the other JSAs feel it is so important to deal with people's anger about the shutdown before tackling any other issues. No employer wants to hire someone with an ax to grind, and no spouse wants to live with a bear.

But anger is more than just a hot-tempered feeling. As anthropologist Robert Solomon observes, getting angry expresses a particular way of interpreting the world: "[It] is essentially a judgmental emotion, a perception of an offense. It consists of a series of concepts and judgments that among other ingredients, involve the concept of blame. Getting angry is making an indictment (whether overtly or not)."[3] When Kenosha's dislocated autoworkers "get in touch" with their anger and "get it out" into the open where it can be discussed by the group, they are doing more than letting off steam. Cultural perceptions are taking shape, judgmental interpretations are being hammered out, and a renewed sense of moral order is under construction.

Politics of Meaning

The shift from manufacturing to services has irrevocably altered the cultural and political landscape of American society. American culture is not homogeneous, however, and there is considerable internal disagreement over the nature and meaning of this transition. Anthropologist Clifford Geertz argues that there is a *cultural* "politics of meaning" that frequently finds its clearest expression outside the economic and political spheres of life: "[Internal cultural diversity can be seen in] the bitter combat of groups who see in one another rivals not merely for political and economic power, but for the right to define truth, justice, beauty, and morality, the very nature of reality. [This can be called] 'the struggle for the real,' the attempt to impose upon the world a particular conception of how things at bottom are and how men are therefore obliged to act."[4]

The cultural conflict we see in Kenosha is precisely this kind of "struggle for the real." Autoworkers and middle-class professionals confront each other over very different notions about how social value should be calculated and who is qualified to speak for the common good of the community. Autoworkers are faced with the challenge of finding new ways to express old values, while at the same time the legitimacy of these values is being disputed in American society at large.[5] Industrial change of the magnitude we are witnessing today is a profound disruption not just of individual lives, but of the values that have long shaped the cultural identity of manufacturing communities throughout the United States.

People who were once able to fulfill their obligations to family, community, and nation with minimal schooling and thirty years of manual labor in a manufacturing industry have become culturally "deviant" within the life span of a single generation. Blue-collar workers who entered the factories in the 1960s and 1970s are no longer perceived as the hardworking, self-sacrificing immigrants of their parents' or grandparents' generation.[6] Working in a factory to provide a middle-class life for your family is no longer considered a legitimate goal. America's industrial workers are today more often the target of national—and now even international—ridicule, censure, and blame.[7] Few factory workers are able to shake the stereotype of being lazy, illiterate, and overpaid. Their tastes, leisure activities, and political views are parodied by the popular media and "upper classes" as tacky, materialistic, narrow-minded, and reactionary.[8] The home life they provide for their children is dismissed or deplored by educators, psychologists, and other "liberal" social critics as authoritarian, provincial, and culturally impoverished.[9]

What was once a fundamental segment of the American economic structure—heavy industry and durable goods manufacturing—has now become a marginal part of the national portfolio. As this sector of the economy gives way to the new "knowledge industries," workers in this sector are being superseded as well. In America's new image of itself as a postindustrial society, individuals still employed in basic manufacturing industries look like global benchwarmers in the competitive markets of the modern world. Industrial change has come to be seen as a transition for the country as a whole—a national rite of passage, if you will—that demands a thoroughgoing transformation of our cultural character.

Old categories have collapsed, and familiar boundaries have become blurred. People who once stood at the center of things now seem out of place. The shifting of cultural boundaries essentially "reclassifies" elements of social life and creates new categories of experience. The rules have been changed in the middle of the game, and new notions of deviance are being culturally manufactured.[10] For those who find themselves suddenly reclassified, the experience can be devastating. Messages about moral worth are conveyed in the changing face of the urban landscape, and workers like Bill Sorensen are shocked by what they see:

> There's been very effective community propaganda to put down and blame the victim. I can express in a few sentences what I feel out in the community. "They had it too good for too long, so, good! They *deserve* what they got. If they hadn't been so greedy, maybe Chrysler would have stayed. So now anything bad that happens to them, they deserve. And it can't be bad enough for those people because they had it too good for so long. They made so much more money than I did, so they really deserve to suffer now." I get that feeling out there. It's out there. [Being a blue-collar town] is something people pooh-pooh. Somehow they think that somebody with dirt under their fingernails is intellectually and artistically inferior. Like they have no soul, they're just blue-collar workers. Get those nice yuppies in here and they'll make it a nice clean place!

The same war of images is waged over the airwaves, as Connie Miller will attest. The way the news makes it look, she says angrily, autoworkers are "people that try to do the *least* possible work for the *most* money." Obviously some people in town must think this is what autoworkers are like—especially if the only source for their impressions is the evening news! But this image is totally unlike the people she knows:

> The news always portrayed us all as such a bunch of bums. It really galls us. There's maybe 1 percent rowdy people in the workforce, and the [news reporters] would always go to the bars and interview *them!* The rest are nice family people, you know? People that worked there for thirty years and they had nice families and their kids had nice families. The majority of those people are good, honest family people, hardworking, who deserved every penny they got. And we just were not portrayed that way at all.

The realization that other people think you are inferior can also be picked up through dealings with formal organizations like the courts, prospective employers, social service agencies, or the schools. Frequently, judgments about moral worth are delivered inadvertently, through actions that infringe on your freedom or civil rights. Local school authorities seemed particularly adept at this sort of guerrilla warfare. As you might expect, workers keep close tabs on the attitudes their children pick up in school about the superiority of people who have an education. Their own, largely negative, memories of school are never far from their minds when they find themselves dealing with school officials now, as adults, when presumably they are on an equal social footing.

After the shutdown was announced, the superintendent of Kenosha schools received enough complaints about what children were hearing from teachers—stories of traumatized youngsters coming home in tears, fearing the worst—that he issued a moratorium on all classroom discussions of the plant closing. These complaints came from autoworkers, not white-collar parents. Several parents told me that their kids were being frightened to the point of hysteria by teachers who exulted over the coming of the new marina, oblivious to the fact that hundreds of little ears picked up only the news that their parents' place of employment was going to be destroyed and that their families would soon have no money.

The superintendent's moratorium may have spared some heartache, but it did little to address the underlying conflict between educators and blue-collar parents. Subterranean antagonisms continue to pop up in incidents that seem minor enough in the telling but carry decades of accumulated baggage. Even gestures ostensibly designed to ensure the schools' "neutrality" on the plant-closing issue are rarely seen as such by the parents involved. Assembler Sally Nolan tells of this run-in with her sons' junior-high principal:

> [The union] sold Iacocca buttons [that said]: Lie-Acocca. When my kids went to school . . . I had put one on their jackets, but the principal wouldn't let them wear them. I was very upset; I says, "I let them wear this." And he says, "That's not nice." And I says, "Well, he did lie. [The schools] don't think he lied? I know he lied." [My kids] didn't wear their buttons anymore, but they didn't feel it was anything to be ashamed of wearing. That really upset me. And [the principal] even had relatives that worked in the plant!

Scenes like these are mortifying to blue-collar parents. In one stroke they discover not only that people in high places disagree with them, but that these very same people can simply deny them freedom of speech. Workers naturally feel they have a right to express their beliefs and values and to raise their children to uphold the same morality. The principal's action in this scenario—however well intentioned it might have been—is interpreted by blue-collar parents as an affront to their authority and standing in the community.

By far the most common experience autoworkers have is a kind of "overheard indictment" to which no effective response seems possible, since they are not personally the intended audience of the insult. This is probably the most demoralizing way blue-collar workers pick up clues about how others view them. Standing in the checkout line at the supermarket or spreading a blanket for a family picnic at the beach, workers become unwitting eavesdroppers on other people's condemnation of their way of life. Sadly enough, the effect of these purloined messages is a kind of self-imposed social segregation in which autoworkers come to feel that certain public places are off-limits to people like them. Donna Clausen tells a story that poignantly captures the nature of such encounters:

> Before the decision [not to sue] was made, three of my friends and I would go to a little restaurant downtown and have soup for lunch. Real nice little place, we enjoyed going there. One time we heard one of the owners telling all these people from wherever they were from, "Oh yes, [that plant's] been an eyesore all these years; I can't wait to see it go." I'm getting mad, but my friends are saying to me, "Come on, Donna, come on, [cool down]," cuz they know my temper. All of a sudden my friend that is usually quiet, she just let him have it! For years this [restaurant owner] sold AMC cars. For years that's how he made his living! Which now he don't. But yet he could sit there and tell all these people in their business suits and their fancy dresses that [the plant] has been nothing but an eyesore, a problem to the city, and we're gonna get rid of it—*even* before the final decision was made about it! All's I was just gonna say, is "*Where'd* you get your bread and butter from for all these years? By selling the *eyesore* cars." Oh, he made me so mad! We never went back in there again.

Through social interactions like these, media images, the contrived "neutrality" of formal organizations, and the symbolic transformation of the city's image, autoworkers have gained a clear sense of how they are devalued by middle-class professionals. Were the nature of culture such that people adopt whatever system of meaning happens to dominate the society they live in, workers should now be "converting" to the culture of the mind and heading off to school in droves. But this is not happening. In the "struggle for the real" they are, instead, looking hard at their own values—hard at how they believe things, at bottom, really are—and they are not prepared to discard the cultural codes that brought them to this point in their lives and made them who they are. Not yet at least. For culture is not something that can be shucked off like a tattered overcoat. It can only be patched and mended, as Yeats might say, as "Soul clap its hands and sing, and louder sing / For every tatter in its mortal dress."[11]

Moral Ambiguity

"I see trouble down the road," says Joe Gordon. We have just been talking about the choice he will have to make between going back to school for a degree in counseling and returning to work at Chrysler's Motor Division when, and if, current high-seniority workers retire and laid-off workers are called back to take their place. A callback, if it comes, could be a year from now, maybe two years. And beyond that, no one can say for sure how long the Motor Division, with nine hundred to one thousand employees, will remain in operation.

Joe knows the salary he can expect to receive in the field of social service counseling will never amount to what he could make in the plant:

> I say the pay doesn't bother me, but it does. I could keep my house. I'm lucky, I have only fourteen years left on the mort- gage, and even if I had to work at seven dollars an hour, [the mortgage is] low enough that I could pay it off. But I couldn't do things with my family: I couldn't take vacations; I'd have trouble buying cars. And the retirement wouldn't be there. If I go back and finish my time out in the Motor Division, at age fifty-one, I can go out with a 30-year retirement and full benefits. Then I could use the excuse that, well, then I'm go- ing to go on with my life and go back to school. But at age fifty-one, I may say, "Why quit? I'm only fifty-one, I'll stay here ten more years."

Joe has no trouble putting his finger on what lies at the root of this dilemma: "My obligations to my family as opposed to my obligations to myself." These are the basic—and potentially contradictory— moral commitments that he feels all dislocated workers must grapple with as they try to figure out what to do now that the plant has closed.

> [The need to balance these commitments], that's more or less what I'm trying to get across to the people in this pro- gram—and I'm struggling with it myself. Number one, you have to go and talk to your family about what you're going to do with the rest of your life. You can't do it [on your own]; you owe [it to] your family to [let them] help make a decision.

But then after your family makes a decision, you have to say, "I owe it to myself what I'm going to do; it's my life. You know I'll always take care of you, but maybe I won't be making fifteen dollars an hour; maybe I'm going to be happy now and make eight dollars an hour." And that's where I'm struggling right now, [trying to decide] what I'm going to do.

Joe attaches special value to the goal of supporting his family and also to the goal of developing his ability to help others. When Joe was a shop steward, these goals didn't seem mutually exclusive: it was possible to serve both moral objects simultaneously simply by working in the plant. Now the tasks required to serve one goal (earning an income that will maintain his family's present standard of living) seem to conflict with the endeavors required to serve the other goal (working in a job where he is helping others). Not only does it seem that these goals are now suddenly incompatible, the problem cannot be solved simply by choosing between them or by giving one priority.

Even if Joe were to say that supporting his family is more important to him than helping others, there is no guarantee that he will be called back to the engine plant (or that it will remain open much longer). There is even less chance that he will find another job in manufacturing that will pay enough to support the lifestyle his family now enjoys. Even if Joe were to say that finding a personally satisfying job is more important to him than maintaining his present lifestyle, there is always the possibility that the social service jobs available to him may not offer the kind of satisfaction he desires. With a two-year degree from a local community college, he could get state certification to counsel people with alcohol and other drug addictions (AODA). But Joe fears he would quickly become discouraged with chemical dependency rehabilitation because "the success rate is so low." The kind of counseling he thinks he would like to do, some kind of family therapy, requires a four-year bachelor's degree at the least, and Joe isn't sure he can justify the expenditure of money and time that earning these credentials would require. "I may find out," he worries, "that I'm going in the totally wrong direction two years from now."

As Joe talks about his future possibilities, weighing his career options on one hand and his responsibilities to his family on the other, I am struck by the way he continues to frame the choice between work devoted to helping others and work devoted to supporting others. The basic conflict, as he sees it, is between self-fulfillment and duty to family. By categorizing his work in this way, Joe has set up his choice as a contest between selfishness and altruism. Because Joe is so uncomfortable with the thought of putting his own interests ahead of his family's well-being, he feels he will probably not pursue further schooling and a career in counseling—on the grounds that it would be too selfish. Somehow, in his moral calculations, what began as a desire to help others quickly gets transformed into an unacceptable desire to advance himself.[12] Why throw money at a college degree if two years down the road he might change his mind about the kind of work he wants to do? Wouldn't it be better—a less ambiguous demonstration of moral worth—to spend that money making life as nice as possible for his wife and two teenage daughters?

Joe's dilemma is a good example of how hard it is to translate the morality of shopfloor culture into a code of conduct for a new life outside the factory gates. Moral understandings built up among coworkers in the assembly plant are being tested in new situations, and commonsense cultural categories don't always give meaning to the world in the way they once did. In the plant, Joe could honor a moral commitment to both of his goals simultaneously, simply by performing his duties as a union steward. Outside the plant, he is now engaged in pursuits—working as a JSA during the day and going to school at night—that serve, at least for the time being, both his goals. But the situation feels highly unstable. Self-doubt picks away at his self-esteem and sense of purpose. Images of classroom failure and humiliation float into view, only to be crowded out by the disappointed and resentful faces of spouse and children.

When Joe projects himself into the future, no matter what he imagines himself doing—working in another factory, counseling at a rehabilitation center, or taking classes at the university—his heart sinks at the premonition that he will just be going through the motions and not really enjoying whatever it is he chooses to do. Inexplicably, the goals he once held dear have lost their light and luster. Over the murky waters of an uncharted sea, they no longer stand out like brilliant stars in the night, giving him a sense of his place in the order of things. Somehow goals held for a lifetime got lost along with the job that once served them. As a result, Joe has a hard time feeling confident that he is doing the right thing.

The culture of the mind has a relentlessly corrosive effect on workers' self-esteem. Precisely because prevailing opinion holds autoworkers *responsible* for their misfortune, they are forced to question a fundamental component of their self-worth. Drawn down "that very well-lit back alley where one keeps assignations with oneself,"[13] they have to ask themselves if maybe people are right, maybe they *have* done something to deserve what's happening to them now. Was the plant closing truly an event beyond their control? Or was there something they could have done to prevent it, some reason they must now hold themselves accountable for their fate?

Tom Sheppard speaks for many autoworkers who struggle with the issue of self-respect:

> A lot of people look down on us because of the money we made. And like I say, I didn't *choose* to make this money. If I had my way, we wouldn't be making fourteen dollars an hour. I've said that from day one, and I'm sure I've pissed a lot of people off by sayin' it, but there ain't no way in hell that I'm worth fourteen dollars an hour to put parts on a car. Especially when you look at . . . they cut back on nurses, they cut back on education. I'm making fourteen dollars an hour and a nurse is going to save somebody's life for six dollars an hour? I mean, where's the priorities here?

Tom knows that other people think he is overpaid, and he feels a sense of guilt about this.[14] But he cannot bring himself to take *moral* responsibility for the wage levels negotiated in his union contract. He had no control over this, he insists. Indeed, if Tom did not limit his responsibility in some way, guilt and self-blame would rise to unbearable levels. Should he have quit in protest? Sent part of his paycheck back to the company?

All systems of morality must make a distinction between free will and determinism—between what is intentional and what is inevitable. "Concepts of free will permit persons to take credit for their accomplishments," observes sociologist Robert Wuthnow, while "concepts of determinism give them an 'out' for their failures."[15] Clearly, as autoworkers' powerful critique of American industry and government attests, they do not blame themselves for the shutdown itself. But the culture of the mind can slip around this first line of defense and undermine the distinction between free will and determinism in another way: the state of the economy may not be within their control, but the state of their minds certainly is. In this system of morality, workers have no one but themselves to blame for the loss of their jobs and their present standard of living: they did not get an education when they should have.

Joe Gordon feels compelled to overlook nothing in his search for a coherent understanding of the situation in which he finds himself:

> I think what [the closing] has done is . . . it's forced everybody to turn around and to look back into themselves now and see how you've been BS-ing yourself for years. Because now that I say, "Yeah, [becoming a counselor] is what I want to do with my life . . ." you know, why didn't I do it [before]? . . . I never

had to be here right now. I could have a long time ago chosen another field. I *could* have gone back to school. So if you really examine what happened and you want to blame somebody for this whole thing: I blame myself. And I think everybody's doing that. I don't know if they're doing it the same way. Maybe they're even doing it harsher than I'm doing it, or maybe they're doing it easier than I'm doing it, because everybody does it in their own way. But I find [the way things are] hard to deal with. I keep thinking, *Why?*

It's hard to reconcile Joe's harsh self-appraisal with what he has also told us about the satisfactions of union work and the warm family life his factory job supported. But as autoworkers juggle values drawn from the culture of the hands with others drawn from the culture of the mind, there are inconsistencies and agonizing trade-offs. Rich memories fall by the way, only to be replaced by a searing sense of shame. For this reason most workers are not willing to abandon their core values entirely. If they were to accept the idea that education is the true measure of social worth, they would have to concede that anyone with a college degree was their superior and deserving of higher wages. Few are willing to go that far. As Al Tirpak says defiantly:

We're worth fifteen dollars an hour because we're producing a product that can be sold on the market that'll produce that fifteen dollars an hour. Of course, in the equation of what people pay for a car, labor is only about 10 percent of the cost. We are a minor cost to the employer; we are not a major cost. I think that being a human being entitles somebody to be able to put food in their stomach and a roof over their head and clothes on their back. There oughta be some floor, some minimum that everybody is entitled to, simply because they are a human being. And if they're willing to do some work, they should get paid that amount. I don't know if you want to [base a person's value] strictly on education. You can send someone to school for twelve years and they can still be doing something that's socially undesirable and not very worthwhile for society. I don't know if they should get paid *just* because they had an education. In my mind, yuppie means *young unproductive parasite.* We're gonna have an awful lot of yuppies here in Kenosha that say they are doing something worthwhile when, really, they aren't. You can't have a viable economy just frying hamburgers for each other and doing each other's wash.

In the culture of the hands, social value derives from the production of things that most people can't make for themselves, because

either special skills or collective efforts are involved. To many autoworkers, the proliferation of service-sector jobs is an enigma. Why are
millions of jobs being created to do things that most people should be
able to do for themselves?[16] Does society really need these kinds of
services? Obviously some people want to pay paltry wages to have others do these things for them, but what kind of creature lives off the
labor of others? Only a parasite, of course. Truly productive labor is
measured both by what people are willing to pay for the final product
and by how it contributes to the good of the whole society.

Mary Cleveland rejects the idea that autoworkers have been nothing but a flat tire on the wheel of progress, or that they have held
the whole community hostage to their self-interest. She does this by
pointing to the physical sacrifice workers make and how they have
contributed to the common good, even if other people refuse to acknowledge it:

> Every person, you work in there for any length of time, comes
> out with a disability. They never go in with the same body that
> they have after working there five years. [With such injuries
> it's not easy] for these people to find another job. People do
> not understand what these people do. All we read in the pa-
> per [is that we] are people on sick leave, we abuse drugs, we're
> an alcoholic environment. Those people that worked in there,
> they *worked* for what they did. I look at it this way: If those
> people made fourteen dollars, Joe Blow down the street that
> got eight dollars, he wouldn't be getting eight dollars if that
> other guy didn't get fourteen dollars. [Everybody's wages] all
> have to kinda come up. Where my son works, he's a super-
> visor in a small factory, his boss had to raise the wages in
> order to pay more to get the skilled people in order to keep
> them. Like I told my son, if it weren't for AMC, they never
> would have raised [those wages]. I says we help other people
> whether they see it or not. We pay taxes. Somebody's gonna
> have to pick up them taxes.

From this vantage point, self-worth is based on what you do for
others in your community and how, as in the system of collective reliance on the line, your efforts make life a little better for those around
you. If new politicians justify their vision of Kenosha's future by appealing to the common good, autoworkers counter that claim with
their own ideas about what constitutes the common good.[17] Bill Sorensen argues that Kenosha's "blue-collar ethic" made the city what it
is today. Carthage College and the University of Wisconsin–Parkside
would not even be *in* Kenosha, Bill says, if it weren't for the support
of the blue-collar community:

I really feel slapped in the face when people rejoice that it's not going to be a blue-collar town anymore. And they are [rejoicing]; I hear it, and I resent it. Essentially, the blue-collar mentality they complain about is characterized as being regressive. But it really isn't. If you look at this community, historically, things like [the private college and the university extension], the people who pushed for those things were blue-collar workers. This town is so proud of all its parks. But that is part of the blue-collar ethic. The concept of public access—something for everybody to share, all these wonderful things in the community—is a very blue-collar notion. You know, the idea of something for the *common good*. I'm not rich enough to own my own home by the lake, so I'll work to make sure that there are parks on the lake so I can at least go by the lake and enjoy it. Now most of the lakefront will be privately owned.

To understand the meaning of industrial change in the United States, we need to focus on how people make sense of their lives in the face of ambiguous or shifting cultural rules. The social response to changing economic conditions can never be guided, or regulated, by one system of morality. Moral behavior, after all, can never be reduced to a single system of unchanging cultural meanings. People have to be rule makers, not just rule followers. "Morality," writes sociologist Alan Wolfe, is "neither a fixed set of rules handed down unchanging by powerful structures nor something made up on the spot. It is a negotiated process through which individuals, by reflecting periodically on what they have done in the past, try to ascertain what they ought to do next."[18]

A lack of consensus about the proper response to economic change doesn't mean that American society is in a state of decline or moral collapse. Rather than seeing moral "disorder" in national debates over deindustrialization and the value of industrial labor, I see a situation of "nonorder." We need to look beyond the traditional dichotomy of "order" versus "chaos" and recognize what anthropologist Renato Rosaldo calls an intermediate, more creative zone of cultural life. This zone of "nonorder" is characterized by improvisation—all the spontaneous, experimental things people do when plans go awry and expectations are not met.[19] For in addition to generating goals, expectations, and guidelines for action, our cultural systems endow us with the capacity to bend rules and tolerate contradictions, so that we can go about our daily lives in meaningful ways even when the future is uncertain—as indeed, contrary to our fondest hopes, it always is.

American Primitive

The building itself is something I'll miss. That building is older than I am. My whole concept of this city is [that] this city has been that big factory downtown. When they tear it down, my whole concept of what this city is, physically as well as psychologically, is gonna be drastically altered. It's gonna be this huge gaping hole where this huge chunk of my life was . . . literally, just a huge gaping hole.

BILL SORENSEN, TOOL AND DIE MAKER

When they start tearing [the plant] down, I'm going to go get a brick. I would just keep it. My kids know Mama spent fifteen years of her life [in the plant] working, and to tell my future grandkids about it. You know, tell them that it was a place where we worked, and that when they tore the building down, Grandma went and got herself a brick. For all that I put in there. I figure I at least deserve a brick.

DONNA CLAUSEN, ASSEMBLER

For several weeks after the rambling turn-of-the-century buildings were completely demolished, all that remained standing along the lakefront was a lone factory smokestack, thrusting up out of the debris, looking vulnerable and oddly ridiculous against the barren skyline. This, the most dangerous part of the demolition, had to be saved for last. The surrounding area had to be cleared and evacuated before it came down since, like a giant sequoia, no one could be too sure just which way it might fall.

173

The demolition of the auto plant's 250-foot smokestack marked the end of an era for Kenosha. Photo by Brian Passino and the *Kenosha News*.

I was back in New York City the day they blew up that smokestack. Friends tell me it was quite an event. Traffic was stopped on nearby streets, and the usually desolate downtown area was alive with nervous expectation as people gathered from all around to witness the passing of an age. Some reserved picnic spots hours in advance, set up folding chairs, and uncorked bottles of champagne. Boats dotted the shoreline, flung out in an arc across the water like the audience at a Greek theater. People relaxed on makeshift bleachers of tailgates and beer coolers, while overhead a helicopter circled in slow loops, poised to capture the moment for the evening news. The news clipping I have shows the smokestack seconds after the explosives were detonated. In this picture there are no dramatic tongues of fire, no billowing clouds of smoke, no showers of sparks or flying concrete. It is simply a picture of a smokestack, broken in half, falling out of the sky.

Anthropologists are supposed to understand rituals like these. We pride ourselves on being able to plumb the depths of strange and fantastic rites—no matter how grotesque or comical—and extract a nugget of truth, some deep insight that will illuminate the essence of the culture at hand. Implicit in this view of ritual is the notion that cultural systems do in fact have an essential core, some set of ideas about the world that people agree upon unequivocally.[1] But how are we to understand rituals in which people seriously disagree about the future direction their society should take and what its basic rules should be? What does it mean to know that the spectacle of the falling smokestack did not have the same meaning for all who gathered to watch it?

The Vanishing Primitive

Rituals bring us together because they dramatize, often in vivid ways, something about the moral order of the society we live in. But the lesson we draw from this dramatization is far from uniform. We each come to a ritual with a certain set of expectations about how social life should be ordered and where we as individuals fit into the scheme of things. Plant closings, as a national ritual, communicate to all of us a sense that our society is changing in new and important ways. We may disagree about the cause of these changes, and not all of us may believe those changes are a good thing. But few of us dispute that the changes are occurring. The ritual symbols of a plant closing are not about the causes of change, or even about the desirability of change. Rather, I think the symbolism of a plant closing is about the *meaning of change* itself. The abandonment, gentrification, and outright destruction of old factory buildings signifies not just social change, but a particular kind of social change. When chrome and glass skyscrapers rise out of the rubble of an industrial plant, when bombed-out factories are left to crumble in urban wastelands where vibrant communities once thrived, the message is not just about the inevitability of change, but about the obsolescence of the past.

Change, as anthropologist Colin Turnbull points out, can be of two kinds. There is the kind of nondirectional change that societies undergo as part of a sensitive, nondisruptive response to a changing natural environment, and there is *unidirectional* change—the kind of drastic social reorganization that comes about in response to technologically dominant cultures.[2] Turnbull is concerned with changes experienced by the Mbuti Pygmies of Zaire, but his insight applies to the concept of social change more generally. Cultural adaptation to change—be it environmental, social, or economic—doesn't necessarily involve "progress," "advancement," or "evolution" in any form. Cultural systems may change in response to economic and environmental conditions without abandoning core values or insisting on a future that is radically different from the past. This kind of stability through change has characterized hunting and gathering societies for hundreds of thousands of years. Yet we are not accustomed to thinking about this form of cultural adaptation as change. When we look at the once remarkably stable cultures of people like the Mbuti, we see static, unchanging, "primitive" societies. We are much more inclined to think of change in Turnbull's second sense, that is, change as a means of adapting to the technology and cultural practices of "advanced" societies like our own. Thus, the people who experience "real" change are those who must abandon their past ways of life in order to survive. This kind of adaptation means giving up traditional values, assimilating to a new moral order, and learning to live as the members of the most powerful societies do. Change, from this perspective, means making other people more like us.

Images of the primitive, notions of change, and ideas about the past have often been conflated in Western cultures. The small-scale societies anthropologists encountered during the period of colonial expansion were classified as "primitive" because they appeared to be holdovers from prehistoric times, examples of how "we," as "civilized" people, must have lived in the remote, unrecorded past. This way of understanding cultural differences, as anthropologist Johannes Fabian shows, seriously confuses notions of time and space. The farther away from Western centers of commerce tribal peoples lived, the "earlier" the stage in cultural evolution they were presumed to represent.[3]

What is remarkable about this concept is its denial of the coeval existence that made the study of these living cultures possible in the first place. What, apart from our conquest of their lands and interest in their resources, made them relics of a bygone day?[4] Both cultures had survived, each in its own way, into the modern age. Yet rather than seeing their social organization and exotic practices as evidence of the great variety of cultural forms, anthropologists and others perceived non-Western peoples as doomed to extinction or conquest. In one encounter after another, the Darwinian perception of primitive cultures as maladaptive "species" became, as we now know, a self-fulfilling prophecy.

Oddly enough, as other cultures around the world have come to seem more and more like our contemporaries—consuming Western goods and desiring a Western standard of living—people within our own society appear less and less modern—less able, that is, to keep up with the demands of a postindustrial society. Today the concept of cultural "otherness" depends less on geographical distance than on the notion of social or economic distance. Competition in the global economy between and among "advanced" and "developing" nations has provided an international scale for the way we evaluate the value of different forms of labor here in the United States. The globalization of basic manufacturing has driven home the realization that the kind of labor typically performed by blue-collar workers in the industrial Midwest can now be done for a fraction of the cost by "Third World" workers in Mexico or the industrializing countries of the Pacific Rim. In this new symbolic universe, dislocated factory workers in America have fallen to their "natural" level in the capitalist world economy; and like other "primitive" social forms, they are portrayed as a vanishing breed, the contemporary representatives of a dying way of life.

In the ritual symbolism of postindustrial society, industrial workers have become the new American primitive. They are people who work with their hands in a society that increasingly values work done with the mind. Their social distance from the new cultural ideal is measured and legitimated by educational credentials. If they wish to survive in the modern age and claim a place in the middle class, it is said, they will have to educate themselves to do the kind of work demanded of people living in a postindustrial society. The kind of social change required is clearly unidirectional: blue-collar workers must adapt to the cultural forms practiced by the dominant social groups in American society and other countries around the world. The nation's industrial past plays no part in our vision of the future, and the artifacts of this vanishing culture carry no special meaning in the present. Smokestacks do not stand as monuments to a venerable age in American history, and paralleling the fall of communism elsewhere in the world, the image of the manual laborer is no longer glorified.

Remembrance of Things Past

Anthropologists have always been "on location" during periods of sweeping social change and cultural conflict. Our ethnographic tradition grew out of the profound ethical concerns that arose when different cultural systems came into contact and those with the more powerful technologies were able to dominate or supersede others. In one way or another, anthropologists have always found themselves living among and coming to care for people on the "wrong" side of history. Our immersion in these vanishing ways of life was construed as a source of moral authority when we returned home to Europe or the United States to offer our perspective on global issues and universal human dilemmas. Margaret Mead was, of course, a pioneering figure in this bully pulpit style of anthropology. Drawing on her fieldwork in the South Pacific and elsewhere, she lectured, lobbied, and as a monthly columnist for *Redbook* magazine, spoke directly to the American public about such issues of the day as gender roles, child-rearing practices, intergenerational conflict, and nuclear war.[5]

Ours is a presumptuous enterprise, no matter how broadly we generalize our findings, but the intensive field study of remote and ultimately "disappearing" cultures was always thought to grant a certain authority, if not urgency, to the need to speak for people in less powerful societies as well as for those without power in our own. In recent years, however, the epistemological source of ethnographic authority has increasingly come under attack, largely by critics within the discipline of anthropology itself.[6] This intense self-scrutiny is directed primarily at the long-standing assumption that our interpretation of a cultural "other" can in any meaningful way be objective. Knowledge is power, and the power to "know," define, and deconstruct the cosmology of someone else's culture is not morally neutral or innocent. Anthropologists have always been in danger of playing handmaiden to Western imperialism, to the extent that they appropriate the material and cultural resources of other peoples in ways that reflect our own ethnocentric perception of the universe. Indeed, the very notion that certain ways of life need to be saved or "salvaged" implies that the societies in question have already been tossed on the junk heap of history, and that their sacred myths, artifacts, and other cultural lore are simply there for the taking.

In the context of our developing world system, as anthropologist James Clifford reminds us, the theme of the "vanishing primitive" has often been used to justify the mission of salvage ethnology. Where other cultures are perceived to be too weak, fragmented, or demoralized to speak for themselves, the imperialist anthropologist steps in and presumes to speak "for" them.[7] It is no coincidence, Clifford argues, that many anthropological texts make a point of portraying the society under study as one in decline or in imminent danger of collapse. Rarely do we think it odd that a culture has begun to "vanish" the moment an anthropologist happens upon the scene. Like undertakers in search of new business, anthropologists seem adept at figuring out which ambulances to chase through the world's busy streets. For many of us who have grown critical of traditional forms of ethnographic writing, anthropology's reliance on the trope of decline and salvage not only fails to justify its moral authority, but also results in two contradictory, and equally misleading, portraits of social change. As Mary Louise Pratt points out in her analysis of ethnographic discourse, subjugated peoples tend to be either "historicized" as the victims qua survivors of Western imperialism or "romanticized" as pure and "primal beings virtually untouched by history." In either case, Pratt observes, "they stand doomed to extinction."[8]

Taken together, these historicizing and romanticizing modes of discourse create a curious nostalgia in which "we," as members of the dominant culture, feel a personal sense of loss and yearning for the very societies that our own social system has had a hand in destroying.[9] This form of lament is not limited to anthropological writings about non-Western societies caught in the grip of brutalizing "development" and "modernization" programs. The rhetorical bells toll just as dolorously in the newly emerging ethnography of deindustrialization. As titles like *Rusted Dreams* or *The Magic City* suggest,[10] American industrial workers are also subject to the kind of historicizing and romanticizing imagery that characterizes nostalgic treatments of more distant but nonetheless passing ways of life. Labor historian William Serrin captures the spirit of this genre in a Labor Day editorial for the *New York Times* titled, "Requiem for a Steel Town." Of Homestead, Pennsylvania, victim of a mill shutdown, he writes: "[Homestead] shows America at perhaps its most courageous: how we came from many continents and built towns, the nation, through the hardest work; it also shows what is exceedingly lamentable about us: how we use things up—people and towns among these things—and how we care so little for those we regard as beneath us."[11]

The power and appeal of this reading of deindustrialization are undeniable. Toward this "American tragedy" an attitude of nostalgia seems entirely natural, especially when it is evoked, as in Serrin's piece, in the service of self-critique. We romanticize and valorize the world our immigrant ancestors built, even as we are forced to historicize that world by acknowledging our complicity in a modern world system that has rendered that past, and that way of life, obsolete. A nostalgic attitude appeals to us because it reaffirms our own place in the world as people on the "right" side of history, even (or especially) when the moral dilemmas of life in the modern world give us reason to doubt the new age we are heirs to. With a view of social change as *progress,* our perception of the past is softened to sepia tones and our understanding of the meaning of the past *in the present* is held at bay. "Nostalgia," as historian Christopher Lasch suggests, "evokes the past only to bury it alive."[12]

Contested Meanings

Kenosha's autoworkers did not protest the plant closing because they feared the destruction of blue-collar culture. They fought to save the plant because they valued their jobs and the social life they engendered with family and friends on the shopfloor and in the community.[13] They fought to save the plant because, in a rapidly changing economy, their sense of self-worth and their vision of how the world should be depended on it. Yet as we have seen, two very different ways of thinking about success and individual merit have coexisted in Kenosha for a long time. Middle-class professionals justify their place in the social order by citing their educational credentials as the ultimate measure of the value of the work they do. In contrast, autoworkers point to the market value of their manual labor to legitimize their place in society. The wages they received as workers in a vital American industry are for them the measure of their real worth.

What is interesting to me is that both versions of meritocracy are viable in American society, so long as the economy backs them up. Blue-collar workers who rode the wave of postwar expansion into the middle class had every reason to believe that their prosperity reflected their moral worth. During those years, what was the real value of educational credentials when high-school teachers could look out the windows of their suburban homes and envy the material wealth of the high-school dropout living next door? Right now, thanks to the global restructuring of manufacturing, the credentialism of middle-class professionals appears to be the on winning side of history—in Kenosha, across the country, and at the end of the twentieth century. It would be easy enough to say that educated workers have always known that their yardstick of moral worth has the greatest legitimacy in American society as a whole, and that it was only a matter of time before they would be vindicated. That, certainly, is their version of things. But it's not the lesson I draw from my research.

I still see a contested terrain. Autoworkers chose their way of life within the context of a local economy that supported and validated that choice. Their occupational identity is tied to a cultural system that has been built up over generations, linking family dreams to secure jobs on the shopfloor, the factory to community, and auto work to national strength and pride. For over half a century, Kenosha's autoworkers were able to kick aside mainstream measures of merit. They were able to validate their sense of self-worth by achieving the consumption standards that had become the hallmark of the American middle class in the "happy days" of the 1950s. In the spirit of the Protestant work ethic, they could look at the fleet of cars AMC shipped out and see in the product of their craftsmanship the source of their worldly rewards. Today autoworkers know they cannot simply walk away from the credentialist standards that are applied to everyone in this society. At some level they too accept the idea that college degrees are "badges of ability." At some level we are all like the Scarecrow in the *Wizard of Oz*, believing that without the diploma we have no brains. For in truth we know we are worthy only when a symbol of social worth is conferred upon us—whether by God, the economy, university regents, or a little man behind a curtain. In this moral tautology, the proof of our worthiness is contained in the reward. A changing economy can privilege one form of work over another, but only culture can supply the meaning of that privilege. What we see in America today is not a unitary consensus about technological progress, but a cultural debate about two very different ways of calculating the value of the work we do and the worth of the people we are.

I for one will never forget my exchange with Ralph Harding at the end of our time together. We shake hands and I give him a business card that lists my address at Columbia's Department of Anthropology, where I tell him I can always be reached.

"Columbia, huh?" he says, squinting up over the card as he reads it. "You gonna make a lot of money when you get out?"

I grin in spite of myself. "Doing this? Probably not."

"You're an anthropologist?" he continues, doubtfully. "Why would an anthropologist study something as to the effects of the closing of a plant?"

A fair enough question, after all. "Well," I begin, "as you know, I'm studying industrial problems in American society . . ."

181

[handwritten marginalia: self worth determined by culture = defines the meaning of privilege]

[handwritten note at bottom: the value of the work ↕ the worth of the people.]

"With *an-thro-pol-o-gy* as a major?" he blurts out.

This man is almost old enough to be my father, and I suddenly feel like a coed being taken to task, once again, for my admittedly vague career goals. I think of Margaret Mead carrying youngsters on her back in Samoa, and try to explain. "Anthropologists study people in all sorts of places and societies . . ."

"Yeah," Ralph allows, a bemused expression crossing his face. "But usually you're out in the middle of some desert digging somebody up! I mean, *we're* still walking around," he laughs. "*We* haven't died yet!"

I laugh at his joke too, as I have at so many others that I don't fully understand. But when my eyes meet Ralph's I see the sadness there, the sadness and the fear. And in a funny way I know then, as I watch him turn and leave, what this book will be about.

The Kenosha Workforce

The impact of a plant closing on individual workers, their families, and others in a community will depend in large part on the composition of that particular workforce.[1] At the time of the shutdown, Chrysler's Kenosha operations employed 7,600 salaried and hourly employees. Most of these workers are residents of Kenosha; the rest live in the surrounding communities in southeastern Wisconsin (see table A1). Of the 4,438 hourly employees in the Kenosha workforce, 17 percent are classified as "skilled" and 83 percent as "unskilled." Over 90 percent are white, 5.3 percent are black, and 4 percent are Hispanic. About one in every five autoworkers is female.[2]

Like the workforce in many closing plants, Kenosha's is relatively old (see table A2). More than half the workers are over forty.[3]

Table A1   Demographics of Chrysler Corporation, Kenosha Operations

Residence	Hourly	%	Salaried	%	Total	%
Kenosha	4,438	64.9	540	71.6	4,978	65.5
Racine	1,159	16.9	118	15.7	1,277	16.8
Walworth	53	0.8	8	1.1	61	0.8
Milwaukee[a]	388	5.67	44	5.8	432	5.7
Illinois	428	6.3	24	3.2	452	6.0
Other	376	5.5	20	2.7	396	5.2
Total	6,842		754		7,596	

[a] Milwaukee and surrounding counties.

183

Table A2   Age Distribution of Kenosha Resident
Hourly Workers

Employee Age	Number	Percentage of Total
66+	5	—
60–65	184	4.1
50–59	1,084	24.4
40–49	1,215	27.4
30–39	1,151	34.3
20–29	431	9.7
18–19	4	—

Table A3   Percentage of Civilian Labor Force by Industry,
Kenosha County, 1960–1990

Industry	1960	1970	1980	1990
Agriculture, forestry, fishing, and mining	3.3	0.4	1.8	1.7
Construction	4.7	3.5	4.6	6.1
Manufacturing	49.5	44.1	39.6	27.5
Durable goods	88.4	86.4	84.0	70.8
Nondurable goods	11.6	13.6	16.0	29.2
Transportation, communications, and utilities	3.9	4.0	5.0	5.6
Wholesale trade	1.2	2.2	2.2	3.4
Retail trade	14.1	17.2	16.3	19.0
Finance, insurance, and real estate	1.8	2.3	3.1	4.5
Services	15.0	22.2	24.8	28.9
Public administration	3.4	4.1	2.6	3.4

Source: U.S. Bureau of the Census and *Kenosha County Overall Economic Development Program (OEDP) Plan—1986 Update,* 2d ed. Community Assistance Planning Report 74 (Waukesha, Wis.: SEWRPC, 1986), p. 107, plus 1990 SEWRPC data.

Table A4 Profile of Informants ($N = 45$)

	Number	% of Total
Sex		
Male	35	78
Female	10	22
Age		
60+	2	4
50–59	6	13
40–49	16	36
30–39	21	47
Individual income ($/year)		
<10,000	3	7
10,000–19,999	3	7
20,000–29,999	13	29
30,000–39,999	23	51
40,000–49,999	1	2
50,000–59,999	2	4
Household income ($/year)		
<10,000	1	2
10,000–19,999	1	2
20,000–29,999	7	16
30,000–39,999	21	47
40,000–49,999	6	13
50,000–59,999	6	13
60,000–69,999	1	2
70,000–79,999	1	2
80,000–89,999	1	2

Table A5 Informants' Individual Income by Education and Seniority ($N = 45$)

Individual Income in 1988[a]	Years of Schooling		Years in the Plant		% of Total
	Twelve or Less (N)	Over Twelve (N)	Sixteen or Less (N)	Over Sixteen (N)	
$29,999 or less ($N = 19$)	11	8	10	9	42
Over $30,000 ($N = 26$)	16	10	20	6	58
Percentage of total	60	40	67	33	100

[a] Many autoworkers were laid off from AMC for part of 1988.

Table A6 Informants' Household Income by Sex ($N = 45$)

Household Income	Male (N)	Female (N)	% of Total
Less than $29,999 (N = 9)	9	0	20
$30,000–39,999 (N = 21)	15	6	47
Over $40,000 (N = 15)	11	4	33

Introduction

1. Over the year following the shutdown, I conducted in-depth interviews with autoworkers and a wide range of professionals in the Kenosha area. With the support of United Auto Workers Local 72, I was allowed to conduct an extensive part of my research at the union hall, where the UAW in conjunction with the Job Development and Training Corporation (JDTC) and Wisconsin Job Service agencies had set up an assistance center for dislocated workers. I sat in on group workshops and interviewed many of the former Chrysler workers participating in the UAW-JDTC program. To ensure that my interviews were not skewed in favor of autoworkers willing to seek institutionalized forms of help with their experience of job loss, I also interviewed many autoworkers who had minimal contact with union representatives or the assistance center. I approached these men and women through personal referrals from their family members, friends, or coworkers.

In all, I interviewed forty-five autoworkers during the spring and summer of 1989, with some additional follow-up interviews in the winter and spring of 1990. The dislocated workers I spoke with were either retired or still receiving unemployment benefits at the time of the interview. Since the focus of my research was on the cultural meaning of the shutdown rather than on the social or psychological impact of unemployment per se, my open-ended questions were designed to explore how people were making sense of their situation and did not attempt to elicit quantitative measures of their coping strategies. Informants were free to introduce topics as they saw fit, and most of the rich material on populist nativism emerged in this spontaneous fashion.

Community leaders, social workers, business managers, and local politicians were approached through more formal channels, usually through a letter explaining the nature of my research, followed up with a telephone call to arrange the interview. In addition to the thirty interviews conducted in this manner, I also had the opportunity to interview forty high-school principals, teachers, and guidance counselors during their "free" hours in the school day. Like the interviews with autoworkers, these conversations focused primarily on educators' perceptions of the shutdown and its meaning for the local community.

To protect the confidentiality of all interviews, the identities of my informants have been concealed. There are no "composite" characters or falsified biographies, but the personal names that appear in the text are fictitious unless otherwise noted.

2. On employment figures at Nash, see Richard H. Keehn, "Industry and Business," in *Kenosha in the Twentieth Century: A Topical History,* ed. John A. Neuenschwander (Kenosha, Wis.: Kenosha Bicentennial Commission, 1976), pp. 175–214.

3. One out of every four autoworkers commuted to Kenosha from nearby Racine, Milwaukee, or North Chicago. For an overview of AMC's place in the regional economy, see William F. Thompson, *The History of Wisconsin,* vol. 6, *Continuity and Change, 1940–1965* (Madison: State Historical Society of Wisconsin, 1988).

4. For a sociological study of African Americans and Mexican Americans in Kenosha, see Lyle Shannon and Magdaline Shannon, *Minority Migrants in the Urban Community: Mexican-American and Negro Adjustment to Industrial Society* (Beverly Hills, Calif.: Sage, 1973). On the local history of minority groups, see Jonathan W. Zophy, "Invisible People: Blacks and Mexican Americans," in *Kenosha in the Twentieth Century: A Topical History,* ed. John Neuenschwander (Kenosha, Wis.: Kenosha Bicentennial Commission, 1976), pp. 51–77.

5. Frank Levy, "Incomes, Families, and Living Standards," in *American Living Standards: Threats and Challenges,* ed. Robert E. Litan, Robert Z. Lawrence, and Charles L. Schultz (Washington, D.C.: Brookings Institution, 1988), pp. 114–115.

6. Ibid.; see also Frank Levy, *Dollars and Dreams: The Changing American Income Distribution* (New York: W. W. Norton, 1987).

7. U.S. Bureau of the Census, "Income in 1969 of Families and Persons in the United States," *Current Population Reports,* ser. P-60, no. 75 (Washington, D.C.: Department of Commerce, 1970), and idem, "Money Income in 1973 of Families and Persons in the United States," *Current Population Reports,* ser. P-60, no. 97 (Washington, D.C.: Department of Commerce, 1975), p. 77, table 36, cited in Levy, "Incomes, Families, and Living Standards," p. 127. On the declining investment value of education, see Richard B. Freeman, *The Overeducated American* (New York: Academic Press, 1976).

8. The transition toward a "knowledge" or "information" society was dramatically predicted in 1973 by Daniel Bell in *The Coming of Post-industrial Society: A Venture in Social Forecasting* (New York: Basic Books, 1973).

9. Victor R. Fuchs, *The Service Economy* (New York: National Bureau of Economic Research, 1968).

10. Levy, "Incomes, Families, and Living Standards," p. 116.

11. Robert Wuthnow makes this point in his important book, *Meaning and Moral Order Explorations in Cultural Analysis* (Berkeley and Los Angeles: University of California Press, 1987). The anthropological perspective I take on the problem of moral ambiguity is deeply indebted to Wuthnow's lucid analysis of this subject.

12. On working-class *embourgeoisement* see Eli Ginzberg, *Manpower Agenda* (New York: McGraw-Hill, 1968), and Sar A. Levitan, ed., *Blue-Collar Workers: A Symposium on Middle America* (New York: McGraw-Hill, 1971). On the myth of cultural uniformity in the suburbs see William M. Dobriner, *Class in Suburbia* (Englewood Cliffs, N.J.: Prentice-Hall, 1963), and Bennett M. Berger, *Working Class Suburb: A Study of Auto Workers in Suburbia* (Berkeley and Los Angeles: University of California Press, 1971). On the myth of the affluent worker see Patricia Sexton and Brendan Sexton, *Blue Collars and Hard-Hats: The Working Class and the Future of American Politics* (New York: Random House, 1971), and Andrew Levison, *The Working-Class Majority* (New York: Penguin, 1974). On the emotional strain within blue-collar families see Richard Sennett and Jonathan Cobb, *The Hidden Injuries of Class* (New York: Vintage Books, 1972), and Lillian Breslow Rubin, *Worlds of Pain: Life in the Working Class Family* (New York: Basic Books, 1976).

13. David Halle, *America's Working Man* (Chicago: University of Chicago Press, 1984).

14. The number of people who put in a full day's work but whose income still falls below the poverty level has risen dramatically over the past decade. Since 1978 the number of working people in poverty has risen by 28 percent, according to the Center on Budget and Policy Priorities, "1986 Poverty Graphs and Tables" (Washington, D.C., 1987). For a good discussion of these figures, see Lawrence Mischel, *The State of Working America* (Washington, D.C.: Economic Policy Institute, 1990).

15. See, for example, Lester Thurow, *Head to Head: The Coming Battle among Japan, Europe, and America* (New York: William Morrow, 1992); Robert Kuttner, *The End of Laissez-Faire: National Purpose and the Global Economy after the Cold War* (New York: Alfred A. Knopf, 1991); Robert B. Reich, *The Work of Nations: Preparing Ourselves for Twenty-first Century Capitalism* (New York: Alfred A. Knopf, 1991); Bennett Harrison and Barry Bluestone, *The Great U-Turn: Corporate Restructuring and the Polarizing of America* (New York: Basic Books, 1988).

16. For an important exception, see Katherine S. Newman, *Declining Fortunes: The Withering of the American Dream* (New York: Basic Books, 1993).

17. Eli Chinoy, *Automobile Workers and the American Dream* (New York: Doubleday, 1955).

18. Robert Bellah, Richard Madsen, William M. Sullivan, Ann Swidler, and Steven M. Tipton, *Habits of the Heart: Individualism and Commitment in American Life* (New York: Harper and Row, 1985), p. 27.

19. See Katherine S. Newman, "Turning Your Back on Tradition: Sym-

bolic Analysis and Moral Critique in a Plant Shutdown," *Urban Anthropology* 14, nos. 1–3 (1985): 109–150.

20. Wuthnow, *Meaning and Moral Order,* p. 109.

Chapter One

"Hey Lee" was written by listeners of the Cat Simon radio show in Milwaukee (Star 95, WZTR 95.7 FM). The recording debuted on March 7, 1988, and features a group of Chrysler "line rats" who shout out each repetition of the ballad's chorus.

1. Vast portions of the North American continent were opened to westward expansion when the Erie Canal was completed in 1825. With the signing of the Chicago Treaty in 1833, the Chippewa, Ottawa, and Potawatomi Indians ceded much of the northern Midwest to the United States government. On the competition between Kenosha and other localities to attract settlers and investment capital to southeastern Wisconsin, see Lee D. Dahl, "The Origins of the Conflict between Southport and Racine, in *Kenosha: Historical Sketches,* ed. Nicholas C. Burckel (Kenosha, Wis.: Kenosha Historical Society, 1986), pp. 46–64.

2. John D. Buencker, "Immigration and Ethnic Groups," in *Kenosha in the Twentieth Century: A Topical History,* ed. John A. Neuenschwander (Kenosha, Wis.: Kenosha Bicentennial Commission, 1976), pp. 1–44. Wisconsin's rich farmlands, pine forests, and growing urban areas attracted millions of the German and Scandinavian immigrants who poured through Ellis Island from 1890 to 1900. Germans rapidly became the dominant ethnic group in the state. By the early 1900s the proportion of Germans living in Wisconsin was the largest of any state in the country. For more of this history, see Lavern J. Rippley, *The Immigrant Experience in Wisconsin* (Boston: Twayne, 1985).

3. Before the introduction of Henry Ford's revolutionary assembly line in 1914, automobile production required the skills of craftsmen trained in the bicycle and carriage shops of the Midwest. The first cars were built at fixed work stations by a group of all-around mechanics. On the "deskilling" of this work, see Harry Braverman, *Labor and Monopoly Capital: The Degradation of Work in the Twentieth Century* (New York: Monthly Review Press, 1974), pp. 146–150.

4. Richard Keehn, "Industry and Business," in *Kenosha in the Twentieth Century: A Topical History,* ed. John A. Neuenschwander (Kenosha, Wis.: Kenosha Bicentennial Commission, 1976), pp. 175–214.

5. The six larger automobile manufacturers were Ford, General Motors, Dodge, Willys-Overland, Studebaker, and Hudson.

6. Almost no industrial development occurred outside the city center, and this prompted rapid urban growth. From 1890 to 1920, the number of people living in the city virtually doubled, from 42 to 79 percent. Keehn, "Industry and Business," p. 177.

7. The city grew from 11,606 in 1900 to 50,262 in 1930. At the same time, the population of Kenosha County nearly tripled, from 21,707 to 63,277. Buencker, "Immigration and Ethnic Groups," p. 4.

8. An early study of Kenosha's residential patterns found clear evidence for the clustering of immigrant neighborhoods around major factory sections. Mabel B. Duncan, "Kenosha, Wisconsin: A Study in Urban Choreography" (Ph.D. diss., University of Chicago, 1935).

9. The aldermanic form of government had originally been designed to enable the city's old immigrants—Germans in particular—to control the political machinery. New immigrants, many of whom were not eligible to vote, found it difficult to break into this system. Only about one-third of the foreign-born males in Kenosha were naturalized citizens by 1910. Before women's suffrage, of course, these were the only immigrants who were eligible to vote. Even by 1920, over half of the new immigrants were not naturalized. This did not change until 1950, by which time over 90 percent of the new immigrants had become citizens. John L. Scott, "Union Politics and the City Council Manager Government in Kenosha" (master's thesis, University of Chicago, 1942).

10. John W. Bailey, "Labor's Fight for Security and Dignity," in *Kenosha in the Twentieth Century: A Topical History,* ed. John A. Neuenschwander (Kenosha, Wis.: Kenosha Bicentennial Commission, 1976), pp. 223–264.

11. Kenosha did not fully recover from the depression until the country entered World War II. By 1939 there were still only 8,572 workers employed in manufacturing, substantially below the city's 1929 level of 11,478 and even further below the 1919 level of 13,045. Keehn, "Industry and Business," p. 187.

12. Angela H. Zophy, "UAW Local 72: Assertive Union," in *Kenosha in the Twentieth Century: A Topical History,* ed. John A. Neuenschwander (Kenosha, Wis.: Kenosha Bicentennial Commission, 1976), pp. 297–331.

13. As elsewhere in the United States, the stimulus for union organizing in Kenosha was the 1933 National Industrial Recovery Act included in Roosevelt's New Deal. The critical section of this legislation, section 7(a), upheld the right of workers to organize and bargain collectively through representation of their own choosing. Although the workforce at Nash had been reduced during the depression, it remained the largest in the city. Kenosha's Trades and Labor Council targeted these three thousand workers for its initial organizing efforts.

14. For more on this second strike, see Zophy, "UAW Local 72," p. 305.

15. During the 1930s the AFL was split on the national level between craft unionists and industrial unionists. Kenosha's Local 72 followed the UAW international in its formal affiliation with the Congress of Industrial Organizations (CIO) when the AFL dropped industrial unions from its craft-based organization in 1939.

16. Keehn, "Industry and Business," p. 189. Nash merged with the Kelvinator Company, an appliance manufacturer, in 1937 to form Nash-Kelvinator.

17. These fascinating statistics are available because Kenosha was among ten cities selected by the Women's Bureau of the U.S. Department of Labor in 1944 for a study of the impact of war production on women's labor force

participation. Sylvia R. Weissbrodt, *Women Workers in Ten War Production Areas and Their Postwar Employment Plans,* Bulletin 209 (Washington, D.C.: U.S. Women's Bureau, 1946). The effect of wartime production on working conditions also influenced the new kinds of collective bargaining issues that arose. Among these were demands for the seniority rights of veterans and for the rights of working women. Zophy, "UAW Local 72," p. 315.

18. William F. Thompson, *The History of Wisconsin,* vol. 6, *Continuity and Change, 1940–1965* (Madison: State Historical Society of Wisconsin, 1988), p. 211.

19. "AM Drops to Low Gear," *Business Week,* February 19, 1966.

20. Thompson, *History of Wisconsin,* p. 212.

21. From 1960 to 1980, the number of unemployed men in Kenosha County increased from 2.3 to 7.8 percent of the county's population. The unemployment picture for minorities was even bleaker. In 1980 the minority unemployment rate in Kenosha County was 18.4 percent, almost triple the figure for whites. The number of female unemployed increased from 5 percent to 6.5 percent over the same decades. Data compiled by the Southeastern Wisconsin Regional Planning Commission, *Kenosha County Overall Economic Development Program (OEDP) Plan—1986 Update,* 2d ed. Community Assistance Planning Report (Waukesha, Wis.: SEWRPC, 1986), pp. 112–115.

22. Surprisingly, this decline in manufacturing failed to affect the overall labor force participation rate. From 1970 to 1980 participation remained fairly constant. How could this be when there were so many job losers? The answer lies in the surge of working women. From 1960 to 1980, the female labor force in Kenosha grew from 28.5 percent to 41.6 percent. Over the same period the male participation rate dropped from 71.5 percent to 58.4 percent. Ibid., pp. 99–101.

23. Greater Kenosha Economic Development Corporation Task Force, "The Future of American Motors/Renault in Kenosha," supplement to the *Kenosha News,* March 3, 1985, p. 5.

24. Ibid.

25. Upon appeal by the local unions, the National Labor Relations Board said it would not file formal unfair labor practice charges against AMC if the company and the unions were able to settle their differences. This NLRB action effectively gave the bargaining advantage to the company, allowing it to hold the threat of a shutdown over the heads of union negotiators until the concessions it desired were accepted. Conservative decisions like these by the Reagan-era NLRB have been a major factor in the declining influence of labor unions in the United States today.

26. Renault's purchase of AMC was part of its strategy to become an international car manufacturer and distributor, and the United States is the single largest automotive market in the world. But AMC's Kenosha operations were not a central hub in Renault's enterprise; it could maintain a presence in the United States car market without the Kenosha plant. Renault's goal of reaching long-term profitability by 1987 involved cutting AMC's costs by 25 percent. This led to management downsizing and the plant-closing threats, as

eight hundred white-collar employees were let go and new contracts were sought with Locals 72 and 75 in Wisconsin and Local 12 in Toledo, Ohio. Warren Brown, "French Taking Drastic Steps to Save AMC," reprinted from the *Washington Post* in the *Kenosha News*, June 12, 1985.

27. Management also bristled at the notion that it was under a binding obligation to repay workers' EIP investments, since GM and Ford had gotten the same financial relief from their unions without a restoration or payback arrangement. In addition, company representatives made it clear that without state "incentives" of $100 million, they would be hard pressed to keep the Kenosha and Milwaukee plants open much longer. "Destiny of AMC Unknown," *Kenosha News*, December 31, 1985.

28. The UAW constitution authorizes membership votes in such cases.

29. The bargaining committee nonetheless continued to maintain that the company had not bargained in good faith. As the chairman of the committee explained to the press, "We felt that even though there were many individual items in this agreement that were abhorrent to us, nothing could be gained by a 'no' vote on our part, which could confuse the membership to believe that if the agreement were rejected something better would come and take its place." "AMC, Union Reach New Agreement," *Kenosha News*, June 30, 1985.

30. "AMC, Chrysler Have a Deal," *Kenosha News*, December 31, 1986.

31. "Chrysler Makes Kenosha's Day," *Kenosha News*, December 31, 1987.

32. Daniel Fischer, "American Motors and Chrysler: A Commitment to Excellence," supplement to *Kenosha News*, March 30, 1987.

33. "Chrysler Makes Kenosha's Day," *Kenosha News*, December 31, 1987.

34. "Plant Closing Inevitable, but Shocking," *Kenosha News*, December 31, 1988.

Chapter Two

1. Sections of Jackson's speech were reported in the local newspapers. Quotations cited are from "Jackson Wows 'em at Rally," *Kenosha News*, February 3, 1988; "Rally Puts Focus on Kenosha: City a Symbol in 'Economic Justice' Fight," *Kenosha News*, February 2, 1988; and "Jackson: 'Must Draw the Line Here and Now,'" *Kenosha Labor*, February 5, 1988.

2. Union leaders felt their action was justified by the extraordinary situation they were in. The president of Local 72 argued that Jesse Jackson was the best spokesman autoworkers had on the national level. "In many of the debates, Jesse Jackson mentions Kenosha, Wisconsin, and the injustice of the barracudas," he said when nominating Jackson for the membership's endorsement. "These are the things Jesse Jackson is close to. He cares about the people in Kenosha. Can we say that about all the candidates?" Jacqueline Jackson addressed the crowded union hall on the day of the vote, thanking the autoworkers on behalf of her husband. "In Historic Move, L. 72 Endorses Jackson," *Kenosha Labor*, March 18, 1988.

3. "In Autos, US Makes Strides," *New York Times*, March 24, 1989, pp. D1, D3.

4. Although autoworkers recognized that the media had their own reasons

for wanting to cover the shutdown, they still believed they could use the media to "get their story out" to an uninformed or indifferent public. In a comparable situation, the air traffic controllers studied by Katherine Newman saw their relationship with the media in more adversarial terms. As PATCO saw it, the public had been on their side until it got brainwashed by the media—which appeared to be in bed with the government. Society remained potentially redeemable, the ultimate vindicator, if only strikers could break the media-government stranglehold on their public image. Autoworkers, in contrast, saw the media as a potential ally in their fight against big business–government. The different position of public and private sector employees vis-à-vis the government and business may account for this variation in their moral analysis of the national media. Katherine S. Newman, "PATCO Lives! Stigma, Heroism, and Symbolic Transformations," *Cultural Anthropology* 2, no. 3 (1987): 319–346.

5. "Local 72 Pickets Chrysler in Chicago," *Kenosha News*, February 12, 1988.

6. "We Want Jobs, Not Charity," *Kenosha Labor*, February 19, 1988.

7. Chrysler also promised not to withdraw the fund even if the state and local governments went ahead with their lawsuits. "Chrysler Establishes Kenosha Trust," *Kenosha News*, 17 February 1988; "Chrysler Guarantees Trust Fund," *Kenosha News*, 18 February 1988.

8. Other Chrysler locals were concerned that if Kenosha was shut down entirely Kenosha workers would have the seniority upon their transfer into other Chrysler plants to bump lower-seniority workers out of a job. If, as Chrysler maintained, Kenosha's Motor Division was to remain open, this concern was moot, since the seniority on transfer provision would not apply anyway. But Chrysler officials were refusing to make a firm commitment on the longevity of the engine plant, making it impossible for Local 72 to assure other Chrysler locals that they had nothing to worry about.

9. "Locals Threatening to Strike," *Kenosha News*, February 23, 1988.

10. "Strike Threatened by Auto Workers," *Kenosha News*, February 13, 1988.

11. "Auto Assembly Here until End of 1988," *Kenosha Labor*, April 29, 1988.

12. The decision to extend production in Kenosha reportedly was the result of a meeting between Lee Iacocca and UAW international president Owen Bieber. That meeting had been called to discuss the status of national contract talks in light of the company's plan to transfer its Detroit work to Mexico. But Iacocca issued a statement asserting that his decision to delay the shutdown was based solely on market considerations. "Meetings on Tentative Contract Next Week," *Kenosha Labor*, May 6, 1988.

13. The nature of this transfer also formed the basis of the federal lawsuit that Local 72 filed in February. The suit was based on federal laws prohibiting the use of federal funds to finance projects that increase employment in one place by taking jobs away from somewhere else. Local 72 claimed that Chrysler misled both the city of Detroit and the Department of Housing and Urban

Development (HUD) when it applied for and received $50 million in federal assistance. Chrysler had been given a $15 million Urban Development Action Grant and $35 million in Community Development Block Grant loan guarantees to retool its existing plant and build a replacement. The suit accused Chrysler of applying for funds under the pretense of shifting truck assembly from another Michigan plant to Jefferson Avenue. But instead of bringing in truck production, Chrysler had decided to shift work and jobs out of Kenosha. This transfer was held to be in violation of the Housing and Community Development Act, which prohibits industrial relocations in the use of the Urban Development Action Grant funds. The suit also charged that federal law was violated because HUD and the city of Detroit had not conducted an environmental impact assessment of the Kenosha plant closing, as would normally have been required by Community Development Block Grant regulations. "Local 72 Files Chrysler Lawsuit," *Kenosha Labor*, February 26, 1988; "Local 72 Sues Chrysler for Lost Work," *Kenosha News*, February 27, 1988.

14. The new contract included a four-year commitment to the Motor Division; expanded opportunities for early retirement; increased pension benefits of $135 a month; twenty-four weeks of supplemental unemployment benefits (SUB) for laid-off workers; 100 percent repayment of EIP money; health insurance for two years; company consideration of additional work for Kenosha plants; and a $20 million job bank for laid-off workers. "Union Drops Chrysler Lawsuit," *Kenosha News*, April 11, 1988.

15. "Contracts Ratified, but Fight Not Over Yet," *Kenosha Labor*, May 13, 1988.

16. Common Council of the City of Kenosha, *Official Proceedings* (Kenosha, Wis.: Common Council, February 1, 1988), pp. 34–35. The council unanimously adopted a resolution authorizing the city attorney to investigate a potential breach of contract on the part of Chrysler and to "take appropriate legal action to protect the city's interest, either alone, or in conjunction with the claims of other aggrieved parties."

17. The state attorney general said he was willing to prepare a lawsuit against Chrysler, since the automaker had broken a "clearly enforceable" agreement with its decision to close the Kenosha plant. Maintaining that oral agreements and letters of intent constitute a binding contract, the attorney general claimed the state had evidence that such a contract had been made. The state had been given to understand that Chrysler would continue to produce the two models it moved to Kenosha as long as the cars were selling. In exchange, Wisconsin provided Chrysler with $5 million for job training at the time of model transfers and an additional $1 million in training funds when air bags and motorized seat belts were introduced in the luxury models in 1989 and 1990. Under the impression that Chrysler planned to stay for at least three to five years, the city of Kenosha spent $1 million to resurface parking lots, install new streetlights, and make railroad track improvements on and near Chrysler properties. "Hanaway Says Sue," *Kenosha News*, February 9, 1988; "Thompson 'Leaning' toward Lawsuit," *Kenosha News*, February 11, 1988.

18. "Thompson Says State Serious about Suit," *Kenosha Labor,* March 18, 1988, pp. 1, 10.

19. Congressman Les Aspin and Governor Tommy Thompson, along with other state legislators, signed a public letter to Lee Iacocca in February 1988 imploring him to keep the Kenosha plant open.

20. In the great majority of shutdowns, the villain is not Japan or another low-cost competitor, but the American merger and acquisition mania of the 1980s. Apparently healthy plants are frequently closed as part of a corporation's strategy to reduce overcapacity, increase efficiency, or pay off the loans required for a merger. States and cities are increasingly turning to attorneys and courts to demand retribution. During the 1980s there were several major cases in which local officials attempted to pursue some form of litigation against a departing employer: Otis Elevator in Yonkers, New York; Playschool in Chicago, Illinois; Anchor-Hocking in Clarksburg, West Virginia; and Triangle Industries in Duluth, Minnesota. "To Keep a Business Open, Talk in a Business-like Way," *Minneapolis Star Tribune,* May 16, 1988.

21. The stated purpose of the memorandum is to "lessen the impact, upon the State and its local communities, including the County and the City, of the closing of the assembly and stamping operations at Chrysler's Kenosha Plant." Common Council of the City of Kenosha, *Official Proceedings,* pp. 311–317.

22. "Last Chrysler Leaves Kenosha," *Racine Journal Times,* December 22, 1988.

23. "Retooling for Tomorrow," *Racine Journal Times,* December 12, 1988.

24. "Kenosha Begins to Pick up Pieces of Plant Closing," *St. Paul Pioneer Dispatch,* December 25, 1988.

25. In 1988 Kenosha County had a population of 123,000 and a workforce of 55,000. Wisconsin Department of Industry, Labor and Human Relations, *Affirmative Action Data for Wisconsin, 1989* (Madison, Wis.: Division of Employment and Training Policy and Human Relations, 1989).

26. Pro-growth, supply-side strategies such as these have dominated urban redevelopment initiatives in recent years. See John Mollenkopf, *The Contested City* (Princeton: Princeton University Press, 1983); P. K. Eisinger, *The Rise of Entrepreneurial Society: State and Local Economic Development Policy in the United States* (Madison: University of Wisconsin Press, 1988); and J. R. Logan and H. L. Mototch, *Urban Fortunes: The Political Economy of Place* (Berkeley and Los Angeles: University of California Press, 1987).

27. "Boom County," *Kenosha News,* special report, January 20, 1990.

28. Thomas Moore and Gregory Squires, sociologists at the University of Wisconsin in Milwaukee, have investigated the social costs of the Kenosha shutdown and the ideological assumptions behind the city's current redevelopment initiatives. They conclude that Kenosha is undergoing a process of "uneven development." Although growth has been stimulated in selected sectors of the economy, severe social costs have been imposed on other segments of the population—in particular, minorities, the long-term unemployed, and those who have been forced to settle for jobs at much lower wages. Moore and Squires attribute this pattern of uneven development to a combination

of economic forces and political decisions that have been given legitimacy through an ideology of "privatism" that says, in effect, if it's good for business, it's good for the community. Thomas S. Moore and Gregory D. Squires, "Two Tales of a City: Economic Restructuring and Uneven Development in a Former Company Town," unpublished paper, Dept of Sociology, University of Wisconsin—Milwaukee, December 1990.

29. This increased demand for housing has raised local property values and fueled a housing boom. From 1988 to 1989, the value of new building permits rose from $111 million to $127 million as single-family housing starts jumped from 369 to 521. "Boom County," *Kenosha News,* special report, January 20, 1990; Moore and Squires, "Two Tales of a City," pp. 12–13.

30. "Retail 'Hot Spot' Developing along Interstate 94 Corridor," *Milwaukee Sentinel,* February 25, 1988; Moore and Squires, "Two Tales of a City," p. 13.

31. "Place," observes sociologist Sharon Zukin, "expresses how a spatially connected group of people mediate the demands of cultural identity, state power, and capital accumulation. . . . With the creative destruction of the industrial market economy and the expansion of employment in services, people experience a qualitative shift in the source of social meaning from the sphere of production to consumption." Sharon Zukin, *Landscapes of Power: From Detroit to Disney World* (Berkeley and Los Angeles: University of California Press, 1991), pp. 12, 29.

32. For a thought-provoking discussion of the moral torpor that has gripped Americans who have by all measures "made it," see John Kenneth Galbraith, *The Culture of Contentment* (Boston: Houghton Mifflin, 1992).

Chapter Three

1. Two retirement programs were available to Kenosha autoworkers. The first, called "thirty and out," allowed workers who had thirty years' seniority to retire with a guaranteed income, which worked out to be about $15,050 a year, plus a total insurance program. About 1,800 Chrysler workers were eligible for benefits under this program. Under a second plan, called "special early," workers who were over forty years old and had over ten years' seniority at the time of the shutdown could "grow into" their retirement plan. At age fifty-five, full insurance coverage would be reinstated, and these workers could then begin to draw monthly retirement benefits at a rate calculated by multiplying their total years of service by $26. Since this type of retirement program would cover about half the workers in the plant, it was understandably high on the union's list of contract priorities during negotiations with Chrysler.

2. Dislocated or "displaced" workers are defined as those who had stable employment in jobs with satisfactory pay and every reason to expect continued employment up to retirement, have been laid off with little chance of recall, and are unlikely to find new employment at or near their customary rates of pay using their familiar skills. Under this definition, operatives (production workers) in basic manufacturing account for about half of all displaced workers since 1980. Gary B. Hansen, "Layoffs, Plant-Closings, and

Worker Displacement in America: Serious Problems That Need a National Solution," *Journal of Social Issues* 44, no. 4 (1988): 153–171.

3. Dislocated workers frequently appear to act irresponsibly during the early phases of the job hunt. Employment opportunities are commonly declined in preference for a more desirable, appropriate job, regardless of the low likelihood of finding one. Job counselors often consider this behavior self-defeating and unrealistic. As Ramsay and Joan Liem have suggested, however, this "strategy" can also be seen as a form of resistance to the "job skidding" that has affected many underemployed workers during the 1980s. The jobs resistant workers refuse to take pay significantly less than their previous employment, confer much lower status, and demand a significant accommodation in lifestyle—not only of workers but of their families as well. The Liems argue that the strategies of holding out, turning to part-time work, and exploiting the underground economy are short-term responses to unemployment that reflect survivors' resourcefulness and unwillingness to compromise their integrity. The Liems see in this behavior evidence that the unemployed retain their own priorities and actively dispute the external redefinition of their social status. Ramsay Liem and Joan Liem, "Psychological Effects of Unemployment on Workers and Their Families," *Journal of Social Issues* 44, no. 4 (1988): 87–105.

4. From a psychological perspective, exclusion from employment is a threat to mental health because it frustrates needs that can be met only in the organized, purposeful company of others. Thus psychological studies of unemployment usually focus on the fit (or lack of fit) between jobs loss and human needs. The mental state of the unemployed is most often explained by reference to two basic factors: the sudden drop and steady decline in the standard of living, and the loss of the habitual way of life that having a job entails. How people cope (or fail to cope) with this frustration is the key research problem in most psychological studies of unemployment. Frank Furstenberg, "Work Experience and Family Life," in *Work and the Quality of Life,* ed. J. O'Toole (Cambridge: MIT Press, 1974), pp. 341–360; S. Kasl and S. Cobb, "Some Mental Health Consequences of Plant Closings," in *Mental Health and the Economy,* ed. L. Ferman and J. Gordus (Kalamazoo, Mich.: Upjohn Institute, 1979), pp. 255–300; Marie Jahoda, "Economic Recessions and Mental Health: Some Conceptual Issues," *Journal of Social Issues* 44, no. 4 (1988): 13–23; Patricia Voydanoff and Brenda W. Donnelly, "Economic Distress, Family Coping, and Quality of Family Life," in *Families and Economic Distress: Coping Strategies and Social Policy,* ed. P. Voydanoff and L. Majka (Beverly Hills, Calif.: Sage, 1988), pp. 97–115.

5. This figure is based on data from the government's Displaced Worker Survey for 1979–1983. The earnings loss drops to 20 percent in the next year and remains more or less at that level through the fifth year. Michael Podgursky and Paul Swaim, "Dislocated Workers and Earnings Loss: Estimates from the Dislocated Worker Survey," Department of Economics, University of Massachusetts-Amherst, March 1985.

6. Bennett Harrison and Barry Bluestone, *The Great U-Turn: Corporate Restructuring and the Polarizing of America* (New York: Basic Books, 1993), pp. 121–123.

7. See appendix, table A1, for the income profile of autoworkers who participated in this study.

8. While production jobs in the nation declined 29.7 percent from 1979 to 1984, the decline in Great Lakes rust belt cities was 45.3 percent. Richard Child Hill and Cynthia Negrey, "Deindustrialization in the Great Lakes," *Urban Affairs Quarterly* 22, no. 4 (June 1987): 580–597.

9. Donald L. Barlett and James B. Steele, *America: What Went Wrong?* (Kansas City, Mo.: Andrews and McMeel, 1992), p. 35.

10. Barry Bluestone and Bennett Harrison, *The Deindustrialization of America: Plant Closings, Community Abandonment, and the Dismantling of Basic Industry* (New York: Basic Books, 1982).

11. Overseas investment did not have an adverse impact on domestic employment early in the postwar period. Workers actually benefited from the export of capital, insofar as it kept corporate profits high and gave the unions considerable bargaining flexibility. Only when United States jobs began to be exported along with United States capital did unions start to suffer from the problems of international production and economic integration. For an excellent analysis, see Kim Moody, *An Injury to All: The Decline of American Unionism* (London: Verso Press, 1988).

12. The impact of deindustrialization on communities, workers, and their families is measured by how long it takes for workers dislocated by a mass layoff or plant shutdown to find new employment at comparable pay. Some have argued that deindustrialization is simply a myth. This argument rests on the observation that total manufacturing employment in 1980 remained almost identical to its 1973 level. If there has been no decrease in the total number of industrial workers, so this line of reasoning goes, how can it be said that the country is deindustrializing? As Barry Bluestone has pointed out, however, it is wrong to assume that aggregate employment patterns reflect a situation in which there is perfect interindustry and interregional worker mobility. In other words, workers who lose highly paid union jobs in a particular part of the country still suffer the effects of deindustrialization even if new manufacturing jobs are created in other geographic regions (often at lower nonunion wages). Aggregate, macrolevel data cannot be used as a measure of the social costs incurred by capital flight. Bluestone, "Is Deindustrialization a Myth? Capital Mobility versus Absorptive Capacity in the US Economy," *Annals of the American Academy of Political and Social Science* 475 (September 1984): 39–51.

13. Economists who attribute the loss of good-paying jobs to industrial shifts point to the lower and inherently unequal incomes earned in the service sector. See Robert Kuttner, "The Declining Middle," *Atlantic Monthly* 252 (July 1983): 60–72; Lester C. Thurow, "The Disappearance of the Middle Class, *New York Times*, February 5, 1984; and Barry Bluestone and Bennett

Harrison, "The Great American Job Machine: The Proliferation of Low-Wage Employment in the US Economy," a study prepared for the Joint Economic Committee of the U.S. Congress, Washington, D.C., December 1986. Other economists argue that the newly created jobs are high-status, white-collar jobs that more often than not support a middle-class standard of living. See, for example, *Economic Report of the President*, February 1988, pp. 60–61; Marvin H. Kosters and Murray N. Ross, "A Shrinking Middle Class?" *Public Interest*, no. 90 (Winter 1988): 3–27; and Robert J. Samuelson, "The American Job Machine," *Newsweek*, February 23, 1987.

14. Candee Harris, "The Magnitude of Job Loss from Plant Closings and the Generation of Replacement Jobs: Some Recent Evidence," *Annals of the American Academy of Political and Social Science* 475 (September 1984): 15–27.

15. D. S. Hamermesh, "What Do We Know about Worker Displacement in the US?" *Industrial Relations* 28 (1989): 51–60.

16. Barlett and Steele, *America*, p. 18.

17. Ibid.

18. Mary Lindenstein Walshok, *Blue-Collar Women: Pioneers on the Male Frontier* (New York: Anchor Books, 1981), and Ellen Israel Rosen, *Bitter Choices: Blue-Collar Women in and out of Work* (Chicago: University of Chicago Press, 1987).

19. Women's earnings are systematically below those of men, but as Frank Levy points out, the proportion of women earning more than $20,000 a year rose from 16 percent in 1973 to 27 percent in 1986. This increase in working women's incomes is masked by the substantial decline in the earnings of working men. Frank Levy, *Dollars and Dreams: The Changing American Income Distribution* (New York: W. W. Norton, 1987).

20. Lawrence Mischel and David M. Frankel, *The State of Working America, 1990–91 Edition* (Armonk, N.Y.: Economic Policy Institute, 1991), pp. 93–95.

21. Levy, *Dollars and Dreams*, p. 127.

22. Ibid., pp. 127–128, table 4-4.

23. See appendix, table A2.

24. As anthropologist Carol MacLennan points out, knowledge about the auto industry can be gleaned only from a few broad measures of production and employment compiled by the United States Census and the Bureau of Labor Statistics. Some information about the industry is available through trade publications, but the reporting in these publications is not always consistent, and sources are often unknown. This "black box" is a result of the cultural assumption that, in the right economic environment, business will behave in ways that are beneficial to society as a whole. Given this bias, policy efforts to address industrial problems tend to focus not on matters internal to industry, but on correcting imbalances in society and the economy. As a result, knowledge about the industrial factors that do affect social life is generally lacking. Carol A. MacLennan, "Political Response to Economic Loss: The Automotive Crisis of 1979–1982," *Urban Anthropology* 14, nos. 1–3 (1985): 21–57.

Chapter Four

1. Kenosha operates under a mayoral-aldermanic form of government. The full-time mayor is elected for four years. The seventeen aldermen are elected by wards (each aldermanic district contains two wards) for two-year terms and work part time. Elections take place in even-numbered years.

2. "Kenosha's Future: Citizens Must Learn to Adapt to City's Continuing Rate of Dramatic Change," *Kenosha News*, December 12, 1989.

3. As many political observers have noted, those who experienced the downside of Reagan's economic policies during the 1980s have become increasingly disillusioned with politics and are fast becoming the portion of the electorate least likely to vote. The sad irony is that critical ballot-box decisions have thus been left to the very people who profit from the policies that have brought such hardship for others. Walter Dean Burnham, in *The Current Crisis in American Politics* (New York: Oxford University Press, 1982), quips that nonvoters are America's fastest-growing political party. In *The Politics of Rich and Poor*, Kevin Phillips argues that middle-class and upper-middle-class Americans were the power bloc of the 1980s, accounting for the largest proportions of voter turnout in the 1984 and 1988 presidential elections. See also Frances Fox Piven and Richard A. Cloward, *Democracy Thwarted: Why So Many Americans Don't Vote* (New York: Pantheon, 1988).

4. Herbert Gans, *Middle American Individualism: The Future of Liberal Democracy* (New York: Free Press, 1988), pp. 73–74.

5. This information was made available by the Kenosha city clerk, Department of Voter Registration and Elections.

6. David Halle and Frank Romo point out that the much-discussed decline of the blue-collar vote for Democratic presidential contenders is offset by a far more striking trend—the rising number of blue-collar workers who do not vote at all in presidential elections. Halle and Romo offer this eye-opening statistic: "In 1980, 1984, and 1988, a larger percentage of skilled blue-collar workers did not vote than voted for either the Republican or Democratic candidate; and among less-skilled blue-collar workers in four of the five elections from 1972 to 1988, a larger number did not vote than voted for either the Republican or Democratic candidate." David Halle and Frank Romo, "The Blue-Collar Working Class: Continuity and Change," in *America at Century's End*, ed. Alan Wolfe (Berkeley and Los Angeles: University of California Press, 1991), pp. 152–184.

7. Since Eugene Dorff and Patrick Moran are public figures and the events I am describing are public events, I am using actual names rather than pseudonyms.

8. Canvass of the 1988 mayoral vote is included in the April 1988 *Proceedings of the Common Council* and reported in the *Kenosha News*, April 6, 1988.

9. Occupational ratios were calculated from information published by the Kenosha City Plan Division, "1980 Neighborhood Profiles for the City of Kenosha," Department of City Development, July 1986. These neighborhood profiles are based on information from the 1980 United States Census of Population and Housing. In 1983 the Kenosha City Plan Division participated

in the "Neighborhood Statistics Program" and prepared this breakdown of census data into its own geographic areas.

10. In 1980 operatives composed 28.2 percent, and managerial workers 20.8 percent, of the total population.

11. This incident was picked up by the national news media, and Mayor Dorff was given three minutes to "explain himself" on a talk show produced by the NBC Radio Network. "Dorff Says He Misspoke," *Kenosha News*, February 2, 1988; "Dorff Still Explaining," *Kenosha News*, February 5, 1988.

12. "Moran Victory Shows City Ready for Change: But the New Mayor Should Also Be Cautious," *Kenosha News*, April 6, 1988, p. 4.

13. Alan Ehrenhalt, *The United States of Ambition: Politicians, Power, and the Pursuit of Office* (New York: Random House, 1991).

14. Mary Douglas, *Purity and Danger: An Analysis of Concepts of Pollution and Taboo* (London: Penguin, 1966).

15. Ironically, this "capital as blood" metaphor coexists with the equally powerful idea that economic revitalization depends on "redemption through sacrifice." If only people would tighten their belts a few notches, it is widely believed, the capital available for investment would be increased and, in turn, infused back into the veins of a languishing economy. The centrality of these metaphors in our economic thought, as Block shows, obscures rather than illuminates the structural problems that now beset American interests in the global economy. In the Kenosha case, moreover, this symbolic logic is used to construct a damning critique of blue-collar culture. Evidently the directive to "save" doesn't apply to government officials. Fred Block, "Mirrors and Metaphors: The United States and Its Trade Rivals," in *America at Century's End*, ed. Alan Wolfe (Berkeley and Los Angeles: University of California Press, 1991), pp. 92–111.

16. On the culturally dynamic relationship between history, memory, and desire, see especially Marshall Sahlins, *Islands of History* (Chicago: University of Chicago Press, 1985), and James Clifford, *The Predicament of Culture: Twentieth-Century Ethnography, Literature, and Art* (Cambridge: Harvard University Press, 1988).

17. Department of City Development, *Kenosha Focus 2000* (Kenosha, Wis.: City of Kenosha, October 1987).

18. Quotations are from the text of the *Focus 2000* report itself. These statements were repeated, usually verbatim, in the local press as well as by city officials in public speeches and personal interviews.

19. "Kenosha's Future: Citizens Must Learn to Adapt to City's Continuing Rate of Dramatic Change," *Kenosha News*, December 18, 1989, Op-Ed section.

Chapter Five

1. The tendency to hold oneself responsible for job loss is a remarkable feature of the professional-managerial culture. As Katherine Newman has shown in *Falling from Grace: The Experience of Downward Mobility in the American Middle Class* (New York: Free Press, 1988), the subjective interpretation of downward mobility is not uniform across occupational groups. Business man-

agers are more likely to experience economic dislocation as an "individual" problem than are factory workers, who tend to see their job loss as a "collective" misfortune. Thus, while managers search their souls for a personal flaw that will explain their downfall, blue-collar workers tend to shake their fists at inscrutable gods and attribute their collective predicament to forces beyond their control.

2. Ibid., p. 76.

3. The "bailout" refers to the federally guaranteed loans that saved Chrysler from bankruptcy in the late 1970s. For the whole story, see Robert Reich and John D. Donahue, *New Deals: The Chrysler Revival and the American System* (New York: Times Books, 1985).

4. This clearly is the guiding sentiment behind the more extreme approaches to welfare reform during the Reagan administration. See the budget-cutter's bible written by Charles Murray, *Losing Ground: American Social Policy, 1950–1980* (New York: Basic Books, 1984). The same kind of logic runs through the conservative reaction to muticulturalism, where efforts to acknowledge the contributions of diverse cultural traditions are said to stunt intellectual growth or, in Allan Bloom's notorious phrase, lead to "the closing of the American mind." See his book, *The Closing of the American Mind* (New York: Simon and Schuster, 1987). Bloom believes that a multicultural curriculum merely lets students learn what they want to know rather than challenging them to learn what they need to know.

5. As Frances Fox Piven and Richard A. Cloward argue in *Regulating the Poor: The Functions of Public Welfare* (New York: Vintage Books, 1971), civil disorder on the part of the poor has the power to trigger unprecedented political responses, such as the welfare initiatives of the 1930s and 1960s.

6. The term "status degradation" was coined by sociologist Harold Garfinkel in his classic work, "Conditions of Successful Degradation Ceremonies," *American Journal of Sociology* 61, no. 5 (1956): 420–424. Degradation ceremonies involve "any communicative work between persons whereby the public identity of an actor is looked on as lower in the local scheme of social types." Court trials and public hearings are typical examples. For a degradation ceremony to be successful, Garfinkel observes, it must take the form of a public denunciation. The person whose status is to be degraded must be denounced before witnesses for being "in essence" of a different social type than others in the community. In full view of the public, respected community leaders must deliver a curse that sounds something like this: "I call upon all citizens to bear witness that these people are not one of us, as they claim to be, but are instead, motivated by values and attitudes that the rest of us condemn." Status degradation is a form of "secular communion" insofar as it strengthens the cultural solidarity of the denouncers while excluding the denounced. My use of this concept differs from Garfinkel's in that I emphasize the ritual aspects of transforming a whole cultural identity, not merely one individual's social status.

7. Robert B. Reich, "Ideologies of Survival: The Return of Social Darwinism," *New Republic*, September 27, 1982, pp. 32–37. See also Donald Bellomy,

"'Social Darwinism' Revisited," *Perspectives in American History*, n.s. 1 (1984): 1–129; and Sidney Lens, "Blaming the Victims: Social Darwinism, Is Still the Name of the Game," *Progressive* 44 (August 1980): 27–28.

8. Kevin Phillips, *The Politics of Rich and Poor: Wealth and the American Electorate in the Reagan Aftermath* (New York: Random House, 1990), pp. 59–60, 91–101.

9. It was Spencer, of course, who provided Darwin with the phrase "survival of the fittest." See Richard Hofstadter, *Social Darwinism in American Thought*, rev. ed. (Boston: Beacon Press, 1955); Marvin Harris, *The Rise of Anthropological Theory: A History of Theories of Culture* (New York: Harper and Row, 1968, chap. 5; Raymond Williams, "Social Darwinism," in *The Limits of Human Nature*, ed. Jonathan Benthall (New York: E. P. Dutton, 1974), pp. 115–132; and Robert M. Young, "Darwinism Is Social," in *The Darwinian Heritage*, ed. David Kohn (Princeton: Princeton University Press, 1985), pp. 609–638.

10. Hofstadter, *Social Darwinism*, p. 40.

11. Ibid.

12. Bannister's argument on this point is thought provoking but problematic from a cultural perspective. It's rather like surveying the members of the Ku Klux Klan and, upon discovering that they all deny being racists, concluding that racism doesn't exit. Robert C. Bannister, *Social Darwinism: Science and Myth in Anglo-American Social Thought* (Philadelphia: Temple University Press, 1979). Although the historian Carl Degler doesn't totally reject the existence of social Darwinism as a public philosophy, he does question how influential it could ever have been, given the strong resistance with which Darwinian theory itself was met, especially in the social sciences. See Carl N. Degler, *In Search of Human Nature: The Decline and Revival of Darwinism in American Social Thought* (New York: Oxford University Press, 1991).

13. Robert B. Reich, *The Work of Nations: Preparing Ourselves for Twenty-first Century Capitalism* (New York: Alfred A. Knopf, 1991), p. 37.

14. The classic work here is Claude Lévi-Strauss's "The Story of Asdiwal," in *The Structural Study of Myth and Totemism*, ed. Edmund Leach (London: Tavistock, 1967). A useful review of Kenneth Burke's contributions to cultural studies is Joseph Gusfield's introduction to Kenneth Burke, *On Symbols and Society*, ed. Joseph R. Gusfield (Chicago: University of Chicago Press, 1989), pp. 1–49.

15. In his analysis of western movies, Wright shows how the myth of the western hero who saves society from unscrupulous villains has been used to mediate the enduring conflict in American culture between the values of individualism and community. Will Wright, *Six Guns and Society: A Structural Study of the Western* (Berkeley and Los Angeles: University of California Press, 1975), p. 18.

16. During this project I began to take note of how frequently Darwinian imagery is used in our everyday lives. Here are two of what turned out to be many examples. (1) On a T-shirt worn by army recruits in basic training, a muscular drill sergeant is shown standing over a lowly private, who is doing

push-ups. The caption above the private reads, "No pain, no gain!" The caption above the drill sergeant says, "Only the fittest survive!" (2) An incident that took place in Minneapolis during the summer of 1991: On a billboard overlooking the interstate highway, the management of the Conservatory, an upscale shopping center, put up an advertisement that boasted: "Come to the Conservatory—See How the Fittest Survive!" After being deluged by complaints from outraged motorists, the company eventually painted over this sign.

17. On the individual and social costs of mass unemployment, see Terry F. Buss and F. Steven Redburn, *Shutdown at Youngstown: Public Policy for Mass Unemployment* (Albany: State University of New York Press, 1983); David Bensman and Roberta Lynch, *Rusted Dreams: Hard Times in a Steel Community* (Berkeley and Los Angeles: University of California Press, 1987); Ellen Israel Rosen, *Bitter Choices: Blue-Collar Women in and out of Work* (Chicago: University of Chicago Press, 1987); Gregory Pappas, *The Magic City: Unemployment in a Working-Class Community* (Ithaca: Cornell University Press, 1989). For the cultural dimension of job loss, see Newman, *Falling from Grace.*

18. The model "disaster ethnography" is Kai Erikson's study of the Buffalo Creek flood. Erickson documents in chilling detail the trauma experienced by survivors of a flood that, in a single roaring instant, swept away their homes and loved ones. Kai T. Erikson, *Everything in Its Path: Destruction of Community in the Buffalo Creek Flood* (New York: Simon and Schuster, 1976).

19. Erikson concludes that "traumatization is becoming an increasingly common experience in human life." Ibid., pp. 254, 256.

20. The same, of course, is now being said about the United States auto industry. See Bensman and Lynch, *Rusted Dreams,* pp. 202–203.

Chapter Six

1. The notion that a maladaptive or deviant way of life is "learned" in blue-collar homes is remarkably similar to the idea that poverty is an "inherited" condition among families on public assistance—welfare mothers beget welfare mothers. Oscar Lewis, an anthropologist who did ethnographic fieldwork with poor families in Mexico and Puerto Rico, was one of the first to suggest that there is a "culture of poverty" that poor people in all societies learn and pass along to their children. Lewis argued that poor families develop a distinctive set of adaptations to the conditions of unemployment, low wages, and crowded living conditions. But cultural behaviors that are adaptive in one context (the conditions of poverty) are all too often maladaptive in another (the conditions of prosperity). Therefore children who grow up in poverty learn a "design for living" that effectively perpetuates their low socioeconomic status. Oscar Lewis, *Five Families* (New York: Basic Books, 1959); idem, *The Children of Sanchez* (New York: Random House, 1961); idem, *La Vida* (New York: Random House, 1966). Sociologist Herbert Gans points out that the culture of poverty idea is essentially an argument about social change: it is "about the psychological readiness of people to respond to change, and about the role of culture in change." Herbert Gans, "Culture

and Class in the Study of Poverty: An Approach to Anti-poverty Research," in *On Understanding Poverty: Perspectives from the Social Sciences,* ed. Daniel P. Moynihan (New York: Basic Books, 1968).

2. The defilement of public space is a powerful catalyst for moralistic reflections on the conditions of modern life. Anthropologist Jonathan Reider offers a compelling look at what urban graffiti mean to middle-American ethnic groups living in Canarsie, a section of predominantly white neighborhoods in Brooklyn, New York. For the Jews and Italians of Canarsie, Reider writes, "the spread of the arabesques onto the face of the city marked sinister forces crossing the line between public rules and private whim." Fearful of losing the modest savings they had accumulated in home equity, Canarsians were actively resisting the racial integration of their community and protesting the busing of minority-group children into Canarsie schools. To people who felt threatened by liberal desegregation policies, rising crime rates, and the increasing "permissiveness" of American society, the graffiti scrawled in public places confirm their worst fears about the state of the world. "The ultimate message of graffiti," Reider observes, was that "the public sphere was full of unseen dangers and no longer belonged to the law-abiding." Moreover, not only are graffiti a particularly public expression of moral deviance, the very fact that people were getting away with the defacement—that these looping swirls of profanity have become a permanent feature of the urban landscape—signals a social order on the brink of collapse. Jonathan Reider, *Canarsie: The Jews and Italians of Brooklyn against Liberalism* (Cambridge: Harvard University Press, 1985), p. 61.

3. See Jonathan Kozol's alarming report on the inequities of public-school funding in affluent and less-affluent communities, *Savage Inequalities: Children in America's Schools* (New York: Crown, 1991).

4. Richard Sennett and Jonathan Cobb, *The Hidden Injuries of Class* (New York: Vintage Books, 1972), pp. 179–181.

5. Fred Block, "Mirrors and Metaphors: The United States and Its Trade Rivals," in *America at Century's End,* ed. Alan Wolfe (Berkeley and Los Angeles: University of California Press, 1990), pp. 93–111, and idem, *Postindustrial Possibilities: A Critique of Economic Discourse* (Berkeley and Los Angeles: University of California Press, 1990).

Chapter Seven

1. Within the auto industry as a whole, only about 25 percent of the blue-collar workforce works on the line. For this reason, some writers have argued that line work should not be taken as symbolic of the total character of factory life in the auto industry, and their point is well taken. Since the Kenosha plant was a full-scale assembly plant, however, the line was clearly a central image for this particular workforce.

2. Charles Walker and Robert Guest, *The Man on the Assembly Line* (Cambridge: Harvard University Press, 1952).

3. Robert Blauner, *Alienation and Freedom: The Factory Worker and His Industry* (Chicago: University of Chicago Press, 1964).

4. William Serrin, *The Company and the Union* (New York: Alfred A Knopf, 1973), p. 221.

5. U.S. Department of Health, Education, and Welfare, *Work in America: Report of a Special Task Force to the Secretary of Health, Education and Welfare* (Cambridge: MIT Press, 1973), p. 38.

6. Of course, white-collar workers in large corporations and mass occupations like engineering, accounting, teaching, and so forth may also experience their work in this way. See Harry Braverman, *Labor and Monopoly Capital: The Degradation of Work in the Twentieth Century* (New York: Monthly Review Press, 1974).

7. The term "dehumanization" can also refer to the process by which social structures compel people to act toward others as though they were less than human. This behavior is common among managers, bankers, bosses, bureaucrats, politicians, and workers in social service agencies. See Robert Reiff, "Alienation and Dehumanization," in *Auto Work and Its Discontents*, ed. B. J. Widick (Baltimore: Johns Hopkins University Press, 1976), pp. 45–51.

8. There is far more social interaction on the job than is often reported. In addition to work groups that form along segments of the line, there are those that coalesce for other reasons such as gender, race, or ethnicity, and around shared interest in sports, and card playing, or politics, as well as in-shop drinking or drug use. Another reason for the existence of identifiable groups is that workers tend to stay in the same department for many years, thus perpetuating old ties. See Eli Chinoy, *Automobile Workers and the American Dream* (New York: Doubleday, 1955), p. 124.

9. The concept of teamwork seems to be an integral part of most work cultures, even among ultraindividualist business managers. See Robert Jackall's illuminating study of life inside the corporate world, *Moral Mazes* (New York: Oxford University Press, 1984).

10. Michael Burawoy, *Manufacturing Consent: Changes in the Labor Process under Monopoly Capitalism* (Chicago: University of Chicago Press, 1979), pp. 46–94.

11. In *The UAW and Walter Reuther* (New York: Random House, 1949), p. 21, Irving Howe and B. J. Widick argue that the tedium of the line creates a psychology they call "fighting the line," a feeling that is a mixture of punch-drunk and city-tense: "Implicitly rejecting the idea that he is merely a function of a mechanical process, the worker tries to rebel against it; but not only doesn't the assembly line recognize his rebellion, it even refuses to recognize his separate identity. The psychological result is that the worker's aggression against the line can be released only against himself or other workers." In contrast, I argue that because "letting something go" is a ritualized social behavior, it can indeed be culturally recognized by coworkers as an act of rebellion and thus reduce frustration and stress.

12. The pace of work has been a source of labor disputes since Henry Ford instituted the first assembly line in the early 1900s. The union movement in the auto industry arose out of this constant friction over work standards—"speedup" in the eyes of workers—and the need for an organized

challenge to management's attempts to squeeze additional labor from its workforce. B. J. Widick, "Work in Auto Plants: Then and Now," in *Auto Work and Its Discontents*, ed. B. J. Widick (Baltimore: Johns Hopkins University Press, 1976), p. 14.

13. This form of cooperation is not to be confused with the well-documented practice of "doubling up," in which two workers learn each other's operations so that one worker can perform both jobs while the other takes a break. There are many other ways of making line work tolerable that I do not discuss here. For examples of these, see Stanley Aronowitz, *False Promises: The Shaping of American Working Class Consciousness* (New York: McGraw-Hill, 1973), pp. 23–24; Blauner, *Alienation and Freedom*, pp. 99–100; Frank Marquart, "The Auto Worker," in *Voices of Dissent* (New York: Grove Press, 1958), p. 144; Walker and Guest, *Man on the Assembly Line*, pp. 146–147; Bennett Kreman, "Search for a Better Way of Work: Lordstown, Ohio," in *Humanizing the Workplace*, ed. R. P. Fairfield (Buffalo: Prometheus Books, 1974), pp. 146–147; and Al Nash, "Job Satisfaction: A Critique:" in *Auto Work and Its Discontents*, ed. B. J. Widick (Baltimore: Johns Hopkins University Press, 1976), pp. 81–83.

14. Social structures based on generalized reciprocity are well known to anthropologists as the egalitarian form of social organization found in "primitive" or hunter-gatherer societies. In these small-scale societies, economic exchange takes place according to cultural rules that emphasize altruism and solidarity. In the words of Marshall Sahlins, generalized reciprocity is characterized by "the vagueness of the obligation to reciprocate." See his article "On the Sociology of Primitive Exchange" in *The Relevance of Models for Social Anthropology*, Association for Social Anthropologists Monograph 1 (New York: Praeger, 1965), p. 147. As Morton Fried has observed, however, there continue to be very real pressures for reciprocation in egalitarian systems, but they are largely implicit and set no standards of equivalency or time limits on the return transaction: "Those who can, give and continue to give [while] those who need, take and continue to take." *The Evolution of Political Society: An Essay in Political Anthropology* (New York: Random House, 1967), p. 35.

15. Rick Fantasia, *Cultures of Solidarity: Consciousness, Action, and Contemporary American Workers* (Berkeley and Los Angeles: University of California Press, 1988), p. 25. By "cultures of solidarity," Fantasia means the "social encasement for the expression of working-class solidarity, an emergent cultural form embodying the values, practices, and institutional manifestations of mutuality." This concept allows the consideration of a wider range of cultural practices generated in social struggle than does the more ideational, attitudinal notion of class consciousness.

Chapter Eight
1. In *America's Working Man* (Chicago: University of Chicago Press, 1984), pp. 119–125, David Halle shows how blue-collar workers in an automated chemical plant also take steps to guard shop secrets in their effort to exercise control over the production process. Plant managers know that workers have

this leverage, but they interact with workers and outsiders on the assumption that these sub rosa shenanigans do not exist. Halle argues that managers acquiesce in this power struggle because the production of chemicals requires knowledge of procedural quirks unique to each factory.

2. Alvin Gouldner makes a similar argument in his book, *Patterns of Industrial Bureaucracy: A Case Study of Modern Factory Administration* (New York: Free Press, 1964). Formal organizational charts tend to assume that workers higher up in the hierarchy are more powerful. Gouldner argues that, in fact, people lower down, those who have specialized knowledge about how a machine works, are often extremely powerful. Not only can they bring the entire production process to a grinding halt, they are the only ones who really know how long it takes to repair something.

3. Randall Collins, *The Credential Society: An Historical Sociology of Education and Stratification*, (New York: Academic Press, 1979).

4. Richard Sennett and Jonathan Cobb, *The Hidden Injuries of Class* (New York: Vintage Books, 1972).

5. I distinguish shopfloor culture from that of the mainstream along lines suggested by Collins, *Credential Society*, pp. 60–62. Collins argues that culture is produced in two ways: "indigenously," in the experiences of everyday interactions, and "formally," by specialized culture-producing organizations like churches and schools. Indigenous culture supports "local barter markets" with nontransferable resources, whereas formal culture operates more nearly like a monetary currency with a widely negotiable "store of value." A similar distinction has been suggested by anthropologist Douglas Foley in his analysis of class cultures as forms of "historical speech communities." Foley argues that the collective nature of working-class communities gives rise to a context-bound form of discourse in which people share a stock of background knowledge about each other. "Does the Working Class Have a Culture in the Anthropological Sense?" *Cultural Anthropology* 4, no. 2 (1989): 137–162.

6. Katherine S. Newman, "Turning Your Back on Tradition: Symbolic Analysis and Moral Critique in a Plant Shutdown," *Urban Anthropology* 14, nos. 1–3 (1985): 109–150, found that workers caught in the closing of a Singer Sewing Machine plant also believed that making a quality product could protect them from a shutdown. When the plant closed, workers argued that American industry is failing in the world market because corporate management has abandoned the traditions of craftsmanship, loyalty to the company, and pride in a quality product.

7. Erving Goffman points out that this strategy of in-group alignment is almost universally employed by stigmatized groups in the effort to combat dehumanizing cultural images of their groups. In-groups and out-groups construct mutually exclusive social identities for the stigmatized individual, who is told that "if he adopts the right line (which line depending on who is talking), he will have come to terms with himself and be a whole man; he will be an adult with dignity and respect." In *Stigma: Notes on the Management of Spoiled Identity* (New York: Simon and Schuster, 1963), pp. 112–125, Goffman refers to this form of discourse as "the politics of identity."

8. In *Tally's Corner* (Boston: Little Brown, 1967), Elliot Liebow suggests that black street-corner men develop a set of "shadow values" that resemble those of the mainstream but are more readily realized under conditions of poverty. Carol Stack proposes that the women she studied in *All Our Kin: Strategies for Survival in a Black Community* (New York: Harper and Row, 1974) draw upon a "bicultural model" of social values, attempting to follow mainstream norms when it is feasible but falling back on subcultural coping strategies when necessary. Alternative evaluations of self-worth and social roles appear to be possible when a "deviant" community is also to maintain a strong countercultural ideology, as documented by ethnographer Deborah Goleman Wolf in her study *The Lesbian Community* (Berkeley and Los Angeles: University of California Press, 1980).

9. Refer to the appendix for profiles of the autoworkers who participated in this study.

10. For the chemical workers studied by Halle, *America's Working Man*, pp. 204–208, being a "working man" means doing physical work; dangerous or dirty work; boring and routine work; factory work; closely supervised work. Halle argues that the concept of the workingman contains two related ideas—first, that the labor of workingmen contains these distinctive job features, and second, that unlike workers in the rest of the class structure, workingmen perform labor that is productive. Off the job, however, workers, considered themselves "middle class," since their income enabled them to own homes and enjoy fairly affluent lifestyles.

11. Literacy is a good example of the cultural connection between individual ability and skill. Literacy was considered a skill when few people possessed it. Now that we have come to expect this ability of everyone, is it still a skill?

12. Kenosha autoworkers frequently used the imagery of the western movie in their critique of modern society. The symbolic opposition between civilized society and the wilderness is a key feature of American ideas about individualism, freedom, and group strength, as popularly expressed in the plot of the western. See Will Wright, *Six Guns and Society: A Structural Study of the Western* (Berkeley and Los Angeles: University of California Press, 1975).

13. Sennett and Cobb, *Hidden Injuries*, show how notions of freedom and dignity are closely tied to the same calculations of human worth that make having ability a matter of individual achievement. Mainstream cultural concepts support the belief that educated people have somehow "earned" the freedom to be whatever they wish.

14. In *The Managed Heart: Commercialization of Human Feeling* (Berkeley and Los Angeles: University of California Press, 1983), Arlie Hochschild describes the emotional strain of service sector jobs that put a premium on "personality" and pleasing the customer.

15. In "PATCO Lives! Stigma, Heroism, and Symbolic Transformations," *Cultural Anthropology* 2, no. 3 (1987): 319–346, Katherine Newman observes that the air traffic controllers who lost their jobs in the 1981 strike were able to hold on to their collective dignity long after they no longer worked to-

gether, even in the face of substantial condemnation from outside. Newman argues that this internal sense of worth could be maintained because controllers had established a strong national organization that allowed them to retain their group identity. If this structure had not been perpetuated, the collective integrity it was able to support would most likely have fallen apart.

Chapter Nine

1. In *False Promises: The Shaping of American Working Class Consciousness* (New York: McGraw-Hill, 1973), pp. 406–409, Stanley Aronowitz observes that this generation of industrial workers came to their jobs with radically different expectations than did their parents—about the importance of education (completing high school), the meaning of self-fulfillment, and the belief that consumerism alone could assuage the alienation of severely routinized labor. Aronowitz cautions against overstating how far younger workers have freed themselves from authoritarian structures and ideologies, but he points to ways new sensibilities generated by student protests in the 1960s became a part of mass culture, which was imbibed by working-class youth as well as their middle-class contemporaries.

2. Steelworkers in South Chicago and rubber workers in Barberton, Ohio, felt a similar sense of national pride in their work. Steelworkers saw the mills, and the country as whole, as depending on them to make steel, one of the world's most important commodities. Rubber workers took pride in being associated with an internationally known company (Firestone) and producing an essential commodity. See David Bensman and Roberta Lynch, *Rusted Dreams: Hard Times in a Steel Community* (Berkeley and Los Angeles: University of California Press, 1987), and Gregory Pappas, *The Magic City: Unemployment in a Working-Class Community* (Ithaca: Cornell University Press, 1989).

3. Chinoy concluded that "patriotism," as a form of job satisfaction, ultimately expressed "anti-success" values, which stemmed from an underlying desire to compensate for feelings of failure. The inability to live up to cultural expectations of advancement, he argued, creates a psychological attitude of defensive rationalization in which workers try to redefine the meaning of success.

4. David Halle, *America's Working Man* (Chicago: University of Chicago Press, 1984), pp. 230–241, considers blue-collar nationalism a blend of populism and nativism, both of which rest on a notion of nationality or American citizenship. Mistrust of national leaders can run so deep, Halle observes, that blue-collar nationalism is always in danger of dissolving into unmitigated populism.

5. For a provocative discussion of the ideological divisions in contemporary American society, see James Davison Hunter, *Culture Wars: The Struggle to Define America* (New York: Basic Books, 1991).

6. George McKenna, *American Populism* (New York: Putnam's Sons, 1974).

7. Gans, *Middle American Individualism: The Future of Liberal Democracy* (New York: Free Press, 1988), pp. 60–62.

8. The full poem reads: "Jesse Jackson is the best, / putting Chrysler to the

test. / Iacocca to say the least, / is just another greedy beast. / Jesse put that boy on call, / told him just how far he'd fall. / Now Lee is scared although he's fast, / afraid each step may be his last. / Our Jesse's not a man to cross, / or he'll show Chrysler just who's boss." Published in "Jackson: 'Must Draw the Line Here and Now,'" *Kenosha Labor,* February 5, 1988.

9. Jesse Jackson received 4,997 votes out of 24,072 total votes cast in the presidential primary in the city of Kenosha. This put him in second place among the Democratic contenders, behind Michael Dukakis, who received 10,090 votes. "Ward-by-Ward Vote Totals,' *Kenosha News,* April 6, 1988.

10. Rick Fantasia, *Cultures of Solidarity: Consciousness, Action, and Contemporary American Workers* (Berkeley and Los Angeles: University of California Press, 1988).

11. Rebecca Klatch observes that the conservative movement that grew out of a backlash against the liberalism of the 1960s is composed of some very unlike allies, some espousing a "social conservatism" based on religion and the family, while others embrace a "laissez-faire conservatism" based on the concepts of liberty and individual free will. See her article "Complexities of Conservatism," in *America at Century's End,* ed. Alan Wolfe (Berkeley and Los Angeles: University of California Press, 1991), pp. 361–375. It may be that when social conservatives break away from the economic policies of the New Right, they once again find themselves members of an uneasy coalition—this time with cultural liberals, with whom they also have grave differences of opinion.

12. Quotations are from Jackson's speech, "The Message, the Mission and the Messenger: An Economic Program to Make America Better and to Keep America Strong," in Jesse Jackson, *Keep Hope Alive: Jesse Jackson's 1988 Presidential Campaign,* ed. Frank Clemente and Frank Watkins (Boston: South End Press, 1989).

13. McKenna, *American Populism,* pp. 5–6, also identifies two other tenets or roots of populism: the deification of nature, and a belief in the essentially moral and rational nature of all human beings.

14. See Richard Madsen, "Contentless Consensus," in *America at Century's End,* ed. Alan Wolfe (Berkeley and Los Angeles: University of California Press, 1991), pp. 440–460, for a fascinating discussion of how this myth gives rise to competing notions of "community," all resting on the assumption that communities, like society itself, are formed by voluntary consent.

15. For a classic anthropological account of the symbolism of kinship ties, see David Schneider, *American Kinship: A Cultural Account* (New York: Prentice-Hall, 1968).

16. Katherine S. Newman, "Turning Your Back on Tradition: Symbolic Analysis and Moral Critique in a Plant Shutdown," *Urban Anthropology* 14, nos. 1–3 (1985): 109–150.

Chapter Ten

1. In addition to leading these workshops, JSAs also help fellow workers find new jobs, enroll in retraining programs, and wend their way through the forest of paperwork that protracted periods of unemployment involve. The

Dislocated Workers Assistance Center was set up at the union hall as a joint-partnership program run by the United Auto Workers (UAW) and the Job Development Training Corporation (JDTC). Designed to be a "one-stop shop" to meet as many of a dislocated workers' needs as possible, the UAW-JDTC Center was slated to remain open for at least a year after the shutdown, possibly longer, depending on the availability of government funds. When I began my fieldwork in the spring of 1989, the Center had already been serving workers for several months. It had been set up that fall, just before the shutdown in December 1988.

2. Victor Turner, *The Ritual Process: Structure and Anti-structure* (Ithaca: Cornell University Press, 1969), p. 95.

3. Robert C. Solomon, "Getting Angry: The Jamesian Theory of Emotion in Anthropology," in *Culture Theory: Essays on Mind, Self, and Emotions*, ed. Richard A. Shweder and Robert A. LeVine (Cambridge: Cambridge University Press, 1984), pp. 238–254.

4. Clifford Geertz, *The Interpretation of Cultures* (New York: Basic Books, 1973), p. 316.

5. Malcolm McFee describes the challenge faced by Blackfeet Indians in very similar terms. As I argue in the concluding chapter of this book, the parallels between the problems of culture change in Native American communities and blue-collar industrial communities are striking. Malcolm McFee, *Modern Blackfeet: Montanans on a Reservation* (Prospect Heights, Ill.: Waveland Press, 1972).

6. In contrast to the immigrant generations, baby boomers who began working in factories during the 1960s and 1970s were seen as the radical force behind postwar union demands for higher wages, better working conditions, and greater control over the labor process. In *False Promises: The Shaping of Working Class Consciousness* (New York: McGraw-Hill, 1973), pp. 26–33, Stanley Aronowitz argues that younger workers were responsible for the frequent labor disputes at General Motors' Lordstown plant in the early 1970s. At a time when nonunion workers were being squeezed by inflation, these young union militants appeared to outsiders as spoiled and self-indulgent.

7. I refer here to the remarks made by a Japanese legislative leader in January 1992 and the brouhaha that ensued. Yoshio Sakurauchi, speaker of Japan's lower house of parliament, offered the opinion that America's problems with competitiveness stemmed from having "lazy" workers, a third of whom "cannot even read." News summary "As Ugly Feelings Grow, It's Hard to Separate Facts and Fiction," *New York Times*, January 26, 1992, sec. 4, p. 1. On the erroneous stereotype of lazy, overpaid American workers, see Gilda Haas, *Plant Closures: Myths, Realities and Responses* (Boston: South End Press, 1985).

8. Barbara Ehrenreich chronicles the creation of this working-class stereotype by the media and social sciences following the student rebellions of the 1960s. See chapter 3 in her fascinating book, *Fear of Falling: The Inner Life of the Middle Class* (New York: Pantheon, 1989).

9. For an excellent review of the social science literature on the "authori-

tarian personality," see Christopher Lasch, *The True and Only Heaven: Progress and Its Critics* (New York: W. W. Norton, 1991), pp. 445–450. Lasch links the discovery of this "pathological" personality and family type to a growing perception by postwar liberals of the "antiprogressive" character of the working classes.

10. The manufacturing of deviance, as Kai Erickson has shown, frequently occurs at times when cultural values and codes of conduct are highly ambiguous. In his study of the witch trials in colonial New England, Erickson explains how the persecution of witches and heretics served to clarify and solidify moral boundaries that were unclear, in question, or under dispute. Kai Erickson, *Wayward Puritans: A Study in the Sociology of Deviance* (New York: John Wiley, 1966).

11. William Butler Yeats, "Sailing to Byzantium," in *Modern American and British Poetry*, ed. Louis Untermeyer (New York: Harcourt, Brace, and World, 1955), p. 475.

12. So basic is the cultural injunction against seeking advantage for self over others that Joe feels guilt about his present position as a JSA, even though it seems he is serving the goal of helping others. "I'm given an *unfair* chance," Joe tells me with a sigh. "I'm getting something above and beyond what the other 5,500 people in this plant are getting. I've got a year of breathing room here [as a JSA], where I'm sitting back now, and I can plan my life now. [Everyone else is] confronted with [having to make choices] right now!" That he is helping fellow workers make those choices, often struggling with their problems as though they were his own, is overshadowed by the fact that he has a job and they do not. Clearly, doing something that benefits the self, if it seems to come at other's expense, is not legitimate in Joe's eyes. There is more to this than survivor's guilt—if we mean by that the sense that your success has somehow caused the misfortune of others.

13. Joan Didion, "On Self Respect," in *Slouching toward Bethlehem* (New York: Washington Square Press, 1961), p. 146.

14. The guilt some workers feel about their wages is a complicated emotion indeed. It raises the politically charged question of whether or to what extent labor unions can be held accountable for America's industrial crisis. Even critics sympathetic to labor lament its emphasis on securing an inflation-proof wage instead of attending to more urgent issues like competitiveness and job security. See, for example, Thomas Geoghegan, *Which Side Are You On? Trying to Be for Labor When It's Flat on Its Back* (New York: Farrar, Straus and Giroux, 1991).

15. Robert Wuthnow, *Meaning and Moral Order: Explorations in Cultural Analysis* (Berkeley and Los Angeles: University of California Press, 1987), p. 77.

16. The gendered nature of this work goes unacknowledged by blue-collar and white-collar men alike. The notion that "people" could do many service-sector jobs for themselves implicitly assumes that there is or ought to be a woman at home performing these services. White-collar men are more apt to attribute the rise of service industries to the increased participation of women

in the workforce, but on the home front they still expect their working wives to do the lion's share of the housework. See Arlkie Hochschild, *The Second Shift: Working Parents and the Revolution at Home* (New York: Viking Penguin, 1989).

17. For an excellent ethnographic study of how notions of "the common good" can justify the claims of competing interest groups, see Richard Madsen, "Contentless Consensus," in *America at Century's End*, ed. Alan Wolfe, (Berkeley and Los Angeles: University of California Press, 1991).

18. Alan Wolfe, *Whose Keeper? Social Science and Moral Obligations* (Berkeley and Los Angeles: University of California Press, 1989), pp. 218, 216.

19. Renato Rosaldo, *Culture and Truth: The Remaking of Social Analysis* (Boston: Beacon Press, 1989), pp. 102–103.

Conclusion

1. Ritual symbols, in Durkheim's famous formulation, hold a society together by dramatizing the sentiments and values its people have in common: "If left to themselves individual consciousnesses are closed to each other; they can communicate only by means of signs which express their internal states. If the communication established between them is to become a real communication, that is to say, a fusion of all particular sentiments into one common sentiment, the signs expressing them must themselves be fused into one single and unique resultant. It is the appearance of this that informs individuals that they are in harmony and makes them conscious of their moral unity." Emile Durkheim, *The Elementary Forms of the Religious Life* (New York: Free Press, 1965), p. 262. For a useful analysis of Durkheim's approach to the problem of moral order in complex societies, see Robert Bellah's introduction to *Emile Durkheim on Morality and Society: Selected Writings*, ed. Robert N. Bellah, (Chicago: University of Chicago Press, 1973), pp. ix–lv.

2. Colin M. Turnbull, *The Mbuti Pygmies: Change and Adaptation* (Fort Worth, Tex.: Holt, Rinehart, and Winston, 1983), p. 15.

3. Johannes Fabian, *Time and the Other: How Anthropology Makes Its Object* (New York: Columbia University Press, 1983).

4. In *Living Arctic: Hunters of the Canadian North* (Seattle: University of Washington Press, 1987), Hugh Brody makes this point with reference to current cultural attitudes toward the land claims of aboriginal peoples in Canada.

5. Many of Margaret Mead's lectures and *Redbook* articles have been collected in volumes edited by her longtime collaborator and friend, Rhoda Metraux. See Margaret Mead, *Some Personal Views*, ed. Rhoda Metraux (New York: Walker, 1979), and Margaret Mead and Rhoda Metraux, *Aspects of the Present* (New York: William Morrow, 1980).

6. Not surprisingly, Mead's work was one of the first targets of this intra-disciplinary critique; see Derek Freeman, *Margaret Mead and Samoa: The Making and Unmaking of an Anthropological Myth* (Cambridge: Harvard University Press, 1983). For less sensational writings in this vein see George E. Marcus and Michael M. J. Fischer, *Anthropology as Cultural Critique: An Experimental*

Moment in the Human Sciences (Chicago: University of Chicago Press, 1986); James Clifford and George E. Marcus, eds., *Writing Culture: The Poetics and Politics of Ethnography* (Berkeley and Los Angeles: University of California Press, 1986); and Clifford Geertz, *Works and Lives: The Anthropologist as Author* (Stanford: Stanford University Press, 1988).

7. James Clifford, *The Predicament of Culture: Twentieth-Century Ethnography, Literature, and Art* (Cambridge: Harvard University Press, 1988).

8. Mary Louise Pratt, "Fieldwork in Common Places," in Clifford and Marcus, *Writing Culture*, p. 48.

9. In *Culture and Truth: The Remaking of Social Analysis* (Boston: Beacon Press, 1989), chap. 3, Renato Rosaldo refers to this process of yearning for what one has destroyed as "imperialist nostalgia."

10. David Bensmen and Roberta Lynch, *Rusted Dreams: Hard Times in a Steel Community* (Berkeley and Los Angeles: University of California Press, 1987); and Gregory Pappas, *The Magic City: Unemployment in a Working-Class Community* (Ithaca: Cornell University Press, 1989).

11. William Serrin, "Requiem for a Steel Town," *New York Times*, September 5, 1988. See also William Serrin, *Homestead: The Glory and Tragedy of an American Steel Town* (New York: Random House, 1992).

12. Christopher Lasch, *The True and Only Heaven: Progress and Its Critics* (New York: W. W. Norton, 1991), p. 118.

13. Reflecting on the creation of an indigenous African American culture in the Caribbean, anthropologists Sidney Mintz and Richard Price make the point that traumatic social change such as war or enslavement acts to destroy not "cultures," but the *social contexts* within which people's affective ties are formed and thrive. "People ordinarily do not long for a lost 'cultural heritage' in the abstract," Mintz and Price observe, "but for the immediately experienced personal relationships, developed in a specific cultural and institutional setting." It is the destruction of traditional forms of association, the collapse of social networks, and the estrangement of family and friends that people mourn in the aftermath of traumatic change. Sidney W. Mintz and Richard Price, *The Birth of African-American Culture: An Anthropological Perspective* (Boston: Beacon Press, 1992), p. 47.

Appendix

1. Using data collected by the U.S. Department of Transportation, Carol MacLennan shows that different types of auto plants (assembly, trim, iron foundry, etc.) in different environments (center city, rural, suburban) tend to employ workforces with different gender, age, and racial compositions. "Political Response to Economic Loss: The Automotive Crisis of 1979–1982," *Urban Anthropology* 14, nos. 1–3 (1985): 21–57. A plant's individual history will also shape the characteristics of its workforce, and these features in turn will have a direct bearing on the reemployment problems that workers and their community face.

2. Richard H. Keehn, "Impact of Chrysler Closing on the Kenosha Economy," unpublished paper, third draft, Department of Economics, University of Wisconsin–Parkside, Kenosha, 1988.

3. The age distribution of 1,159 hourly workers living in Racine is virtually identical. The only significant difference in workforce composition between Kenosha and Racine is that a much higher percentage of minority-group workers live in Racine. Of the Racine hourly employees, 32 percent are black and 6.4 percent are Hispanic. Richard H. Keehn, "Impact of Chrysler Closing on Racine County," unpublished paper, first draft, Department of Economics, University of Wisconsin-Parkside, Kenosha, 1988.

Index

Index

middle class: ambiguity of membership in, 59, 210 n.10; definitions of, xx–xxi, 34; vanishing, 33 fig. 4, 39, 199–200 n.13

Midwest: income polarization in, 34, 35 table 1; industrial job loss in, 37, 199 n.8

military strength, industrial production and, 137–138

Mintz, Sidney, 216 n.13

Modern Times, 106

Moore, Thomas, 196–197 n.28

morality, 93, 98; culture and, 46–47; and free will versus determinism, 168–169; marketplace and, xix; as negotiated process, 171. *See also* moral order

moral obligation, 32, 92, 94; competing goals, 165–167; national strength and, 138

moral order, 59–61, 77, 93, 128, 160; in doubt, xxiii–xxiv; populism and, 139; ritual and, xxiv–xxv, 175, 215 n.1. *See also* principle of order

moral worth, 45–46, 107, 109; autoworkers' sense of, 167–171; educators' sense of, 95–97; judgments about, 162–165; measurement of, 74, 180–181

Moran, Patrick, 27, 56–57, 60, 69–70

mortification of the body, 132

Motor Division, 17, 194 n.8, 195 n.14

Motor Trend, 11

myth, 76, 81–82 (*see also* social Darwinism); of national origins, 147–149; of western hero, 204 n.15

Nash, Charles, 4, 7

Nash Lafayette, 7

Nash Motors, 4–6; becomes AMC, 8; impact of depression on, 5, 191 n.11; strikes at, 7; wartime production at, xvii, 7–8, 191–192 n.17

nation: as family, 137; restoration of, 139, 142

National Association for the Advancement of Colored People (NAACP), xviii

National Industrial Recovery Act, 191 n.13

national interest, 146–147

National Labor Advisory Board (NLAB), 7, 192 n.25

national purpose, 138–139, 146

nativism, 140–141

Newman, Katherine, 74, 193–194 n.4, 202–203 n.1, 209 n.6, 210–211 n.15

nonorder, 171

nostalgia, 179–180

occupational distribution, education and, 41–43, 42 figs. 8–9

order, moral. *See* moral order

overheard indictment, 164

past: meaning of, 83; obsolescence of, 176; symbols of, 54; white-collar understanding of, 61

PATCO, 193–194 n.4, 210–211 n.15

Phillips, Kevin, 79

place, meaning of, 28, 197 n.31

plant closing: impact of, 183; interpretations of, 59, 89, 209 n.6; meaning of, 175–176; as morality play, 90–91; as ritual, xxiv–xxv, 79; studies of, 83; symbolism of, 54. *See also* deindustrialization; ritual

Plymouth Gran Fury, 15

Plymouth Horizon, 15, 16, 24

polarization of incomes, 34

political labor, 121–122

politics of meaning, 160–161, 164–165

populism, 139–142, 146–147, 211 n.4

postindustrial society, 26, 42, 71–73, 77, 134; ritual symbolism of, 177; view of industrial workers in, 161

postwar affluence, xx, 180

poverty: culture of, 205–206 n.1; working people in, 189 n.14

Pratt, Mary Louise, 179

Price, Richard, 216 n.13

primitive, concept of, 176–177, 179

principle of order, 81–82

profile of informants, 185 tables A4, A5, 186 table A6

progress, 54–55, 75, 176, 180. *See also* social Darwinism

protectionism, 75–76

Protestant work ethic, 74, 151–152, 181

quality ratings, of Kenosha autoworkers, 17, 152–153

222

Index

Racine, Wisconsin, Chrysler workers residing in, 183 table A1, 217 n.3
Rainbow Coalition, 143
Rambler: AMC, 8; Jeffery, xvii, 4
Rand, Ayn, 65
Reich, Robert, 81
Reider, Jonathan, 206 n.2
Renault, 13; importance of Kenosha operations to, 192–193 n.26; partnership with AMC, 11
"Requiem for a Steel Town, " 179
research methods, 187–188 n.1
retirement benefits, 30–31, 197 n.1
ritual, xxiv, 79; contested meanings and, 175–176; rite of passage, 59; symbols, 215 n.1
Romo, Frank, 201 n.6
Rosaldo, Renato, 171, 216 n.9
Rusted Dreams, 83, 179

Sahlins, Marshall, 208 n.14
Sakurauchi, Yoshio, 213 n.7
salvage ethnology, 178–179
self-respect, 95–98, 167–169
seniority, 30–31, 194 n.8
Senett, Richard, 97, 122
Serrin, William, 179
shopfloor culture, 103, 107, 112; distinguished from mainstream, 209 n.5; egalitarian nature of, 114–115; games in, 110–111 (*see also* shop secrets); individualism and, 116–118, 122–123, 131
shop secrets, 118, 120, 123–124, 208–209 n.1
Shutdown at Youngstown, 83
skill, 116–118, 120, 123–124, 130–131, 210 n.11
skilled workers, 107–108, 118–120; percentage of Kenosha workforce, 183
social change, 213 n.5, 216 n.13; forms of, 176–177
social contract, 142, 147–150
social Darwinism, 76, 79–82
social disorder, 83–84, 151, 171
social value: cultural conflict and, 161; of industrial labor, 128–129, 169–170; inflated sense of, 73, 77
Solomon, Robert, 160
Southport, Wisconsin. *See* Kenosha

special interests, 142–143
Spencer, Herbert, 80
Squires, Gregory, 196–197 n.28
Stack, Carol, 210 n.8
stagnant wages, xviii–xix, xxi, 34, 36 fig. 5
status degradation, 79, 203 n.6
stigmatized identity, 126, 209 n.7
stress awareness, 156–157
stroking, 113
struggle for the real. *See* politics of meaning
success ethic, xix, 46, 211 n.3; basic premise of, xxi; economic contraction and, xxii

teamwork, 110, 207 n.9
Thompson, Tommy, 1, 15, 25, 66, 196 n.19
tradition of opportunity. *See* success ethic
trust fund, 22
Turnbull, Colin, 176
Turner, Victor, 159

UAW-JDTC program. *See* Dislocated Workers Assistance Center
unions: abuse of rights, 94; declining influence of, 53–54, 192 n.25; industrial crisis and, 214 n.14; interference in free market, 78–79
United Auto Workers (UAW), 7, 18, 24–25. *See also* Local 72
unskilled workers, 71, 107–108; percentage of Kenosha workforce, 183
upward mobility, 78, 127; during postwar years, xix

vanishing middle class, 39; controversy over, 199–200 n.13; income distribution and, 33 fig. 4
vanishing primitive, 179
voting patterns: in America, 201 n.3; of blue-collar workers, 201 n.6; in Kenosha's mayoral election, 56–59, 57 fig 10, 58 fig. 11; of middle Americans, 55

wage gap, education and, xix, 39, 40 fig. 7
Wisconsin legislature: breach of contract